Lincoln

Abraham Lincoln, An Account Of His Personal Life, Especially Of Its Springs Of Action As Revealed And Deepened By The Ordeal Of War

by

Nathaniel W. Stephenson

LINCOLN
Abraham Lincoln,
An Account of His Personal Life,
Especially of Its Springs of Action as
Revealed and Deepened by the Ordeal of War
by Nathaniel W. Stephenson

Copyright © 2023

ISBN: 978-93-59321-41-7

Published by

DOUBLE 9 BOOKS
2/13-B, Ansari Road, Daryaganj
New Delhi – 110002
info@double9books.com
www.double9books.com
Tel. 011-40042856

ABOUT THE AUTHOR

Nathaniel W. Stephenson, the renowned author of "Abraham Lincoln and the Union, " is celebrated for his literary prowess and profound ability to bridge the realms of history and nonfiction. His magnum opus, this book, stands as a testament to his exceptional storytelling skills. With a brilliant pen, he weaves intricate narratives that resonate deeply with readers, fostering a connection not only with the past but also with each other. Stephenson's writing is a symphony of creativity and passion, effortlessly introducing readers to a diverse spectrum of emotions and historical events. His prose is both elegant and approachable, inviting readers of all backgrounds to immerse themselves in his remarkable tales. Through his works, he manages to make history come alive, enabling us to comprehend the complexities of the past and the intricacies of human nature. In "Abraham Lincoln and the Union, " Nathaniel W. Stephenson's craftsmanship shines brightly, offering a captivating and insightful exploration of a pivotal moment in American history. His contributions to the world of nonfiction literature are a gift to all who seek to understand, connect, and appreciate the rich tapestry of human experience.

CONTENTS

I
THE CHILD OF THE FOREST

Of first importance in the making of the American people is that great forest which once extended its mysterious labyrinth from tide-water to the prairies when the earliest colonists entered warily its sea-worn edges a portion of the European race came again under a spell it had forgotten centuries before, the spell of that untamed nature which created primitive man. All the dim memories that lay deep in subconsciousness; all the vague shadows hovering at the back of the civilized mind; the sense of encompassing natural power, the need to struggle single-handed against it; the danger lurking in the darkness of the forest; the brilliant treachery of the forest sunshine glinted through leafy secrecies; the Strange voices in its illimitable murmur; the ghostly shimmer of its glades at night; the lovely beauty of the great gold moon; all the thousand wondering dreams that evolved the elder gods, Pan, Cybele, Thor; all this waked again in the soul of the Anglo-Saxon penetrating the great forest. And it was intensified by the way he came, — singly, or with but wife and child, or at best in very small company, a mere handful. And the surrounding presences were not only of the spiritual world. Human enemies who were soon as well armed as he, quicker of foot and eye, more perfectly noiseless in their tread even than the wild beasts of the shadowy coverts, the ruthless Indians whom he came to expel, these invisible presences were watching him, in a fierce silence he knew not whence. Like as not the first signs of that menace which was everywhere would be the hiss of the Indian arrow, or the crack of the Indian rifle, and sharp and sudden death.

Under these conditions he learned much and forgot much. His deadly need made him both more and less individual than he had been, released him from the dictation of his fellows in daily life while it enforced relentlessly a uniform method of self-preservation. Though the unseen world became more and more real, the understanding of it faded. It became chiefly a matter of emotional perception, scarcely at all a matter of philosophy. The morals of the forest Americans were those of audacious, visionary beings loosely hound together by a comradeship in peril. Courage, cautiousness, swiftness, endurance, faithfulness, secrecy, — these were the forest virtues. Dreaming, companionship, humor, — these were the forest luxuries.

From the first, all sorts and conditions were ensnared by that silent land, where the trails they followed, their rifles in their hands, had been trodden hard generation after generation by the feet of the Indian warriors. The best and the worst of England went into that illimitable resolvent, lost themselves, found themselves, and issued from its shadows, or their children did, changed both for good and ill, Americans. Meanwhile the great forest, during two hundred years, was slowly vanishing. This parent of a new people gave its life to its offspring and passed away. In the early nineteenth century it had withered backward far from the coast; had lost its identity all along the north end of the eastern mountains; had frayed out toward the sunset into lingering tentacles, into broken minor forests, into shreds and patches.

Curiously, by a queer sort of natural selection, its people had congregated into life communities not all of one pattern. There were places as early as the beginning of the century where distinction had appeared. At other places life was as rude and rough as could be imagined. There were innumerable farms that were still mere "clearings," walled by the forest. But there were other regions where for many a mile the timber had been hewn away, had given place to a ragged continuity of farmland. In such regions especially if the poorer elements of the forest, spiritually speaking, had drifted thither—the straggling villages which had appeared were but groups of log cabins huddled along a few neglected lanes. In central Kentucky, a poor new village was Elizabethtown, unkempt, chokingly dusty in the dry weather, with muddy streams instead of streets during the rains, a stench of pig-sties at the back of its cabins, but everywhere looking outward glimpses of a lovely meadow land.

At Elizabethtown in 1806 lived Joseph Hanks, a carpenter, also his niece Nancy Hanks. Poor people they were, of the sort that had been sucked into the forest in their weakness, or had been pushed into it by a social pressure they could not resist; not the sort that had grimly adventured its perils or gaily courted its lure. Their source was Virginia. They were of a thriftless, unstable class; that vagrant peasantry which had drifted westward to avoid competition with slave labor. The niece, Nancy, has been reputed illegitimate. And though tradition derives her from the predatory amour of an aristocrat, there is nothing to sustain the tale except her own appearance. She had a bearing, a cast of feature, a tone, that seemed to hint at higher social origins than those of her Hanks relatives. She had a little schooling; was of a pious and emotional turn of mind; enjoyed those amazing "revivals" which now and then gave an outlet to the pent-up religiosity of the village; and she was almost handsome.(1)

History has preserved no clue why this girl who was rather the best of her sort chose to marry an illiterate apprentice of her uncle's, Thomas Lincoln, whose name in the forest was spelled "Linkhorn." He was a shiftless fellow, never succeeding at anything, who could neither read nor write. At the time of his birth, twenty-eight years before, his parents—drifting, roaming people, struggling with poverty—were dwellers in the Virginia mountains. As a mere lad, he had shot an Indian—one of the few positive acts attributed to him—and his father had been killed by Indians. There was a "vague tradition" that his grandfather had been a Pennsylvania Quaker who had wandered southward through the forest mountains. The tradition angered him. Though he appears to have had little enough—at least in later years— of the fierce independence of the forest, he resented a Quaker ancestry as an insult. He had no suspicion that in after years the zeal of genealogists would track his descent until they had linked him with a lost member of a distinguished Puritan family, a certain Mordecai Lincoln who removed to New Jersey, whose descendants became wanderers of the forest and sank speedily to the bottom of the social scale, retaining not the slightest memory of their New England origin.(2) Even in the worst of the forest villages, few couples started married life in less auspicious circumstances than did Nancy and Thomas. Their home in one of the alleys of Elizabethtown was a shanty fourteen feet square.(3) Very soon after marriage, shiftless Thomas gave up carpentering and took to farming. Land could be had almost anywhere for almost nothing those days, and Thomas got a farm on credit near where now stands Hodgenville. Today, it is a famous place, for there, February 12, 1809, Abraham Lincoln, second child, but first son of Nancy and Thomas, was born.(4)

During most of eight years, Abraham lived in Kentucky. His father, always adrift in heart, tried two farms before abandoning Kentucky altogether. A shadowy figure, this Thomas; the few memories of him suggest a superstitious nature in a superstitious community. He used to see visions in the forest. Once, it is said, he came home, all excitement, to tell his wife he had seen a giant riding on a lion, tearing up trees by the roots; and thereupon, he took to his bed and kept it for several days.

His son Abraham told this story of the giant on the lion to a playmate of his, and the two boys gravely discussed the existence of ghosts. Abraham thought his father "didn't exactly believe in them," and seems to have been in about the same state of mind himself. He was quite sure he was "not much" afraid of the dark. This was due chiefly to the simple wisdom of a good woman, a neighbor, who had taught him to think of the night as a great room that God had darkened even as his friend darkened a room in her house by hanging something over the window.(5)

The eight years of his childhood in Kentucky had few incidents. A hard, patient, uncomplaining life both for old and young. The men found their one deep joy in the hunt. In lesser degree, they enjoyed the revivals which gave to the women their one escape out of themselves. A strange, almost terrible recovery of the primitive, were those religious furies of the days before the great forest had disappeared. What other figures in our history are quite so remarkable as the itinerant frontier priests, the circuit-riders as they are now called, who lived as Elijah did, whose temper was very much the temper of Elijah, in whose exalted narrowness of devotion, all that was stern, dark, foreboding—the very brood of the forest's innermost heart—had found a voice. Their religion was ecstasy in homespun, a glory of violent singing, the release of a frantic emotion, formless but immeasurable, which at all other times, in the severity of the forest routine, gave no sign of its existence.

A visitor remembered long afterward a handsome young woman who he thought was Nancy Hanks, singing wildly, whirling about as may once have done the ecstatic women of the woods of Thrace, making her way among equally passionate worshipers, to the foot of the rude altar, and there casting herself into the arms of the man she was to marry.(6) So did thousands of forest women in those seasons when their communion with a mystic loneliness was confessed, when they gave tongue as simply as wild creatures to the nameless stirrings and promptings of that secret woodland where Pan was still the lord. And the day following the revival, they were again the silent, expressionless, much enduring, long-suffering forest wives, mothers of many children, toilers of the cabins, who cooked and swept and carried fuel by sunlight, and by firelight sewed and spun.

It can easily be understood how these women, as a rule, exerted little influence on their sons. Their imaginative side was too deeply hidden, the nature of their pleasures too secret, too mysterious. Male youth, following its obvious pleasure, went with the men to the hunt. The women remained outsiders. The boy who chose to do likewise, was the incredible exception. In him had come to a head the deepest things in the forest life: the darkly feminine things, its silence, its mysticism, its secretiveness, its tragic patience. Abraham was such a boy. It is said that he astounded his father by refusing to own a gun. He earned terrible whippings by releasing animals caught in traps. Though he had in fullest measure the forest passion for listening to stories, the ever-popular tales of Indian warfare disgusted him. But let the tale take on any glint of the mystery of the human soul—as of Robinson Crusoe alone on his island, or of the lordliness of action, as in Columbus or Washington—and he was quick with interest. The stories of talking animals out of Aesop fascinated him.

In this thrilled curiosity about the animals was the side of him least intelligible to men like his father. It lives in many anecdotes: of his friendship with a poor dog he had which he called "Honey"; of pursuing a snake through difficult thickets to prevent its swallowing a frog; of loitering on errands at the risk of whippings to watch the squirrels in the tree-tops; of the crowning offense of his childhood, which earned him a mighty beating, the saving of a fawn's life by scaring it off just as a hunter's gun was leveled. And by way of comment on all this, there is the remark preserved in the memory of another boy to whom at the time it appeared most singular, "God might think as much of that little fawn as of some people." Of him as of another gentle soul it might have been said that all the animals were his brothers and sisters.(7)

One might easily imagine this peculiar boy who chose to remain at home while the men went out to slay, as the mere translation into masculinity of his mother, and of her mothers, of all the converging processions of forest women, who had passed from one to another the secret of their mysticism, coloring it many ways in the dark vessels of their suppressed lives, till it reached at last their concluding child. But this would only in part explain him. Their mysticism, as after-time was to show, he had undoubtedly inherited. So, too, from them, it may be, came another characteristic — that instinct to endure, to wait, to abide the issue of circumstance, which in the days of his power made him to the politicians as unintelligible as once he had been to the forest huntsmen. Nevertheless, the most distinctive part of those primitive women, the sealed passionateness of their spirits, he never from childhood to the end revealed. In the grown man appeared a quietude, a sort of tranced calm, that was appalling. From what part of his heredity did this derive? Was it the male gift of the forest? Did progenitors worthier than Thomas somehow cast through him to his alien son that peace they had found in the utter heart of danger, that apparent selflessness which is born of being ever unfailingly on guard?

It is plain that from the first he was a natural stoic, taking his whippings, of which there appear to have been plenty, in silence, without anger. It was all in the day's round. Whippings, like other things, came and went. What did it matter? And the daily round, though monotonous, had even for the child a complement of labor. Especially there was much patient journeying back and forth with meal bags between his father's cabin and the local mill. There was a little schooling, very little, partly from Nancy Lincoln, partly from another good woman, the miller's kind old mother, partly at the crudest of wayside schools maintained very briefly by a wandering teacher who soon wandered on; but out of this schooling very little result beyond the mastery of the A B C.(8) And even at this age, a pathetic eagerness to learn, to invade the wonder of the printed book! Also a marked keenness of observation. He observed things which his elders overlooked. He had a better sense of direction, as when he corrected his father and others who were taking the wrong short-cut to a burning house. Cool, unexcitable, he was capable of presence of mind. Once at night when the door of the cabin was suddenly thrown open and a monster appeared on the threshold, a spectral thing in the darkness, furry, with the head of an ox, Thomas Lincoln shrank back aghast; little Abraham, quicker-sighted and quicker-witted, slipped behind the creature, pulled at its furry mantle, and revealed a forest Diana, a bold girl who amused herself playing demon among the shadows of the moon.

Seven years passed and his eighth birthday approached. All this while Thomas Lincoln had somehow kept his family in food, but never had he money in his pocket. His successive farms, bought on credit, were never paid for. An incurable vagrant, he came at last to the psychological moment when he could no longer impose himself on his community. He must take to the road in a hazard of new fortune. Indiana appeared to him the land of promise. Most of his property—such as it was—except his carpenter's tools, he traded for whisky, four hundred gallons. Somehow he obtained a rattletrap wagon and two horses.

The family appear to have been loath to go. Nancy Lincoln had long been ailing and in low spirits, thinking much of what might happen to her children after her death. Abraham loved the country-side, and he had good friends in the miller and his kind old mother. But the vagrant Thomas would have his way. In the brilliancy of the Western autumn, with the ruined woods flaming scarlet and gold, these poor people took their last look at the cabin that had been their wretched shelter, and set forth into the world.(9)

II
THE MYSTERIOUS YOUTH

Vagrants, or little better than vagrants, were Thomas Lincoln and his family making their way to Indiana. For a year after they arrived they were squatters, their home an "open-faced camp," that is, a shanty with one wall missing, and instead of chimney, a fire built on the open side. In that mere pretense of a house, Nancy Lincoln and her children spent the winter of 1816-1817. Then Thomas resorted to his familiar practice of taking land on credit. The Lincolns were now part of a "settlement" of seven or eight families strung along a little stream known as Pigeon Creek. Here Thomas entered a quarter-section of fair land, and in the course of the next eleven years succeeded — wonderful to relate — in paying down sufficient money to give him title to about half.

Meanwhile, poor fading Nancy went to her place. Pigeon Creek was an out-of-the-way nook in the still unsettled West, and Nancy during the two years she lived there could not have enjoyed much of the consolation of her religion. Perhaps now and then she had ghostly council of some stray circuit-rider. But for her the days of the ecstasies had gone by; no great revival broke the seals of the spirit, stirred its deep waters, along Pigeon Creek. There was no religious service when she was laid to rest in a coffin made of green lumber and fashioned by her husband. Months passed, the snow lay deep, before a passing circuit-rider held a burial service over her grave. Tradition has it that the boy Abraham brought this about very likely, at ten years old, he felt that her troubled spirit could not have peace till this was done. Shadowy as she is, ghostlike across the page of history, it is plain that she was a reality to her son. He not only loved her but revered her. He believed that from her he had inherited the better part of his genius. Many years after her death he said, "God bless my mother; all that I am or ever hope to be I owe to her."

Nancy was not long without a successor. Thomas Lincoln, the next year, journeyed back to Kentucky and returned in triumph to Indiana, bringing as his wife, an old flame of his who had married, had been widowed, and was of a mind for further adventures. This Sarah Bush Lincoln, of less distinction than Nancy, appears to have been steadier-minded and stronger-willed. Even before this, Thomas had left the half-faced camp and moved into a cabin. But such a cabin! It had neither door, nor window, nor floor. Sally Lincoln required her husband to make of it a proper house—by the standards of Pigeon Creek. She had brought with her as her dowry a wagonload of furniture. These comforts together with her strong will began a new era of relative comfort in the Lincoln cabin.(1)

Sally Lincoln was a kind stepmother to Abraham who became strongly attached to her. In the rough and nondescript community of Pigeon Creek, a world of weedy farms, of miserable mud roads, of log farm-houses, the family life that was at least tolerable. The sordid misery described during her regime emerged from wretchedness to a state of by all the recorders of Lincoln's early days seems to have ended about his twelfth year. At least, the vagrant suggestion disappeared. Though the life that succeeded was void of luxury, though it was rough, even brutal, dominated by a coarse, peasant-like view of things, it was scarcely by peasant standards a life of hardship. There was food sufficient, if not very good; protection from wind and weather; fire in the winter time; steady labor; and social acceptance by the community of the creekside. That the labor was hard and long, went without saying. But as to that—as of the whippings in Kentucky—what else, from the peasant point of view, would you expect? Abraham took it all with the same stoicism with which he had once taken the whippings. By the unwritten law of the creekside he was his father's property, and so was his labor, until he came of age. Thomas used him as a servant or hired him out to other farmers. Stray recollections show us young Abraham working as a farm-hand for twenty-five cents the day, probably with "keep" in addition; we glimpse him slaughtering hogs skilfully at thirty-one cents a day, for this was "rough work." He became noted as an axman.

In the crevices, so to speak, of his career as a farm-hand, Abraham got a few months of schooling, less than a year in all. A story that has been repeated a thousand times shows the raw youth by the cabin fire at night doing sums on the back of a wooden shovel, and shaving off its surface repeatedly to get a fresh page. He devoured every book that came his way, only a few to be sure, but generally great ones—the Bible, of course, and Aesop, Crusoe, Pilgrim's Progress, and a few histories, these last unfortunately of the poorer sort. He early displayed a bent for composition, scribbling verses that were very poor, and writing burlesque tales about his acquaintances in what passed for a Biblical style.(2)

One great experience broke the monotony of the life on Pigeon Creek. He made a trip to New Orleans as a "hand" on a flatboat. Of this trip little is known though much may be surmised. To his deeply poetic nature what an experience it must have been: the majesty of the vast river; the pageant of its immense travel; the steamers heavily laden; the fleets of barges; the many towns; the nights of stars over wide sweeps of water; the stately plantation houses along the banks; the old French city with its crowds, its bells, the shipping, the strange faces and the foreign speech; all the bewildering evidence that there were other worlds besides Pigeon Creek!

What seed of new thinking was sown in his imagination by this Odyssey we shall never know. The obvious effect in the ten years of his life in Indiana was produced at Pigeon Creek. The "settlement" was within fifteen miles of the Ohio. It lay in that southerly fringe of Indiana which received early in the century many families of much the same estate, character and origin as the Lincolns, — poor whites of the edges of the great forest working outward toward the prairies. Located on good land not far from a great highway, the Ohio, it illustrated in its rude prosperity a transformation that went on unobserved in many such settlements, the transformation of the wandering forester of the lower class into a peasant farmer. Its life was of the earth, earthy; though it retained the religious traditions of the forest, their significance was evaporating; mysticism was fading into emotionalism; the camp-meeting was degenerating into a picnic. The supreme social event, the wedding, was attended by festivities that filled twenty-four hours: a race of male guests in the forenoon with a bottle of whisky for a prize; an Homeric dinner at midday; "an afternoon of rough games and outrageous practical jokes; a supper and dance at night interrupted by the successive withdrawals of the bride and groom, attended by ceremonies and jests of more than Rabelaisian crudeness; and a noisy dispersal next day."(3) The intensities of the forest survived in hard drinking, in the fury of the fun-making, and in the hunt. The forest passion for storytelling had in no way decreased.

In this atmosphere, about eighteen and nineteen, Abraham shot up suddenly from a slender boy to a huge, raw-honed, ungainly man, six feet four inches tall, of unusual muscular strength. His strength was one of the fixed conditions of his development. It delivered him from all fear of his fellows. He had plenty of peculiarities. He was ugly, awkward; he lacked the wanton appetites of the average sensual man. And these peculiarities without his great strength as his warrant might have brought him into ridicule. As it was, whatever his peculiarities, in a society like that of Pigeon Creek, the man who could beat all competitors, wrestling or boxing, was free from molestation. But Lincoln instinctively had another aim in life than mere freedom to be himself. Two characteristics that were so significant in his childhood continued with growing vitality in his young manhood: his placidity and his intense sense of comradeship. The latter, however, had undergone a change. It was no longer the comradeship of the wild creatures. That spurt of physical expansion, the swift rank growth to his tremendous stature, swept him apparently across a dim dividing line, out of the world of birds and beasts and into the world of men. He took the new world with the same unfailing but also unexcitable curiosity with which he had taken the other, the world of squirrels, flowers, fawns.

Here as there, the difference from his mother, deep though their similarities may have been, was sharply evident. Had he been wholly at one with her religiously, the gift of telling speech which he now began to display might have led him into a course that would have rejoiced her heart, might have made him a boy preacher, and later, a great revivalist. His father and elder sister while on Pigeon Creek joined the local Baptist Church. But Abraham did not follow them. Nor is there a single anecdote linking him in any way with the fervors of camp meeting. On the contrary, what little is remembered, is of a cool aloofness.(4) The inscrutability of the forest was his—what it gave to the stealthy, cautious men who were too intent on observing, too suspiciously watchful, to give vent to their feelings. Therefore, in Lincoln there was always a double life, outer and inner, the outer quietly companionable, the inner, solitary, mysterious.

It was the outer life that assumed its first definite phase in the years on Pigeon Creek. During those years, Lincoln discovered his gift of story-telling. He also discovered humor. In the employment of both talents, he accepted as a matter of course the tone of the young ruffians among whom he dwelt. Very soon this powerful fellow, who could throw any of them in a wrestle, won the central position among them by a surer title, by the power to delight. And any one who knows how peasant schools of art arise—for that matter, all schools of art that are vital—knows how he did it. In this connection, his famous biographers, Nicolay and Hay, reveal a certain externality by objecting that a story attributed to him is ancient. All stories are ancient. Not the tale, but the telling, as the proverb says, is the thing. In later years, Lincoln wrote down every good story that he heard, and filed it.(5) When it reappeared it had become his own. Who can doubt that this deliberate assimilation, the typical artistic process, began on Pigeon Creek? Lincoln never would have captured as he did his plowboy audience, set them roaring with laughter in the intervals of labor, had he not given them back their own tales done over into new forms brilliantly beyond their powers of conception. That these tales were gross, even ribald, might have been taken for granted, even had we not positive evidence of the fact. Otherwise none of that uproarious laughter which we may be sure sounded often across shimmering harvest fields while stalwart young pagans, ever ready to pause, leaned, bellowing, on the handles of their scythes, Abe Lincoln having just then finished a story.

Though the humor of these stories was Falstaffian, to say the least, though Lincoln was cock of the walk among the plowboys of Pigeon Creek, a significant fact with regard to him here comes into view. Not an anecdote survives that in any way suggests personal licentiousness. Scrupulous men who in after-time were offended by his coarseness of speech — for more or less of the artist of Pigeon Creek stuck to him almost to the end; he talked in fables, often in gross fables — these men, despite their annoyance, felt no impulse to attribute to him personal habits in harmony with his tales. On the other hand, they were puzzled by their own impression, never wavering, that he was "pureminded." The clue which they did not have lay in the nature of his double life. That part of him which, in our modern jargon, we call his "reactions" obeyed a curious law. They dwelt in his outer life without penetrating to the inner; but all his impulses of personal action were securely seated deep within. Even at nineteen, for any one attuned to spiritual meaning, he would have struck the note of mystery, faintly, perhaps, but certainly. To be sure, no hint of this reached the minds of his rollicking comrades of the harvest field. It was not for such as they to perceive the problem of his character, to suspect that he was a genius, or to guess that a time would come when sincere men would form impressions of him as dissimilar as black and white. And so far as it went the observation of the plowboys was correct. The man they saw was indeed a reflection of themselves. But it was a reflection only. Their influence entered into the real man no more than the image in a mirror has entered into the glass.

III
A VILLAGE LEADER

Though placid, this early Lincoln was not resigned. He differed from the boors of Pigeon Creek in wanting some other sort of life. What it was he wanted, he did not know. His reading had not as yet given him definite ambitions. It may well be that New Orleans was the clue to such stirring in him as there was of that discontent which fanciful people have called divine. Remembering New Orleans, could any imaginative youth be content with Pigeon Creek?

In the spring of 1830, shortly after he came of age, he agreed for once with his father whose chronic vagrancy had reasserted itself. The whole family set out again on their wanderings and made their way in an oxcart to a new halting place on the Sangamon River in Illinois. There Abraham helped his father clear another piece of land for another illusive "start" in life. The following spring he parted with his family and struck out for himself. (1) His next adventure was a second trip as a boatman to New Orleans. Can one help suspecting there was vague hope in his heart that he might be adventuring to the land of hearts' desire? If there was, the yokels who were his fellow boatmen never suspected it. One of them long afterward asserted that Lincoln returned from New Orleans fiercely rebellious against its central institution, slavery, and determined to "hit that thing" whenever he could.

The legend centers in his witnessing a slave auction and giving voice to his horror in a style quite unlike any of his authentic utterances. The authority for all this is doubtful.(2) Furthermore, the Lincoln of 1831 was not yet awakened. That inner life in which such a reaction might take place was still largely dormant. The outer life, the life of the harvest clown, was still a thick insulation. Apparently, the waking of the inner life, the termination of its dormant stage, was reserved for an incident far more personal that fell upon him in desolating force a few years later.

Following the New Orleans venture, came a period as storekeeper for a man named Denton Offut, in perhaps the least desirable town in Illinois — a dreary little huddle of houses gathered around Rutledge's Mill on the

Sangamon River and called New Salem.(3) Though a few of its people were of a better sort than any Lincoln had yet known except, perhaps, the miller's family in the old days in Kentucky — and still a smaller few were of fine quality, the community for the most part was hopeless. A fatality for unpromising neighborhoods overhangs like a doom the early part of this strange life. All accounts of New Salem represent it as predominantly a congregation of the worthless, flung together by unaccountable accident at a spot where there was no genuine reason for a town's existence. A casual town, created by drifters, and void of settled purpose. Small wonder that ere long it vanished from the map; that after a few years its drifting congregation dispersed to every corner of the horizon, and was no more. But during its brief existence it staged an episode in the development of Lincoln's character. However, this did not take place at once. And before it happened, came another turn of his soul's highway scarcely less important. He discovered, or thought he discovered, what he wanted. His vague ambition took shape. He decided to try to be a politician. At twenty-three, after living in New Salem less than a year, this audacious, not to say impertinent, young man offered himself to the voters of Sangamon County as a candidate for the Legislature. At this time that humility which was eventually his characteristic had not appeared. It may be dated as subsequent to New Salem — a further evidence that the deep spiritual experience which closed this chapter formed a crisis. Before then, at New Salem as at Pigeon Creek, he was but a variant, singularly decent, of the boisterous, frolicking, impertinent type that instinctively sought the laxer neighborhoods of the frontier. An echo of Pigeon Creek informed the young storekeeper's first state paper, the announcement of his candidacy, in the year 1832. His first political speech was in a curious vein, glib, intimate and fantastic: "Fellow citizens, I presume you all know who I am. I am humble Abraham Lincoln. I have been solicited by many friends to become a candidate for the Legislature. My politics are short and sweet like the old woman's dance. I am in favor of a national bank. I am in favor of the internal improvement system and a high protective tariff. These are my sentiments and political principles. If elected, I shall be thankful; if not it will be all the same."(4)

However, this bold throw of the dice of fortune was not quite so impertinent as it seems. During the months when he was in charge of Offut's grocery store he had made a conquest of New Salem. The village grocery in those days was the village club. It had its constant gathering of loafers all of whom were endowed with votes. It was the one place through which passed the whole population, in and out, one time or another. To a clever storekeeper it gave a chance to establish a following. Had he, as Lincoln had, the gift of story-telling, the gift of humor, he was a made man.

Pigeon Creek over again! Lincoln's wealth of funny stories gave Offut's grocery somewhat the role of a vaudeville theater and made the storekeeper as popular a man as there was in New Salem.

In another way he repeated his conquest of Pigeon Creek. New Salem had its local Alsatia known as Clary's Grove whose insolent young toughs led by their chief, Jack Armstrong, were the terror of the neighborhood. The groceries paid them tribute in free drinks. Any luckless storekeeper who incurred their displeasure found his store some fine morning a total wreck. Lincoln challenged Jack Armstrong to a duel with fists. It was formally arranged. A ring was formed; the whole village was audience; and Lincoln thrashed him to a finish. But this was only a small part of his triumph. His physical prowess, joined with his humor and his companionableness; entirely captivated Clary's Grove. Thereafter, it was storekeeper Lincoln's pocket borough; its ruffians were his body-guard. Woe to any one who made trouble for their hero.

There were still other causes for his quick rise to the position of village leader. His unfailing kindness was one; his honesty was another. Tales were related of his scrupulous dealings, such as walking a distance of miles in order to correct a trifling error he had made, in selling a poor woman less than the proper weight of tea. Then, too, by New Salem standards, he was educated. Long practice on the shovel at Pigeon Creek had given him a good handwriting, and one of the first things he did at New Salem was to volunteer to be clerk of elections. And there was a distinct moral superiority. Little as this would have signified unbacked by his giant strength since it had that authority behind it his morality set him apart from his followers, different, imposing. He seldom, if ever, drank whisky. Sobriety was already the rule of his life, both outward and inward. At the same time he was not censorious. He accepted the devotion of Clary's Grove without the slightest attempt to make over its bravoes in his own image. He sympathized with its ideas of sport. For all his kindliness to humans of every sort much of his sensitiveness for animals had passed away. He was not averse to cock fighting; he enjoyed a horse race.(5) Altogether, in his outer life, before the catastrophe that revealed him to himself, he was quite as much in the tone of New Salem as ever in that of Pigeon Creek. When the election came he got every vote in New Salem except three.(6)

But the village was a small part of Sangamon County. Though Lincoln received a respectable number of votes elsewhere, his total was well down in the running. He remained an inconspicuous minority candidate.

Meanwhile Offut's grocery had failed. In the midst of the legislative campaign, Offut's farmer storekeeper volunteered for the Indian War with Black Hawk, but returned to New Salem shortly before the election without having once smelled powder. Since his peers were not of a mind to give him immediate occupation in governing, he turned again to business. He formed a partnership with a man named Berry. They bought on credit the wreck of a grocery that had been sacked by Lincoln's friends of Clary's Grove, and started business as "General Merchants," under the style of Berry & Lincoln. There followed a year of complete unsuccess. Lincoln demonstrated that he was far more inclined to read any chance book that came his way than to attend to business, and that he had "no money sense." The new firm went the way of Offut's grocery, leaving nothing behind it but debt. The debts did not trouble Berry; Lincoln assumed them all. They formed a dreadful load which he bore with his usual patience and little by little discharged. Fifteen years passed before again he was a free man financially.

A new and powerful influence came into his life during the half idleness of his unsuccessful storekeeping. It is worth repeating in his own words, or what seems to be the fairly accurate recollection of his words: "One day a man who was migrating to the West, drove up in front of my store with a wagon which contained his family and household plunder. He asked me if I would buy an old barrel for which he had no room in his wagon, and which he said contained nothing of special value. I did not want it but to oblige him I bought it and paid him, I think, a half a dollar for it. Without further examination I put it away in the store and forgot all about it Sometime after, in overhauling things, I came upon the barrel and emptying it upon the floor to see what it contained, I found at the bottom of the rubbish a complete edition of Blackstone's Commentaries. I began to read those famous works, and I had plenty of time; for during the long summer days when the farmers were busy with their crops, my customers were few and far between. The more I read, the more intensely interested I became. Never in my whole life was my mind so thoroughly absorbed. I read until I devoured them."(7)

The majesty of the law at the bottom of a barrel of trash discovered at a venture and taking instant possession of the discoverer's mind! Like the genius issuing grandly in the smoke cloud from the vase drawn up out of the sea by the fisher in the Arabian tale! But this great book was not the only magic casket discovered by the idle store-keeper, the broken seals of which released mighty presences. Both Shakespeare and Burns were revealed to him in this period. Never after did either for a moment cease to be his companion. These literary treasures were found at Springfield twenty miles from New Salem, whither Lincoln went on foot many a time to borrow books.

His subsistence, after the failure of Berry & Lincoln, was derived from the friendliness of the County Surveyor Calhoun, who was a Democrat, while Lincoln called himself a Whig. Calhoun offered him the post of assistant. In accepting, Lincoln again displayed the honesty that was beginning to be known as his characteristic. He stipulated that he should be perfectly free to express his opinions, that the office should not be in any respect, a bribe. This being conceded, he went to work furiously on a treatise upon surveying, and astonishingly soon, with the generous help of the schoolmaster of New Salem, was able to take up his duties. His first fee was "two buckskins which Hannah Armstrong 'fixed' on his pants so the briers would not wear them out."(8)

Thus time passed until 1834 when he staked his only wealth, his popularity, in the gamble of an election. This time he was successful. During the following winter he sat in the Legislature of Illinois; a huge, uncouth, mainly silent member, making apparently no impression whatever, very probably striking the educated members as a nonentity in homespun.(9)

In the spring of 1835, he was back in New Salem, busy again with his surveying. Kind friends had secured him the office of local postmaster. The delivery of letters was now combined with going to and fro as a surveyor. As the mail came but once a week, and as whatever he had to deliver could generally be carried in his hat, and as payment was in proportion to business done, his revenues continued small. Nevertheless, in the view of New Salem, he was getting on.

And then suddenly misfortune overtook him. His great adventure, the first of those spiritual agonies of which he was destined to endure so many, approached. Hitherto, since childhood, women had played no part in his story. All the recollections of his youth are vague in their references to the feminine. As a boy at Pigeon Creek when old Thomas was hiring him out, the women of the settlement liked to have him around, apparently because he was kindly and ever ready to do odd jobs in addition to his regular work. However, until 1835, his story is that of a man's man, possibly because there was so much of the feminine in his own make-up. In 1835 came a change. A girl of New Salem, a pretty village maiden, the best the poor place could produce, revealed him to himself. Sweet Ann Rutledge, the daughter of the tavern-keeper, was his first love. But destiny was against them. A brief engagement was terminated by her sudden death late in the summer of 1835. Of this shadowy love-affair very little is known, — though much romantic fancy has been woven about it. Its significance for after-time is in Lincoln's "reaction." There had been much sickness in New Salem the summer in which Ann died. Lincoln had given himself freely as nurse — the depth of his companionableness thus being proved — and was in an overwrought condition when his sorrow struck him. A last interview with the dying girl, at which no one was present, left him quite unmanned. A period of violent agitation followed. For a time he seemed completely transformed. The sunny Lincoln, the delight of Clary's Grove, had vanished. In his place was a desolated soul—a brother to dragons, in the terrible imagery of Job—a dweller in the dark places of affliction. It was his mother reborn in him. It was all the shadowiness of his mother's world; all that frantic reveling in the mysteries of woe to which, hitherto, her son had been an alien. To the simple minds of the villagers with their hard-headed, practical way of keeping all things, especially love and grief, in the outer layer of consciousness, this revelation of an emotional terror was past understanding. Some of them, true to their type, pronounced him insane. He was watched with especial vigilance during storms, fogs, damp gloomy weather, "for fear of an accident." Surely, it was only a crazy man, in New Salem psychology, who was heard to say, "I can never be reconciled to have the snow, rains and storms beat upon her grave."(10)

In this crucial moment when the real base of his character had been suddenly revealed—all the passionateness of the forest shadow, the unfathomable gloom laid so deep at the bottom of his soul—he was carried through his spiritual eclipse by the loving comprehension of two fine friends. New Salem was not all of the sort of Clary's Grove. Near by on a farm, in a lovely, restful landscape, lived two people who deserve to be remembered, Bowlin Green and his wife. They drew Lincoln into the seclusion of their home, and there in the gleaming days of autumn, when everywhere in the near woods flickered downward, slowly, idly, the falling leaves golden and scarlet, Lincoln recovered his equanimity.(11) But the hero of Pigeon Creek, of Clary's Grove, did not quite come hack. In the outward life, to be sure, a day came when the sunny story-teller, the victor of Jack Armstrong, was once more what Jack would have called his real self. In the inner life where alone was his reality, the temper which affliction had revealed to him was established. Ever after, at heart, he was to dwell alone, facing, silent, those inscrutable things which to the primitive mind are things of every day. Always, he was to have for his portion in his real self, the dimness of twilight, or at best, the night with its stars, "never glad, confident morning again."

IV
REVELATIONS

From this time during many years almost all the men who saw beyond the surface in Lincoln have indicated, in one way or another, their vision of a constant quality. The observers of the surface did not see it. That is to say, Lincoln did not at once cast off any of his previous characteristics. It is doubtful if he ever did. His experience was tenaciously cumulative. Everything he once acquired, he retained, both in the outer life and the inner; and therefore, to those who did not have the clue to him, he appeared increasingly contradictory, one thing on the surface, another within. Clary's Grove and the evolutions from Clary's Grove, continued to think of him as their leader. On the other hand, men who had parted with the mere humanism of Clary's Grove, who were a bit analytical, who thought themselves still more analytical, seeing somewhat beneath the surface, reached conclusions similar to those of a shrewd Congressman who long afterward said that Lincoln was not a leader of men but a manager of men. (1) This astute distinction was not true of the Lincoln the Congressman confronted; nevertheless, it betrays much both of the observer and of the man he tried to observe. In the Congressman's day, what he thought he saw was in reality the shadow of a Lincoln that had passed away, passed so slowly, so imperceptibly that few people knew it had passed. During many years following 1835, the distinction in the main applied. So thought the men who, like Lincoln's latest law partner, William H. Herndon, were not derivatives of Clary's Grove. The Lincoln of these days was the only one Herndon knew. How deeply he understood Lincoln is justly a matter of debate; but this, at least, he understood—that Clary's Grove, in attributing to Lincoln its own idea of leadership, was definitely wrong. He saw in Lincoln, in all the larger matters, a tendency to wait on events, to take the lead indicated by events, to do what shallow people would have called mere drifting. To explain this, he labeled him a fatalist.(2) The label was only approximate, as most labels are. But Herndon's effort to find one is significant. In these years, Lincoln took the initiative—when he took it at all—in a way that most people did not recognize. His spirit was ever aloof. It was only the every-day, the external Lincoln that came into practical contact with his fellows.

This is especially true of the growing politician. He served four consecutive terms in the Legislature without doing anything that had the stamp of true leadership. He was not like either of the two types of politicians that generally made up the legislatures of those days—the men who dealt in ideas as political counters, and the men who were grafters without in their naive way knowing that they were grafters. As a member of the Legislature, Lincoln did not deal in ideas. He was instinctively incapable of graft A curiously routine politician, one who had none of the earmarks familiar in such a person. Aloof, and yet, more than ever companionable, the power he had in the Legislature—for he had acquired a measure of power—was wholly personal. Though called a Whig, it was not as a party man but as a personal friend that he was able to carry through his legislative triumphs. His most signal achievement was wholly a matter of personal politics. There was a general demand for the removal of the capital from its early seat at Vandalia, and rivalry among other towns was keen. Sangamon County was bent on winning the prize for its own Springfield. Lincoln was put in charge of the Springfield strategy. How he played his cards may be judged from the recollections of another member who seems to have anticipated that noble political maxim, "What's the Constitution between friends?" "Lincoln," he says, "made Webb and me vote for the removal, though we belonged to the southern end of the state. We defended our vote before our constituents by saying that necessity would ultimately force the seat of government to a central position; but in reality, we gave the vote to Lincoln because we liked him, because we wanted to oblige our friend, and because we recognized him as our leader."(3)

And yet on the great issues of the day he could not lead them. In 1837, the movement of the militant abolitionists, still but a few years old, was beginning to set the Union by the ears. The illegitimate child of Calvinism and the rights of man, it damned with one anathema every holder of slaves and also every opponent of slavery except its own uncompromising adherents. Its animosity was trained particularly on every suggestion that designed to uproot slavery without creating an economic crisis, that would follow England's example, and terminate the "peculiar institution" by purchase. The religious side of abolition came out in its fury against such ideas. Slave-holders were Canaanites. The new cult were God's own people who were appointed to feel anew the joy of Israel hewing Agag asunder. Fanatics, terrible, heroic, unashamed, they made two sorts of enemies—not only the partisans of slavery, but all those sane reformers who, while hating slavery, hated also the blood-lust that would make the hewing of Agag a respectable device of political science. Among the partisans of slavery were the majority of the Illinois Legislature. Early in 1837, they passed resolutions condemning abolitionism. Whereupon it was revealed—not that anybody at the time cared to know the fact, or took it to heart—that among the other sort of the enemies of abolition was our good young friend, everybody's good friend, Abe Lincoln. He drew up a protest against the Legislature's action; but for all his personal influence in other affairs, he could persuade only one member to sign with him. Not his to command at will those who "recognized him as their leader" in the orthodox political game—so discreet, in that it left principles for some one else to be troubled about! Lincoln's protest was quite too far out of the ordinary for personal politics to endure it. The signers were asked to proclaim their belief "that the institution of slavery is founded on both injustice and bad policy; but that the promulgation of abolition doctrines tends rather to promote than to abate its evils."(4)

The singular originality of this position, sweeping aside as vain both participants in the new political duel, was quite lost on the little world in which Lincoln lived. For after-time it has the interest of a bombshell that failed to explode. It is the dawn of Lincoln's intellect. In his lonely inner life, this crude youth, this lover of books in a village where books were curiosities, had begun to think. The stages of his transition from mere story-telling yokel—intellectual only as the artist is intellectual, in his methods of handling—to the man of ideas, are wholly lost. And in this fact we have a prophecy of all the years to come. Always we shall seek in vain for the early stages of Lincoln's ideas. His mind will never reveal itself until the moment at which it engages the world. No wonder, in later times, his close associates pronounced him the most secretive of men; that one of the keenest of his observers said that the more you knew of Lincoln, the less you knew of him. (5)

Except for the handicap of his surroundings, his intellectual start would seem belated; even allowing for his handicap, it was certainly slow. He was now twenty-eight. Pretty well on to reveal for the first time intellectual power! Another characteristic here. His mind worked slowly. But it is worth observing that the ideas of the protest were never abandoned. Still a third characteristic, mental tenacity. To the end of his days, he looked askance at the temper of abolitionism, regarded it ever as one of the chief evils of political science. And quite as significant was another idea of the protest which also had developed from within, which also he never abandoned.

On the question of the power of the national government with regard to slavery, he took a position not in accord with either of the political creeds of his day. The Democrats had already formulated their doctrine that the national government was a thing of extremely limited powers, the "glorified policeman" of a certain school of publicists reduced almost to a minus quantity. The Whigs, though amiably vague on most things except money-making by state aid, were supposed to stand for a "strong central government". Abolitionism had forced on both parties a troublesome question, "What about slavery in the District of Columbia, where the national government was supreme?" The Democrats were prompt in their reply: Let the glorified policeman keep the peace and leave private interests, such as slave-holding, alone. The Whigs evaded, tried not to apply their theory of "strong" government; they were fearful lest they offend one part of their membership if they asserted that the nation had no right to abolish slavery in the District, fearful of offending others if they did not. Lincoln's protest asserted that "the Congress of the United States has the power, under the Constitution, to abolish slavery in the District of Columbia but the power ought not to be exercised, unless at the request of the District." In other words, Lincoln, when suddenly out of the storm and stress that followed Ann's death his mentality flashes forth, has an attitude toward political power that was not a consequence of his environment, that sets him apart as a type of man rare in the history of statesmanship. What other American politician of his day—indeed, very few politicians of any day— would have dared to assert at once the existence of a power and the moral obligation not to use it? The instinctive American mode of limiting power is to deny its existence. Our politicians so deeply distrust our temperament that whatever they may say for rhetorical effect, they will not, whenever there is any danger of their being taken at their word, trust anything to moral law. Their minds are normally mechanical. The specific, statutory limitation is the only one that for them has reality. The truth that temper in politics is as great a factor as law was no more comprehensible to the politicians of 1837 than, say Hamlet or The Last Judgment. But just this is what the crude young Lincoln understood. Somehow he had found it in the depths of his own nature. The explanation, if any, is to be found in his heredity. Out of the shadowy parts of him, beyond the limits of his or any man's conscious vision, dim, unexplored, but real and insistent as those forest recesses from which his people came, arise the two ideas: the faith in a mighty governing power; the equal faith that it should use its might with infinite tenderness, that it should be slow to compel results, even the result of righteousness, that it should be tolerant of human errors, that it should transform them slowly, gradually, as do the gradual forces of nature, as do the sun and the rain.

And such was to be the real Lincoln whenever he spoke out, to the end. His tonic was struck by his first significant utterance at the age of twenty-eight. How inevitable that it should have no significance to the congregation of good fellows who thought of him merely as one of their own sort, who put up with their friend's vagary, and speedily forgot it.

The moment was a dreary one in Lincoln's fortunes. By dint of much reading of borrowed books, he had succeeded in obtaining from the easy-going powers that were in those days, a license to practise law. In the spring of 1837 he removed to Springfield. He had scarcely a dollar in his pocket. Riding into Springfield on a borrowed horse, with all the property he owned, including his law books, in two saddlebags, he went to the only cabinet-maker in the town and ordered a single bedstead. He then went to the store of Joshua F. Speed. The meeting, an immensely eventful one for Lincoln, as well as a classic in the history of genius in poverty, is best told in Speed's words: "He came into my store, set his saddle-bags on the counter and inquired what the furnishings for a single bedstead would cost. I took slate and pencil, made a calculation and found the sum for furnishings complete, would amount to seventeen dollars in all. Said he: 'It is probably cheap enough, but I want to say that, cheap as it is, I have not the money to pay; but if you will credit me until Christmas, and my experiment here as a lawyer is a success, I will pay you then. If I fail in that I will probably never pay you at all.' The tone of his voice was so melancholy that I felt for him. I looked up at him and I thought then as I think now that I never saw so gloomy and melancholy a face in my life. I said to him: 'So small a debt seems to affect you so deeply, I think I can suggest a plan by which you will be able to attain your end without incurring any debt. I have a very large room and a very large double bed in it, which you are perfectly welcome to share with me if you choose.' 'Where is your room?' he asked. 'Up-stairs,' said I, pointing to the stairs leading from the store to my room.

Without saying a word, he took his saddle-bags on his arm, went upstairs, set them down on the floor, came down again, and with a face beaming with pleasure and smiles exclaimed, 'Well, Speed, I'm moved.'"(6)

This was the beginning of a friendship which appears to have been the only one of its kind Lincoln ever had. Late in life, with his gifted private secretaries, with one or two brilliant men whom he did not meet until middle age, he had something like intimate comradeship. But even they did not break the prevailing solitude of his inner life. His aloofness of soul became a fixed condition. The one intruder in that lonely inner world was Speed. In the great collection of Lincoln's letters none have the intimate note except the letters to Speed. And even these are not truly intimate with the exception of a single group inspired all by the same train of events. The deep, instinctive reserve of Lincoln's nature was incurable. The exceptional group of letters involve his final love-affair. Four years after his removal to Springfield, Lincoln became engaged to Miss Mary Todd. By that time he had got a start at the law and was no longer in grinding poverty. If not yet prosperous, he had acquired "prospects"—the strong likelihood of better things to come so dear to the buoyant heart of the early West.

Hospitable Springfield, some of whose best men had known him in the Legislature, opened its doors to him. His humble origin, his poor condition, were forgiven. In true Western fashion, he was frankly put on trial to show what was in him. If he could "make good" no further questions would be asked. And in every-day matters, his companionableness rose to the occasion. Male Springfield was captivated almost as easily as New Salem.

But all this was of the outer life. If the ferment within was constant between 1835 and 1840, the fact is lost in his taciturnity. But there is some evidence of a restless emotional life.

In the rebound after the woe following Ann's death, he had gone questing after happiness—such a real thing to him, now that he had discovered the terror of unhappiness—in a foolish half-hearted courtship of a bouncing, sensible girl named Mary Owens, who saw that he was not really in earnest, decided that he was deficient in those "little links that make up a woman's happiness," and sent him about his business—rather, on the whole, to his relief.(7) The affair with Miss Todd had a different tone from the other. The lady was of another world socially. The West in those days swarmed with younger sons, or the equivalents of younger sons, seeking their fortunes, whom sisters and cousins were frequently visiting.

Mary Todd was sister-in-law to a leading citizen of Springfield. Her origin was of Kentucky and Virginia, with definite claims to distinction. Though a family genealogy mounts as high as the sixth century, sober history is content with a grandfather and great grandfather who were military men of some repute, two great uncles who were governors, and another who was a cabinet minister. Rather imposing contrasted with the family tree of the child of Thomas Lincoln and Nancy Hanks! Even more significant was the lady's education. She had been to a school where young ladies of similar social pretensions were allowed to speak only the French language. She was keenly aware of the role marked out for her by destiny, and quite convinced that she would always in every way live up to it.

The course of her affair with Lincoln did not run smooth. There were wide differences of temperament; quarrels of some sort—just what, gossip to this day has busied itself trying to discover—and on January 1, 1841, the engagement was broken. Before the end of the month he wrote to his law partner apologizing for his inability to be coherent on business matters. "For not giving you a general summary of news, you must pardon me; it is not in my power to do so. I am now the most miserable man living. If what I feel were distributed to the whole human family, there would not be one cheerful face on earth. Whether I shall ever be better, I can not tell. I awfully forebode I shall not. To remain as I am is impossible. I must die or be better, it appears to me . . . a change of scene might help me."

His friend Speed became his salvation. Speed closed out his business and carried Lincoln off to visit his own relations in Kentucky. It was the devotion of Bowlin Green and his wife over again. But the psychology of the event was much more singular. Lincoln, in the inner life, had progressed a long way since the death of Ann, and the progress was mainly in the way of introspection, of self-analysis. He had begun to brood. As always, the change did not reveal itself until an event in the outward life called it forth like a rising ghost from the abyss of his silences. His friends had no suspicion that in his real self, beneath the thick disguise of his external sunniness, he was forever brooding, questioning, analyzing, searching after the hearts of things both within and without..

"In the winter of 1840 and 1841," writes Speed, "he was unhappy about the engagement to his wife—not being entirely satisfied that his heart was going with his hand. How much he suffered then on that account, none knew so well as myself; he disclosed his whole heart to me. In the summer of 1841 I became engaged to my wife. He was here on a visit when I courted her; and strange to say, something of the same feeling which I regarded as so foolish in him took possession of me, and kept me very unhappy from the time of my engagement until I was married. This will explain the deep interest he manifested in his letters on my account.... One thing is plainly discernible; if I had not been married and happy, far more happy than I ever expected to be, he would not have married."

Whether or not Speed was entirely right in his final conclusion, it is plain that he and Lincoln were remarkably alike in temperament; that whatever had caused the break in Lincoln's engagement was repeated in his friend's experience when the latter reached a certain degree of emotional tension; that this paralleling of Lincoln's own experience in the experience of the friend so like himself, broke tip for once the solitude of his inner life and delivered him from some dire inward terror. Both men were deeply introspective. Each had that overpowering sense of the emotional responsibilities of marriage, which is bred in the bone of certain hyper-sensitive types—at least in the Anglo-Saxon race. But neither realized this trait in himself until, having blithely pursued his impulse to the point of committal, his spiritual conscience suddenly awakened and he asked of his heart, "Do I truly love her? Am I perfectly sure the emotion is permanent?"

It is on this speculation that the unique group of the intimate letters to Speed are developed. They were written after Lincoln's return to Springfield, while Speed was wrestling with the demon of self-analysis. In the period which they cover, Lincoln delivered himself from that same demon and recovered Serenity. Before long he was writing: "I know what the painful point with you is at all times when you are unhappy; it is an apprehension that you do not love her as you should. What nonsense! How came you to court her? Was it because you thought she deserved it and that you had given her reason to expect it? If it was for that, why did not the same reason make you court Ann Todd, and at least twenty others of whom you can think, to whom it would apply with greater force than to her? Did you court her for her wealth? Why, you said she had none. But you say you reasoned yourself into it. What do you mean by that? Was it not that you found yourself unable to reason yourself out of it?" And much more of the same shrewd sensible sort,—a picture unintentionally of his own state of mind no less than of his friend's.

This strange episode reveals also that amid Lincoln's silences, while the outward man appeared engrossed in everyday matters, the inward man had been seeking religion. His failure to accept the forms of his mother's creed did not rest on any lack of the spiritual need. Though undefined, his religion glimmers at intervals through the Speed letters. When Speed's fiancee fell ill and her tortured lover was in a paroxysm of remorse and grief, Lincoln wrote: "I hope and believe that your present anxiety and distress about her health and her life must and will forever banish those horrid doubts which I know you sometimes felt as to the truth of your affection for her. If they can once and forever be removed (and I feel a presentment that the Almighty has sent your present affliction expressly for that object) surely nothing can come in their stead to fill their immeasurable measure of misery. . . Should she, as you fear, be destined to an early grave, it is indeed a great consolation to know she is so well prepared to meet it."

Again he wrote: "I was always superstitious. I believe God made me one of the instruments of bringing you and your Fanny together, which union I have no doubt lie had foreordained. Whatever He designs He will do for me yet. 'Stand still and see the salvation of the Lord' is my text now."

The duality in self-torture of these spiritual brethren endured in all about a year and a half, and closed with Speed's marriage. Lincoln was now entirely delivered from his demon. He wrote Speed a charming letter, serene, affectionate, touched with gentle banter, valiant though with a hint of disillusion as to their common type. "I tell you, Speed, our forebodings (for which you and I are peculiar) are all the worst sort of nonsense. . You say you much fear that that elysium of which you have dreamed so much is never to be realized. Well, if it shall not, I dare swear it will not be the fault of her who is now your wife. I have no doubt that it is the peculiar misfortune of both you and me to dream dreams of elysium far exceeding all that anything earthly can realize."(8)

V
PROSPERITY

How Lincoln's engagement was patched up is as delicious an uncertainty, from gossip's point of view, as how it had been broken off. Possibly, as many people have asserted, it was brought about by an event of which, in the irony of fate, Lincoln ever after felt ashamed.(1) An impulsive, not overwise politician, James Shields, a man of many peculiarities, was saucily lampooned in a Springfield paper by some jaunty girls, one of whom was Miss Todd.

Somehow, — the whole affair is very dim, — Lincoln acted as their literary adviser. Shields demanded the name of his detractor; Lincoln assumed the responsibility; a challenge followed. Lincoln was in a ridiculous position. He extricated himself by a device which he used more than once thereafter; he gravely proposed the impossible. He demanded conditions which would have made the duel a burlesque — a butcher's match with cavalry broadswords. But Shields, who was flawlessly literal, insisted. The two met and only on the dueling ground was the quarrel at last talked into oblivion by the seconds. Whether this was the cause of the reconciliation with Miss Todd, or a consequence, or had nothing to do with it, remains for the lovers of the unimportant to decide. The only sure fact in this connection is the marriage which took place November 4, 1842.(2)

Mrs. Lincoln's character has been much discussed. Gossip, though with very little to go on, has built up a tradition that the marriage was unhappy. If one were to believe the half of what has been put in print, one would have to conclude that the whole business was a wretched mistake; that Lincoln found married life intolerable because of the fussily dictatorial self-importance of his wife. But the authority for all these tales is meager. Not one is traceable to the parties themselves. Probably it will never be known till the end of time what is false in them, what true. About all that can be disengaged from this cloud of illusive witnesses is that Springfield wondered why Mary Todd married Lincoln. He was still poor; so poor that after marriage they lived at the Globe Tavern on four dollars a week. And the lady had been sought by prosperous men! The lowliness of Lincoln's origin went ill with her high notions of her family's importance. She was downright, high-tempered, dogmatic, but social; he was devious, slow to wrath, tentative, solitary; his very appearance, then as afterward, was against him. Though not the hideous man he was later made out to be—the "gorilla" of enemy caricaturists—he was rugged of feature, with a lower lip that tended to protrude. His immense frame was thin and angular; his arms were inordinately long; hands, feet and eyebrows were large; skin swarthy; hair coarse, black and generally unkempt. Only the amazing, dreamful eyes, and a fineness in the texture of the skin, redeemed the face and gave it distinction.(3) Why did precise, complacent Miss Todd pick out so strange a man for her mate? The story that she married him for ambition, divining what he was to be—like Jane Welsh in the conventional story of Carlyle—argues too much of the gift of prophecy. Whatever her motive, it is more than likely that she was what the commercialism of to-day would call an "asset." She had certain qualities that her husband lacked. For one, she had that intuition for the main chance which shallow people confound with practical judgment. Her soul inhabited the obvious; but within the horizon of the obvious she was shrewd, courageous and stubborn. Not any danger that Mary Lincoln would go wandering after dreams, visions, presences, such as were drifting ever in a ghostly procession at the back of her husband's mind. There was a danger in him that was to grow with the years, a danger that the outer life might be swamped by the inner, that the ghosts within might carry him away with them, away from fact—seeking-seeking. That this never occurred may be fairly credited, or at least very plausibly credited, to the firm-willed, the utterly matter-of-fact little person he had married. How far he enjoyed the mode of his safe-guarding is a fruitless speculation.

Another result that may, perhaps, be due to Mary Lincoln was the improvement in his fortunes. However, this may have had no other source than a distinguished lawyer whose keen eyes had been observing him since his first appearance in politics. Stephen T. Logan "had that old-fashioned, lawyer-like morality which was keenly intolerant of any laxity or slovenliness of mind or character." He had, "as he deserved, the reputation of being the best nisi prius lawyer in the state."(4) After watching the gifted but ill-prepared young attorney during several years, observing the power he had of simplification and convincingness in statement, taking the measure of his scrupulous honesty — these were ever Lincoln's strong cards as a lawyer — Logan made him the surprising offer of a junior partnership, which was instantly accepted. That was when his inner horizon was brightening, shortly before his marriage. A period of great mental energy followed, about the years 1842 and 1843. Lincoln threw himself into the task of becoming a real lawyer under Logan's direction. However, his zeal flagged after a time, and when the partnership ended four years later he had to some extent fallen back into earlier, less strenuous habits. "He permitted his partner to do all the studying in the preparation of cases, while he himself trusted to his general knowledge of the law and the inspiration of the surroundings to overcome the judge or the jury."(5) Though Lincoln was to undergo still another stimulation of the scholarly conscience before finding himself as a lawyer, the four years with Logan were his true student period. If the enthusiasm of the first year did not hold out, none the less he issued from that severe course of study a changed man, one who knew the difference between the learned lawyer and the unlearned. His own methods, to be sure, remained what they always continued to be, unsystematic, not to say slipshod. Even after he became president his lack of system was at times the despair of his secretaries.(6) Herndon, who succeeded Logan as his partner, and who admired both men, has a broad hint that Logan and Lincoln were not always an harmonious firm. A clash of political ambitions is part explanation; business methods another. "Logan was scrupulously exact and used extraordinary care in the preparation of papers. His words were well chosen, and his style of composition was stately and formal."(7) He was industrious and very thrifty, while Lincoln had "no money sense." It must have annoyed, if it did not exasperate his learned and formal partner, when Lincoln signed the firm name to such letters as this: "As to real estate, we can not attend to it. We are not real estate agents, we are lawyers. We recommend that you give the charge of it to Mr. Isaac S. Britton, a trustworthy man and one whom the Lord made on purpose for such business."(8)

Superficial observers, then and afterward, drew the conclusion that Lincoln was an idler. Long before, as a farm-hand, he had been called "bone idle."(9) And of the outer Lincoln, except under stress of need, or in spurts of enthusiasm, as in the earlier years with Logan, this reckless comment had its base of fact. The mighty energy that was in Lincoln, a tireless, inexhaustible energy, was inward, of the spirit; it did not always ramify into the sensibilities and inform his outer life. The connecting link of the two, his mere intelligence, though constantly obedient to demands of the outer life, was not susceptible of great strain except on demand of the spiritual vision. Hence his attitude toward the study of the law. It thrilled and entranced him, called into play all his powers—observation, reflection, intelligence—just so long as it appeared in his imagination a vast creative effort of the spiritual powers, of humanity struggling perilously to see justice done upon earth, to let reason and the will of God prevail. It lost its hold upon him the instant it became a thing of technicalities, of mere learning, of statutory dialectics.

The restless, inward Lincoln, dwelling deep among spiritual shadows, found other outlets for his energy during these years when he was establishing himself at the bar. He continued to be a voracious reader. And his reading had taken a skeptical turn. Volney and Paine were now his intimates. The wave of ultra-rationalism that went over America in the 'forties did not spare many corners of the land. In Springfield, as in so many small towns, it had two effects: those who were not touched by it hardened into jealous watchfulness, and their religion naturally enough became fiercely combative; those who responded to the new influence became a little affected philosophically, a bit effervescent. The young men, when of serious mind, and all those who were reformers by temperament, tended to exalt the new, to patronize, if not to ridicule the old. At Springfield, as at many another frontier town wracked by its growing pains, a Young Men's Lyceum confessed the world to be out of joint, and went to work glibly to set it right. Lincoln had contributed to its achievements. An oration of his on "Perpetuation of Our Free Institutions,"(10) a mere rhetorical "stunt" in his worst vein now deservedly forgotten, so delighted the young men that they asked to have it printed—quite as the same sort of young men to-day print essays on cubism, or examples of free verse read to poetry societies. Just what views he expressed on things in general among the young men and others; how far he aired his acquaintance with the skeptics, is imperfectly known. (11) However, a rumor got abroad that he was an "unbeliever," which was the easy label for any one who disagreed in religion with the person who applied it. The rumor was based in part on a passage in an address on temperance. In 1842, Lincoln, who had always been abstemious, joined that Washington Society which aimed at a reformation in the use of alcohol. His address was delivered at the request of the society. It contained this passage, very illuminating in its light upon the generosity, the real humility of the speaker, but scarcely tactful, considering the religious susceptibility of the hour: "If they (the Christians) believe as they profess, that Omnipotence condescended to take on himself the form of sinful man, and as such die an ignominious death, surely they will not refuse submission to the infinitely lesser condescension for the temporal and perhaps eternal salvation of a large, erring and unfortunate class of their fellow creatures! Nor is the condescension very great. In my judgment such of us as have never fallen victims have been spared more from the absence of appetite than from any mental or moral superiority over those who have. Indeed, I believe, if we take habitual drunkards as a class, their heads and their hearts will bear an advantageous comparison with those of any other class."(12) How like that remark attributed to another great genius, one whom Lincoln in some respects resembled, the founder of Methodism, when he said of a passing drunkard: "There goes John Wesley, except for the Grace of God." But the frontier zealots of the 'forties were not of the Wesley type. The stories of Lincoln's skeptical interests, the insinuations which were promptly read into this temperance address, the fact that he was not a church-member, all these were seized upon by a good but very narrow man, a devoted, illiterate evangelist, Peter Cartwright.

In 1846, this religious issue became a political issue. The Whigs nominated Lincoln for Congress. It was another instance of personal politics. The local Whig leaders had made some sort of private agreement, the details of which appear to be lost, but according to which Lincoln now became the inevitable candidate.(13) He was nominated without opposition. The Democrats nominated Cartwright.

Two charges were brought against Lincoln: that he was an infidel, and that he was — of all things in the world! — an aristocrat. On these charges the campaign was fought. The small matter of what he would do at Washington, or would not do, was brushed aside. Personal politics with a vengeance! The second charge Lincoln humorously and abundantly disproved; the first, he met with silence.

Remembering Lincoln's unfailing truthfulness, remembering also his restless ambition, only one conclusion can be drawn from this silence. He could not categorically deny Cartwright's accusation and at the same time satisfy his own unsparing conception of honesty. That there was no real truth in the charge of irreligion, the allusions in the Speed letters abundantly prove. The tone is too sincere to be doubted; nevertheless, they give no clue to his theology. And for men like Cartwright, religion was tied up hand and foot in theology. Here was where Lincoln had parted company from his mother's world, and from its derivatives. Though he held tenaciously to all that was mystical in her bequest to him, he rejected early its formulations. The evidence of later years reaffirms this double fact. The sense of a spiritual world behind, beyond the world of phenomena, grew on him with the years; the power to explain, to formulate that world was denied him. He had no bent for dogma. Ethically, mystically, he was always a Christian; dogmatically he knew not what he was. Therefore, to the challenge to prove himself a Christian on purely dogmatic grounds, he had no reply. To attempt to explain what separated him from his accusers, to show how from his point of view they were all Christian—although, remembering their point of view, he hesitated to say so—to draw the line between mysticism and emotionalism, would have resulted only in a worse confusion. Lincoln, the tentative mystic, the child of the starlit forest, was as inexplicable to Cartwright with his perfectly downright religion, his creed of heaven or hell—take your choice and be quick about it!—as was Lincoln the spiritual sufferer to New Salem, or Lincoln the political scientist to his friends in the Legislature.

But he was not injured by his silence. The faith in him held by too many people was too well established. Then, as always thereafter, whatever he said or left unsaid, most thoughtful persons who came close to him sensed him as a religious man. That was enough for healthy, generous young Springfield. He and Cartwright might fight out their religious issues when they pleased, Abe should have his term in Congress. He was elected by a good majority.(14)

VI
UNSATISFYING RECOGNITION

Lincoln's career as a Congressman, 1847-1849, was just what might have been expected — his career in the Illinois Legislature on a larger scale. It was a pleasant, companionable, unfruitful episode, with no political significance. The leaders of the party did not take him seriously as a possible initiate to their ranks. His course was that of a loyal member of the Whig mass. In the party strategy, during the debates over the Mexican War and the Wilmot Proviso, he did his full party duty, voting just as the others did. Only once did he attempt anything original — a bill to emancipate the slaves of the District, which was little more than a restatement of his protest of ten years before — and on this point Congress was as indifferent as the Legislature had been. The bill was denied a hearing and never came to a vote before the House.(1)

And yet Lincoln did not fail entirely to make an impression at Washington. And again it was the Springfield experience repeated. His companionableness was recognized, his modesty, his good nature; above all, his story-telling. Men liked him. Plainly it was his humor, his droll ways, that won them; together with instant recognition of his sterling integrity.

"During the Christmas holidays," says Ben Perley Poore, "Mr. Lincoln found his way into the small room used as the Post Office of the House, where a few genial reconteurs used to meet almost every morning after the mail had been distributed into the members' boxes, to exchange such new stories as any of them might have acquired since they had last met. After modestly standing at the door for several days, Mr. Lincoln was reminded of a story, and by New Year's he was recognized as the champion story-teller of the Capital. His favorite seat was at the left of the open fireplace, tilted back in his chair with his long legs reaching over to the chimney jamb."(2)

In the words of another contemporary, "Congressman Lincoln was very fond of howling and would frequently. . . meet other members in a match game at the alley of James Casparus. . . . He was an awkward bowler, but played the game with great zest and spirit solely for exercise and amusement, and greatly to the enjoyment and entertainment of the other players, and by reason of his criticisms and funny illustrations. . . . When it was known that he was in the alley, there would assemble numbers of people to witness the fun which was anticipated by those who knew of his fund of anecdotes and jokes. When in the alley, surrounded by a crowd of eager listeners, he indulged with great freedom in the sport of narrative, some of which were very broad."(3)

Once, at least, he entertained Congress with an exhibition of his humor, and this, oddly enough, is almost the only display of it that has come down to us, first hand. Lincoln's humor has become a tradition. Like everything else in his outward life, it changed gradually with his slow devious evolution from the story-teller of Pigeon Creek to the author of the Gettysburg Oration. It is known chiefly through translation. The "Lincoln Stories" are stories someone else has told who may or may not have heard them told by Lincoln. They are like all translations, they express the translator not the original—final evidence that Lincoln's appeal as a humorist was in his manner, his method, not in his substance. "His laugh was striking. Such awkward gestures belonged to no other man. They attracted universal attention from the old sedate down to the schoolboy."(4) He was a famous mimic.

Lincoln is himself the authority that he did not invent his stories. He picked them up wherever he found them, and clothed them with the peculiar drollery of his telling. He was a wag rather than a wit. All that lives in the second-hand repetitions of his stories is the mere core, the original appropriated thing from which the inimitable decoration has fallen off. That is why the collections of his stories are such dreary reading,—like Carey's Dante, or Bryant's Homer. And strange to say, there is no humor in his letters. This man who was famous as a wag writes to his friends almost always in perfect seriousness, often sadly. The bit of humor that has been preserved in his one comic speech in Congress,—a burlesque of the Democratic candidate of 1848, Lewis Cass,—shorn as it is of his manner, his tricks of speech and gesture, is hardly worth repeating.(5)

Lincoln was deeply humiliated by his failure to make a serious impression at Washington.(6) His eyes opened in a startled realization that there were worlds he could not conquer. The Washington of the 'forties was far indeed from a great capital; it was as friendly to conventional types of politician as was Springfield or Vandalia. The man who could deal in ideas as political counters, the other man who knew the subtleties of the art of graft, both these were national as well as local figures. Personal politics were also as vicious at Washington as anywhere; nevertheless, there was a difference, and in that difference lay the secret of Lincoln's failure. He was keen enough to grasp the difference, to perceive the clue to his failure. In a thousand ways, large and small, the difference came home to him. It may all be symbolized by a closing detail of his stay. An odd bit of incongruity was the inclusion of his name in the list of managers of the Inaugural Ball of 1849. Nothing of the sort had hitherto entered into his experience. As Mrs. Lincoln was not with him he joined "a small party of mutual friends" who attended the ball together. As one of them relates, "he was greatly interested in all that was to be seen and we did not take our departure until three or four o'clock in the morning."(7) What an ironic picture—this worthy provincial, the last word for awkwardness, socially as strange to such a scene as a little child, spending the whole night gazing intently at everything he could see, at the barbaric display of wealth, the sumptuous gowns, the brilliant uniforms, the distinguished foreigners, and the leaders of America, men like Webster and Clay, with their air of assured power, the men he had failed to impress. This was his valedictory at Washington. He went home and told Herndon that he had committed political suicide.(8) He had met the world and the world was too strong for him.

And yet, what was wrong? He had been popular at Washington, in the same way in which he had been popular at Springfield. Why had the same sort of success inspired him at Springfield and humiliated him at Washington? The answer was in the difference between the two worlds. Companionableness, story-telling, at Springfield, led to influence; at Washington it led only to applause. At Springfield it was a means; at Washington it was an end. The narrow circle gave the good fellow an opportunity to reveal at his leisure everything else that was in him; the larger circle ruthlessly put him in his place as a good fellow and nothing more. The truth was that in the Washington of the 'forties, neither the inner nor the outer Lincoln could by itself find lodgment. Neither the lonely mystical thinker nor the captivating buffoon could do more than ripple its surface. As superficial as Springfield, it lacked Springfield's impulsive generosity. To the long record of its obtuseness it had added another item. The gods had sent it a great man and it had no eyes to see. It was destined to repeat the performance.

And so Lincoln came home, disappointed, disillusioned. He had not succeeded in establishing the slightest claim, either upon the country or his party. Without such claim he had no ground for attempting reelection. The frivolity of the Whig machine in the Sangamon region was evinced by their rotation agreement. Out of such grossly personal politics Lincoln had gone to Washington; into this essentially corrupt system he relapsed. He faced, politically, a blank wall. And he had within him as yet, no consciousness of any power that might cleave the wall asunder. What was he to do next?

At this dangerous moment—so plainly the end of a chapter—he was offered the governorship of the new Territory of Oregon. For the first time he found himself at a definite parting of the ways, where a sheer act of will was to decide things; where the pressure of circumstance was of secondary importance.

In response to this crisis, an overlooked part of him appeared. The inheritance from his mother, from the forest, had always been obvious. But, after all, he was the son not only of Nancy and of the lonely stars, but also of shifty, drifty Thomas the unstable. If it was not his paternal inheritance that revived in him at this moment of confessed failure, it was something of the same sort. Just as Thomas had always by way of extricating himself from a failure taken to the road, now Abraham, at a psychological crisis, felt the same wanderlust, and he threatened to go adrift. Some of his friends urged him to accept. "You will capture the new community," said they, "and when Oregon becomes a State, you will go to Washington as its first Senator." What a glorified application of the true Thomasian line of thought. Lincoln hesitated—hesitated—

And then the forcible little lady who had married him put her foot down. Go out to that far-away backwoods, just when they were beginning to get on in the world; when real prosperity at Springfield was surely within their grasp; when they were at last becoming people of importance, who should be able to keep their own carriage? Not much!

Her husband declined the appointment and resumed the practice of law in Springfield.(9)

VII
THE SECOND START

Stung by his failure at Washington, Lincoln for a time put his whole soul into the study of the law. He explained his failure to himself as a lack of mental training.(1) There followed a repetition of his early years with Logan, but with very much more determination, and with more abiding result.

In those days in Illinois, as once in England, the judges held court in a succession of towns which formed a circuit. Judge and lawyers moved from town to town, "rode the circuit" in company,—sometimes on horseback, sometimes in their own vehicles, sometimes by stage. Among the reminiscences of Lincoln on the circuit, are his "poky" old horse and his "ramshackle" old buggy. Many and many a mile, round and round the Eighth Judicial Circuit, he traveled in that humble style. What thoughts he brooded on in his lonely drives, he seldom told. During this period the cloud over his inner life is especially dense. The outer life, in a multitude of reminiscences, is well known. One of its salient details was the large proportion of time he devoted to study.

"Frequently, I would go out on the circuit with him," writes Herndon. "We, usually, at the little country inn, occupied the same bed. In most cases, the beds were too short for him and his feet would hang over the footboard, thus exposing a limited expanse of shin bone. Placing his candle at the head of his bed he would read and study for hours. I have known him to stay in this position until two o'clock in the morning. Meanwhile, I and others who chanced to occupy the same room would be safely and soundly asleep. On the circuit, in this way, he studied Euclid until he could with ease demonstrate all the propositions in the six books. How he could maintain his equilibrium or concentrate his thoughts on an abstract mathematical problem, while Davis, Logan, Swett, Edwards and I, so industriously and volubly filled the air with our interminable snoring, was a problem none of, us—could ever solve."(2)

A well-worn copy of Shakespeare was also his constant companion.

He rose rapidly in the profession; and this in spite of his incorrigible lack of system. The mechanical side of the lawyer's task, now, as in the days with Logan, annoyed him; he left the preparation of papers to his junior partner, as formerly he left it to his senior partner. But the situation had changed in a very important way. In Herndon, Lincoln had for a partner a talented young man who looked up to him, almost adored him, who was quite willing to be his man Friday. Fortunately, for all his adoration, Herndon had no desire to idealize his hero. He was not disturbed by his grotesque or absurd sides.

"He was proverbially careless as to his habits," Herndon writes. "In a letter to a fellow lawyer in another town, apologizing for his failure to answer sooner, he explains: 'First, I have been very busy in the United States Court; second, when I received the letter, I put it in my old hat, and buying a new one the next day, the old one was set aside, so the letter was lost sight of for the time.' This hat of Lincoln's—a silk plug—was an extraordinary receptacle. It was his desk and his memorandum book. In it he carried his bank-book and the bulk of his letters. Whenever in his reading or researches, he wished to preserve an idea, he jotted it down on an envelope or stray piece of paper and placed it inside the lining; afterwards, when the memorandum was needed, there was only one place to look for it." Herndon makes no bones about confessing that their office was very dirty. So neglected was it that a young man of neat habits who entered the office as a law student under Lincoln could not refrain from cleaning it up, and the next visitor exclaimed in astonishment, "What's happened here!" (3)

"The office," says that same law student, "was on the second floor of a brick building on the public square opposite the courthouse. You went up a flight of stairs and then passed along a hallway to the rear office which was a medium sized room. There was one long table in the center of the room, and a shorter one running in the opposite direction forming a T and both were covered with green baize. There were two windows which looked into the back yard. In one corner was an old-fashioned secretary with pigeonholes and a drawer; and here Mr. Lincoln and his partner kept their law papers. There was also a bookcase containing about two hundred volumes of law and miscellaneous books." The same authority adds, "There was no order in the office at all." Lincoln left all the money matters to Herndon. "He never entered an item on the account book. If a fee was paid to him and Herndon was not there, he would divide the money, wrap up one part in paper and place it in his partner's desk with the inscription, 'Case of Roe versus Doe, Herndon's half.' He had an odd habit of reading aloud much to his partner's annoyance. He talked incessantly; a whole forenoon would sometimes go by while Lincoln occupied the whole time telling stories."(4)

On the circuit, his story-telling was an institution. Two other men, long since forgotten, vied with him as rival artists in humorous narrative. These three used to hold veritable tournaments. Herndon has seen "the little country tavern where these three were wont to meet after an adjournment of court, crowded almost to suffocation, with an audience of men who had gathered to witness the contest among the members of the strange triumvirate. The physicians of the town, all the lawyers, and not infrequently a preacher, could be found in the crowd that filled the doors and windows. The yarns they spun and the stories they told would not bear repetition here, but many of them had morals which, while exposing the weakness of mankind, stung like a whiplash. Some were, no doubt, a thousand years old, with just enough of verbal varnish and alterations of names and date to make them new and crisp. By virtue of the last named application, Lincoln was enabled to draw from Balzac a 'droll story' and locating it 'in Egypt' (Southern Illinois) or in Indiana, pass it off for a purely original conception. . . I have seen Judge Treat, who was the very impersonation of gravity itself, sit up till the last and laugh until, as he often expressed it, 'he almost shook his ribs loose.' The next day he would ascend the bench and listen to Lincoln in a murder trial with all the seeming severity of an English judge in wig and gown."(5)

Lincoln enjoyed the life on the circuit. It was not that he was always in a gale of spirits; a great deal of the time he brooded. His Homeric nonsense alternated with fits of gloom. In spite of his late hours, whether of study or of story-telling, he was an early riser. "He would sit by the fire having uncovered the coals, and muse and ponder and soliloquize."(6) Besides his favorite Shakespeare, he had a fondness for poetry of a very different sort — Byron, for example. And he never tired of a set of stanzas in the minor key beginning: "Oh, why should the spirit of mortal be proud?"(7)

The hilarity of the circuit was not by any means the whole of its charm for him. Part of that charm must have been the contrast with his recent failure at Washington. This world he could master. Here his humor increased his influence; and his influence grew rapidly. He was a favorite of judges, jury and the bar. Then, too, it was a man's world. Though Lincoln had a profound respect for women, he seems generally to have been ill at ease in their company. In what his friends would have called "general society" he did not shine. He was too awkward, too downright, too lacking in the niceties. At home, though he now owned a house and was making what seemed to him plenty of money, he was undoubtedly a trial to Mrs. Lincoln's sense of propriety. He could not rise with his wife, socially. He was still what he had become so long before, the favorite of all the men — good old Abe Lincoln that you could tie to though it rained cats and dogs. But as to the ladies! Fashionable people calling on Mrs. Lincoln, had been received by her husband in his shirt-sleeves, and he totally unabashed, as oblivious of discrepancy as if he were a nobleman and not a nobody.(8) The dreadful tradition persists that he had been known at table to put his own knife into the butter.

How safe to assume that many things were said commiserating poor Mrs. Lincoln who had a bear for a husband. And some people noticed that Lincoln did not come home at week-ends during term-time as often as he might. Perhaps it meant something; perhaps it did not. But there could be no doubt that the jovial itinerant life of the circuit was the life for him — at least in the early 'fifties. That it was, and also that he was becoming known as a lawyer, is evinced by his refusal of a flattering invitation to enter a prosperous firm in Chicago.

Out of all this came a deepening of his power to reach and impress men through words. The tournament of the story-tellers was a lawyers' tournament. The central figure was reading, studying, thinking, as never in his life before. Though his fables remained as broad as ever, the merely boisterous character ceased to predominate. The ethical bent of his mind came to the surface. His friends were agreed that what they remembered chiefly of his stories was not the broad part of them, but the moral that was in them.(9) And they had no squeamishness as critics of the art of fable-making.

His ethical sense of things, his companionableness, the utterly non-censorious cast of his mind, his power to evolve yarns into parables — all these made him irresistible with a jury. It was a saying of his: "If I can divest this case of technicalities and swing it to the jury, I'll win it."(10)

But there was not a trace in him of that unscrupulousness usually attributed to the "jury lawyer." Few things show more plainly the central unmovableness of his character than his immunity to the lures of jury speaking. To use his power over an audience for his own enjoyment, for an interested purpose, for any purpose except to afford pleasure, or to see justice done, was for him constitutionally impossible. Such a performance was beyond the reach of his will. In a way, his nature, mysterious as it was, was also the last word for simplicity, a terrible simplicity. The exercise of his singular powers was irrevocably conditioned on his own faith in the moral justification of what he was doing. He had no patience with any conception of the lawyer's function that did not make him the devoted instrument of justice. For the law as a game, for legal strategy, he felt contempt. Never under any conditions would he attempt to get for a client more than he was convinced the client in justice ought to have. The first step in securing his services was always to persuade him that one's cause was just He sometimes threw up a case in open court because the course of it had revealed deception on the part of the client. At times he expressed his disdain of the law's mere commercialism in a stinging irony.

"In a closely contested civil suit," writes his associate, Ward Hill Lamon, "Lincoln proved an account for his client, who was, though he did not know it at the time, a very slippery fellow. The opposing attorney then proved a receipt clearly covering the entire cause of action. By the time he was through Lincoln was missing. The court sent for him to the hotel. 'Tell the Judge,' said he, 'that I can't come; my hands are dirty and I came over to clean them.'"(11)

"Discourage litigation," he wrote. "Persuade your neighbors to compromise whenever you can. Point out to them how the nominal winner is often a real loser, in fees, expenses, and waste of time. As a peacemaker, the lawyer has a Superior Opportunity of being a good man. There will still be business enough."(12)

He held his moral and professional views with the same inflexibility with which he held his political views. Once he had settled upon a conviction or an opinion, nothing could move him. He was singularly stubborn, and yet, in all the minor matters of life, in all his merely personal concerns, in everything except his basal ideas, he was pliable to a degree. He could be talked into almost any concession of interest. He once told Herndon he thanked God that he had not been born a woman because he found it so hard to refuse any request made of him. His outer easiness, his lack of self-assertion,—as most people understand self-assertion,—persist in an amusing group of anecdotes of the circuit. Though he was a favorite with the company at every tavern, those little demagogues, the tavern-keepers, quickly found out that he could be safely put upon. In the minute but important favoritism of tavern life, in the choice of rooms, in the assignment of seats at table, in the distribution of delicacies, easy-going Lincoln was ever the first one to be ignored. "He never complained of the food, bed, or lodgings," says a judge of the circuit, David Davis. "If every other fellow grumbled at the bill of fare which greeted us at many of the dingy taverns, Lincoln said nothing."(13)

But his complacency was of the surface only. His ideas were his own. He held to them with dogged tenacity. Herndon was merely the first of several who discerned on close familiarity Lincoln's inward inflexibility. "I was never conscious," he writes, "of having made much of an impression on Mr. Lincoln, nor do I believe I ever changed his views. I will go further and say that from the profound nature of his conclusions and the labored method by which he arrived at them, no man is entitled to the credit of having either changed or greatly modified them."(14)

In these years of the early 'fifties, Herndon had much occasion to test his partner's indifference to other men's views, his tenacious adherence to his own. Herndon had become an Abolitionist. He labored to convert Lincoln; but it was a lost labor. The Sphinx in a glimmer of sunshine was as unassailable as the cheery, fable-loving, inflexible Lincoln. The younger man would work himself up, and, flushed with ardor, warn Lincoln against his apparent conservatism when the needs of the hour were so great; but his only answer would be, "Billy, you are too rampant and spontaneous."(15)

Nothing could move him from his fixed conviction that the temper of Abolitionism made it pernicious. He persisted in classifying it with slavery,—both of equal danger to free institutions. He took occasion to reassert this belief in the one important utterance of a political nature that commemorates this period. An oration on the death of Henry Clay, contains the sentence: "Cast into life when slavery was already widely spread and deeply sealed, he did not perceive, as I think no wise man has perceived, how it could be at once eradicated without producing a greater evil even to the cause of human liberty itself."(16)

It will be remembered that the Abolitionists were never strongly national in sentiment. In certain respects they remind one of the extreme "internationals" of to-day. Their allegiance was not first of all to Society, nor to governments, but to abstract ideas. For all such attitudes in political science,

Lincoln had an instinctive aversion. He was permeated always, by his sense of the community, of the obligation to work in terms of the community. Even the prejudices, the shortsightedness of the community were things to be considered, to be dealt with tenderly. Hence his unwillingness to force reforms upon a community not ripe to receive them. In one of his greatest speeches occurs the dictum: "A universal feeling whether well or ill-founded, can not be safely disregarded."(17) Anticipating such ideas, he made in his Clay oration, a startling denunciation of both the extreme factions of

"Those (Abolitionists) who would shiver into fragments the union of these States, tear to tatters its now 'venerated Constitution, and even burn the last copy of the Bible rather than slavery should continue a single hour; together with all their more halting sympathizers, have received and are receiving their just execration; and the name and opinion and influence of Mr. Clay are fully and, as I trust, effectually and enduringly arrayed against them. But I would also if I could, array his name, opinion and influence against the opposite extreme, against a few, but increasing number of men who, for the sake of perpetuating slavery, are beginning to assail and ridicule the white man's charter of freedom, the declaration that 'all men are created free and equal.'"(18)

In another passage he stated what he conceived to be the central inspiration of Clay. Had he been thinking of himself, he could not have foreshadowed more exactly the basal drift of all his future as a statesman:

"He loved his country partly because it was his own country, and mostly because it was a free country; and he burned with a zeal for its advancement, prosperity, and glory, because he saw in such the advancement, prosperity and glory of human liberty, human right and human nature."(19)

VIII
A RETURN TO POLITICS

Meanwhile, great things were coming forward at Washington. They centered about a remarkable man with whom Lincoln had hitherto formed a curious parallel, by whom hitherto he had been completely overshadowed. Stephen Arnold Douglas was prosecuting attorney at Springfield when Lincoln began the practice of law. They were in the Legislature together. Both courted Mary Todd. Soon afterward, Douglas had distanced his rival. When Lincoln went to the House of Representatives as a Whig, Douglas went to the Senate as a Democrat. While Lincoln was failing at Washington, Douglas was building a national reputation. In the hubbub that followed the Compromise of 1850, while Lincoln, abandoning politics, immersed himself in the law, Douglas rendered a service to the country by defeating a movement in Illinois to reject the Compromise. When the Democratic National Convention assembled in 1852, he was sufficiently prominent to obtain a considerable vote for the presidential nomination.

The dramatic contrast of these two began with their physical appearance. Douglas was so small that he had been known to sit on a friend's knee while arguing politics. But his energy of mind, his indomitable force of character, made up for his tiny proportions. "The Little Giant" was a term of endearment applied to him by his followers. The mental contrast was equally marked. Scarcely a quality in Lincoln that was not reversed in Douglas—deliberation, gradualness, introspection, tenacity, were the characteristics of Lincoln's mind. The mind of Douglas was first of all facile. He was extraordinarily quick. In political Strategy he could sense a new situation, wheel to meet it, throw overboard well-established plans, devise new ones, all in the twinkle of an eye. People who could not understand such rapidity of judgment pronounced him insincere, or at least, an opportunist. That he did not have the deep inflexibility of Lincoln may be assumed; that his convictions, such as they were, did not have an ethical cast may be safely asserted. Nevertheless, he was a great force, an immense human power, that did not change its course without good reason of its own sort. Far more than a mere opportunist. Politically, he summed up a change that was coming over the Democratic party. Janus-like, he had two faces, one for his constituents, one for his colleagues. To the voter he was still a Jeffersonian, with whom the old phraseology of the party, liberty, equality, and fraternity, were still the catch-words. To his associates in the Senate he was essentially an aristocrat, laboring to advance interests that were careless of the rights of man. A later age has accused the Senate of the United States of being the citadel of Big Business. Waiving the latter view, the historian may assert that something suggestive of Big Business appeared in our politics in the 'fifties, and was promptly made at home in the Senate. Perhaps its first definite manifestation was a new activity on the part of the great slave-holders. To invoke again the classifications of later points of view, certain of our historians to-day think they can see in the 'fifties a virtual slavery trust, a combine of slave interests controlled by the magnates of the institution, and having as real, though informal, an existence as has the Steel Trust or the Beef Trust in our own time. This powerful interest allied itself with the capitalists of the Northeast. In modern phraseology, they aimed to "finance" the slave interest from New York. And for a time the alliance succeeded in doing this. The South went entirely upon credit. It bought and borrowed heavily in the East New York furnished the money.

Had there been nothing further to consider, the invasion of the Senate by Big Business in the 'fifties might not have taken place. But there was something else. Slavery's system of agriculture was excessively wasteful. To be highly profitable it required virgin soil, and the financial alliance demanded high profits. Early in the 'fifties, the problem of Big Business was the acquisition of fresh soil for slavery. The problem entered politics with the question how could this be brought about without appearing to contradict democracy? The West also had its incipient Big Business. It hinged upon railways. Now that California had been acquired, with a steady stream of migration westward, with all America dazzled more or less by gold-mines and Pacific trade, a transcontinental railway was a Western dream. But what course should it take, what favored regions were to become its immediate beneficiaries? Here was a chance for great jockeying among business interests in Congress, for slave-holders, money-lenders, railway promoters to manipulate deals to their hearts' content. They had been doing so amid a high complication of squabbling, while Douglas was traveling in Europe during 1853. When he returned late in the year, the unity of the Democratic machine in Congress was endangered by these disputes. Douglas at once attacked the problem of party harmony. He threw himself into the task with all his characteristic quickness, all his energy and resourcefulness.

By this time the problem contained five distinct factors: The upper Northeast wanted a railroad starting at Chicago. The Central West wanted a road from St. Louis. The Southwest wanted a road from New Orleans, or at least, the frustration of the two Northern schemes. Big Business wanted new soil for slavery. The Compromise of 1850 stood in the way of the extension of slave territory.

If Douglas had had any serious convictions opposed to slavery the last of the five factors would have brought him to a standstill. Fortunately for him as a party strategist, he was indifferent. Then, too, he firmly believed that slavery could never thrive in the West because of climatic conditions. "Man might propose, but physical geography would dispose."(1) On both counts it seemed to him immaterial what concessions be made to slavery extension northwestward. Therefore, he dismissed this consideration and applied himself to the harmonization of the four business factors involved. The result was a famous compromise inside a party. His Kansas-Nebraska Bill created two new territories, one lying westward from Chicago; one lying westward from St. Louis. It also repealed the Missouri Compromise and gave the inhabitants of each territory the right to decide for themselves whether or not slavery should be permitted in their midst. That is to say, both to the railway promoter and the slavery financier, it extended equal governmental protection, but it promised favors to none, and left each faction to rise or fall in the free competition of private enterprise. Why — was not this, remembering Douglas's assumptions, a master-stroke?

He had expected, of course, denunciation by the Abolitionists. He considered it immaterial. But he was not in the least prepared for what happened. A storm burst. It was fiercest in his own State. "Traitor," "Arnold," "Judas," were the pleasant epithets fired at him in a bewildering fusillade. He could not understand it. Something other than mere Abolitionism had been aroused by his great stroke. But what was it? Why did men who were not Abolitionists raise a hue and cry? Especially, why did many Democrats do so? Amazed, puzzled, but as always furiously valiant, Douglas hurried home to join battle with his assailants. He entered on a campaign of speech-making. On October 3, 1854, he spoke at Springfield. His enemies, looking about for the strongest popular speaker they could find, chose Lincoln. The next day he replied to Douglas.

The Kansas-Nebraska Bill had not affected any change in Lincoln's thinking. His steady, consistent development as a political thinker had gone on chiefly in silence ever since his Protest seventeen years before. He was still intolerant of Abolitionism, still resolved to leave slavery to die a natural death in the States where it was established. He defended the measure which most offended the Abolitionists, the Fugitive Slave Law. He had appeared as counsel for a man who claimed a runaway slave as his property.(2) None the less, the Kansas-Nebraska Bill had brought him to his feet, wheeled him back from law into politics, begun a new chapter. The springs of action in is case were the factor which Douglas had overlooked, which in all his calculations he had failed to take into account, which was destined to destroy him.

Lincoln, no less than Douglas, had sensed the fact that money was becoming a power in American politics. He saw that money and slavery tended to become allies with the inevitable result of a shift of gravity in the American social system. "Humanity" had once been the American shibboleth; it was giving place to a new shibboleth-"prosperity." And the people who were to control and administer prosperity were the rich. The rights of man were being superseded by the rights of wealth. Because of its place in this new coalition of non-democratic influences, slavery, to Lincoln's mind, was assuming a new role, "beginning," as he had said, in the Clay oration, "to assail and ridicule the white man's charter of freedom, the declaration that 'all men are created free and equal.'"

That phrase, "the white man's charter of freedom," had become Lincoln's shibboleth. Various utterances and written fragments of the summer of 1854, reveal the intensity of his preoccupation.

"Equality in society beats inequality, whether the latter be of the British aristocratic sort or of the domestic slavery sort"(3)

"If A can prove, however conclusively, that he may of right enslave B, why may not B snatch the same argument and prove equally that he may enslave A? You say A is white and B is black. It is color then; the lighter having the right to enslave the darker? Take care. By this rule you are to be slave to the first man you meet with a fairer skin than your own. You do not mean color exactly? You mean the whites are intellectually the superiors of the blacks, and therefore have the right to enslave them? Take care again. By this rule you are to be slave to the first man you meet with an intellect superior to your own. But, you say, it is a question of interest, and if you make it your interest, you have the right to enslave another. Very well. And if he can make it his interest, he has the right to enslave you."(4)

Speaking of slavery to a fellow lawyer, he said: "It is the most glittering, ostentatious, and displaying property in the world; and now, if a young man goes courting, the only inquiry is how many negroes he or his lady love owns. The love of slave property is swallowing up every other mercenary possession. Its ownership betokened not only the possession of wealth, but indicated the gentleman of leisure who was above and scorned labor."(5)

It was because of these views, because he saw slavery allying itself with the spread of plutocratic ideals, that Lincoln entered the battle to prevent its extension. He did so in his usual cool, determined way.

Though his first reply to Douglas was not recorded, his second, made at Peoria twelve days later, still exists.(6) It is a landmark in his career. It sums up all his long, slow development in political science, lays the abiding foundation of everything he thought thereafter. In this great speech, the end of his novitiate, he rings the changes on the white man's charter of freedom. He argues that the extension of slavery tends to discredit republican institutions, and to disappoint "the Liberal party throughout the world." The heart of his argument is:

"Whether slavery shall go into Nebraska or other new Territories is not a matter of exclusive concern to the people who may go there. The whole nation is interested that the best use shall be made of these Territories. We want them for homes for free white people. This they can not be to any considerable extent, if slavery shall be planted within them. Slave States are places for poor white people to remove from, not remove to. New Free States are the places for poor people to go to and better their condition. For this use the nation needs these Territories."

The speech was a masterpiece of simplicity, of lucidity. It showed the great jury; lawyer at his best. Its temper was as admirable as its logic; not a touch of anger nor of vituperation.

"I have no prejudice against the Southern people," said he. "They are just what we would be in their situation. If slavery did not exist among them, they would not introduce it. If it did now exist among us, we should not instantly give it up. This I believe of the masses North and South.

"When Southern people tell us that they are no more responsible for the origin of slavery than we are, I acknowledge the fact. When it is said that the institution exists and that it is very difficult to get rid of in any satisfactory way, I can understand and appreciate the saying. I surely will not blame them for not doing what I should not know how to do myself. If all earthly power were given me, I should not know what to do as to the existing institution."

His instinctive aversion to fanaticism found expression in a plea for the golden mean in politics.

"Some men, mostly Whigs, who condemn the repeal of the Missouri Compromise, nevertheless hesitate to go for its restoration lest they be thrown in company with the Abolitionists. Will they allow me as an old Whig, to tell them good-humoredly that I think this is very silly. Stand with anybody that stands right. Stand with him while he is right and part with him when he goes wrong. Stand with the Abolitionist in restoring the Missouri Compromise, and stand against him when he attempts to repeal the Fugitive Slave Law. In the latter case you stand with the Southern disunionist. What of that? You are still right. In both cases you are right. In both cases you expose the dangerous extremes. In both you stand on middle ground and hold the ship level and steady. In both you are national, and nothing less than national. This is the good old Whig ground. To desert such ground because of any company is to be less than a Whig-less than a man-less than an American."

These two speeches against Douglas made an immense impression Byron-like, Lincoln waked up and found himself famous. Thereupon, his ambition revived. A Senator was to be chosen that autumn. Why might not this be the opportunity to retrieve his failure in Congress? Shortly after the Peoria speech, he was sending out notes like this to prominent politicians:

"Dear Sir: You used to express a good deal of partiality for me, and if you are still so, now is the time. Some friends here are really for me for the United States Senate, and I should be very grateful if you could make a mark for me among your members (of the Legislature)."(7)

When the Legislature assembled, it was found to comprise four groups: the out-and-out Democrats who would stand by Douglas through thick and thin, and vote only for his nominee; the bolting Democrats who would not vote for a Douglas man, but whose party rancor was so great that they would throw their votes away rather than give them to a Whig; such enemies of Douglas as were willing to vote for a Whig; the remainder.

The Democrats supported Governor Matteson; the candidate of the second group was Lyman Trumbull; the Whigs supported Lincoln. After nine exciting ballots, Matteson had forty-seven votes, Trumbull thirty-five, Lincoln fifteen. As the bolting Democrats were beyond compromise, Lincoln determined to sacrifice himself in order to defeat Matteson. Though the fifteen protested against deserting him, he required them to do so. On the tenth ballot, they transferred their votes to Trumbull and he was elected. (8)

Douglas had met his first important defeat. His policy had been repudiated in his own State. And it was Lincoln who had formulated the argument against him, who had held the balance of power, and had turned the scale.

IX
THE LITERARY STATESMAN

Lincoln had found at last a mode and an opportunity for concentrating all his powers in a way that could have results. He had discovered himself as a man of letters. The great speeches of 1854 were not different in a way from the previous speeches that were without results. And yet they were wholly different. Just as Lincoln's version of an old tale made of that tale a new thing, so Lincoln's version of an argument made of it a different thing from other men's versions. The oratory of 1854 was not state-craft in any ordinary sense. It was art Lincoln the artist, who had slowly developed a great literary faculty, had chanced after so many rebuffs on good fortune. His cause stood in urgent need of just what he could give. It was one of those moments when a new political force, having not as yet any opening for action, finds salvation in the phrase-maker, in the literary artist who can embody it in words.

During the next five years and more, Lincoln was the recognized offset to Douglas. His fame spread from Illinois in both directions. He was called to Iowa and to Ohio as the advocate of all advocates who could undo the effect of Douglas. His fame traveled eastward. The culmination of the period of literary leadership was his famous speech at Cooper Union in February, 1860.

It was inevitable that he should go along with the antislavery coalition which adopted the name of the Republican party. But his natural deliberation kept him from being one of its founders. An attempt of its founders to appropriate him after the triumph at Springfield, in October, 1854, met with a rebuff.(1) Nearly a year and a half went by before he affiliated himself with the new party. But once having made up his mind, he went forward wholeheartedly. At the State Convention of Illinois Republicans in 1856 he made a speech that has not been recorded but which is a tradition for moving oratory. That same year a considerable number of votes were cast for Lincoln for Vice-President in the Republican National Convention.

But all these were mere details. The great event of the years between 1854 and 1860 was his contest with Douglas. It was a battle of wits, a great literary duel. Fortunately for Lincoln, his part was played altogether on his own soil, under conditions in which he was entirely at his ease, where nothing conspired with his enemy to embarrass him.

Douglas had a far more difficult task. Unforeseen complications rapidly forced him to change his policy, to meet desertion and betrayal in his own ranks. These were terrible years when fierce events followed one another in quick succession — the rush of both slave-holders and abolitionists into Kansas; the cruel war along the Wakarusa River; the sack of Lawrence by the pro-slavery party; the massacre by John Brown at Pottawatomie; the diatribes of Sumner in the Senate; the assault on Sumner by Brooks. In the midst of this carnival of ferocity came the Dred Scott decision, cutting under the Kansas-Nebraska Bill, denying to the people of a Territory the right to legislate on slavery, and giving to all slave-holders the right to settle with their slaves anywhere they pleased outside a Free State. This famous decision repudiated Douglas's policy of leaving all such questions to local autonomy and to private enterprise. For a time Douglas made no move to save his policy. But when President Buchanan decided to throw the influence of the Administration on the side of the pro-slavery party in Kansas, Douglas was up in arms. When it was proposed to admit Kansas with a constitution favoring slavery, but which had not received the votes of a majority of the inhabitants, Douglas voted with the Republicans to defeat admission. Whereupon the Democratic party machine and the Administration turned upon him without mercy. He stood alone in a circle of enemies. At no other time did he show so many of the qualities of a great leader. Battling with Lincoln in the popular forum on the one hand, he was meeting daily on the other assaults by a crowd of brilliant opponents in Congress. At the same time he was playing a consummate game of political strategy, struggling against immense odds to recover his hold on Illinois. The crisis would come in 1858 when he would have to go before the Legislature for reelection. He knew well enough who his opponent would be. At every turn there fell across his path the shadow of a cool sinister figure, his relentless enemy. It was Lincoln. On the struggle with Lincoln his whole battle turned.

Abandoned by his former allies, his one hope was the retention of his constituency. To discredit Lincoln, to twist and discredit all his arguments, was for Douglas a matter of life and death. He struck frequently with great force, but sometimes with more fury than wisdom. Many a time the unruffled coolness of Lincoln brought to nothing what was meant for a deadly thrust. Douglas took counsel of despair and tried to show that Lincoln was preaching the amalgamation of the white and black races. "I protest," Lincoln replied, "against the counterfeit logic which says that because I do not want a black woman for a slave, I must necessarily want her for a wife.

I need not have her for either. I can just leave her alone. In some respects she certainly is not my equal; but in her natural right to eat the bread she earns with her own hands without asking leave of any one else, she is my equal and the equal of all others."(2) Any false move made by Douglas, any rash assertion, was sure to be seized upon by that watchful enemy in Illinois. In attempting to defend himself on two fronts at once, defying both the Republicans and the Democratic machine, Douglas made his reckless declaration that all he wanted was a fair vote by the people of Kansas; that for himself he did not care how they settled the matter, whether slavery was voted up or voted down. With relentless skill, Lincoln developed the implications of this admission, drawing forth from its confessed indifference to the existence of slavery, a chain of conclusions that extended link by link to a belief in reopening the African slave trade. This was done in his speech accepting the Republican nomination for the Senate. In the same speech he restated his general position in half a dozen sentences that became at once a classic statement for the whole Republican party: "A house divided against itself can not stand. I believe this government can not endure permanently half slave and half free. I do not expect the Union to be dissolved. I do not expect the house to fall, but I do expect it will cease to be divided. It will become all one thing or all the other. Either the opponents of slavery will arrest the further spread of it and place it where the public mind shall rest in the belief that it is in the course of ultimate extinction; or its advocates will push it forward till it shall become alike lawful in all the States, old as well as new, North as well as South."(3)

The great duel was rapidly approaching its climax. What was in reality no more than the last round has appropriated a label that ought to have a wider meaning and is known as the Lincoln-Douglas Debates. The two candidates made a joint tour of the State, debating their policies in public at various places during the summer and autumn of 1858.

Properly considered, these famous speeches closed Lincoln's life as an orator. The Cooper Union speech was an isolated aftermath in alien conditions, a set performance not quite in his true vein. His brief addresses of the later years were incidental; they had no combative element. Never again was he to attempt to sway an audience for an immediate stake through the use of the spoken word. "A brief description of Mr. Lincoln's appearance on the stump and of his manner when speaking," as Herndon aptly remarks, "may not be without interest. When standing erect, he was six feet four inches high. He was lean in flesh and ungainly in figure. Aside from his sad, pained look, due to habitual melancholy, his face had no characteristic or fixed expression. He was thin through the chest and hence slightly stoop-shouldered. . . . At first he was very awkward and it seemed a real labor to adjust himself to his surroundings. He struggled for a time under a feeling of apparent diffidence and sensitiveness, and these only added to his awkwardness.... When he began speaking his voice was shrill, piping and unpleasant. His manner, his attitude, his dark yellow face, wrinkled and dry, his oddity of pose, his diffident movements; everything seemed to be against him, but only for a short time. . . . As he proceeded, he became somewhat more animated. . . . He did not gesticulate as much with his hands as with his head. He used the latter frequently, throwing it with him, this way and that. . . . He never sawed the air nor rent space into tatters and rags, as some orators do. He never acted for stage effect. He was cool, considerate, reflective — in time, self-possessed and self-reliant. . . . As he moved along in his speech he became freer and less uneasy in his movements; to that extent he was graceful. He had a perfect naturalness, a strong individuality, and to that extent he was dignified. . . . He spoke with effectiveness — and to move the judgment as well as the emotion of men. There was a world of meaning and emphasis in the long, bony finger of the right hand as he dotted the ideas on the minds of his hearers. . . . He always stood squarely on his feet. . . . He neither touched nor leaned on anything for support. He never ranted, never walked backward and forward on the platform. . . . As he proceeded with his speech, the exercise of his vocal organs altered somewhat the pitch of his voice. It lost in a measure its former acute and shrilling pitch and mellowed into a more harmonious and pleasant sound. His form expanded, and notwithstanding the sunken breast, he rose up a splendid and imposing figure. . . . His little gray eyes flashed in a face aglow with the fire of his profound thoughts; and his uneasy movements and diffident manner sunk themselves beneath the wave of righteous indignation that came sweeping over him."(4)

A wonderful dramatic contrast were these two men, each in his way so masterful, as they appeared in the famous debates. By good fortune we have a portrait of Douglas the orator, from the pen of Mrs. Stowe, who had observed him with reluctant admiration from the gallery of the Senate. "This Douglas is the very ideal of vitality. Short, broad, thick-set, every inch of him has its own alertness and motion. He has a good head, thick black hair, heavy black brows, and a keen face. His figure would be an unfortunate one were it not for the animation that constantly pervades it. As it is it rather gives poignancy to his peculiar appearance; he has a small handsome hand, moreover, and a graceful as well as forcible mode of using it. . . . He has two requisites of a debater, a melodious voice and clear, sharply defined enunciation. His forte in debating is his power of mystifying the point. With the most offhand assured airs in the world, and a certain appearance of honest superiority, like one who has a regard for you and wishes to set you right on one or two little matters, he proceeds to set up some point which is not that in question, but only a family connection of it, and this point he attacks with the very best of logic and language; he charges upon it, horse and foot, runs it down, tramples it in the dust, and then turns upon you with 'See, there is your argument. Did I not tell you so? You see it is all stuff.' And if you have allowed yourself to be so dazzled by his quickness as to forget that the routed point is not, after all, the one in question, you suppose all is over with it. Moreover, he contrives to mingle up so many stinging allusions, so many piquant personalities, that by the time he has done his mystification, a dozen others are ready and burning to spring on their feet to repel some direct or indirect attack all equally wide of the point."

The mode of travel of the two contestants heightened the contrast. George B. McClellan, a young engineer officer who had recently resigned from the army and was now general superintendent of the Illinois Central Railroad, gave Douglas his private car and a special train. Lincoln traveled any way he could-in ordinary passenger trains, or even in the caboose of a freight train. A curious symbolization of Lincoln's belief that the real conflict was between the plain people and organized money!

The debates did not develop new ideas. It was a literary duel, each leader aiming to restate himself in the most telling, popular way. For once that superficial definition of art applied: "What oft was thought but ne'er so well expressed." Nevertheless the debates contained an incident that helped to make history. Though Douglas was at war with the Administration, it was not certain that the quarrel might not be made up. There was no other leader who would be so formidable at the head of a reunited Democratic party. Lincoln pondered the question, how could the rift between Douglas and the Democratic machine be made irrevocable? And now a new phase of Lincoln appeared. It was the political strategist He saw that if he would disregard his own chance of election-as he had done from a simpler motive four years before — he could drive Douglas into a dilemma from which there was no real escape. He confided his purpose to his friends; they urged him not to do it. But he had made up his mind as he generally did, without consultation, in the silence of his own thoughts, and once having made it up, he was inflexible.

At Freeport, Lincoln made the move which probably lost him the Senatorship. He asked a question which if Douglas answered it one way would enable him to recover the favor of Illinois but would lose him forever the favor of the slave-holders; but which, if he answered it another way might enable him to make his peace at Washington but would certainly lose him Illinois. The question was: "Can the people of a United States Territory in any lawful way, against the wish of any citizen of the United

States, exclude slavery from its limits prior to the formation of a State Constitution?"(5) In other words, is the Dred Scott decision good law? Is it true that a slave-holder can take his slaves into Kansas if the people of Kansas want to keep him out?

Douglas saw the trap. With his instantaneous facility he tried to cloud the issue and extricate himself through evasion in the very manner Mrs. Stowe has described. While dodging a denial of the court's authority, he insisted that his doctrine of local autonomy was still secure because through police regulation the local legislature could foster or strangle slavery, just as they pleased, no matter "what way the Supreme Court may hereafter decide as to the abstract question whether slavery may or may not go into a Territory under the Constitution."

As Lincoln's friends had foreseen, this matchless performance of carrying water on both shoulders caught the popular fancy; Douglas was reelected to the Senate. As Lincoln had foreseen, it killed him as a Democratic leader; it prevented the reunion of the Democratic party. The result appeared in 1860 when the Republicans, though still a minority party, carried the day because of the bitter divisions among the Democrats. That was what Lincoln foresaw when he said to his fearful friends while they argued in vain to prevent his asking the question at Free-port. "I am killing larger game; the great battle of 1860 is worth a thousand of this senatorial race."(6)

X
THE DARK HORSE

One of the most curious things in Lincoln is the way his confidence in himself came and went. He had none of Douglas's unwavering self-reliance. Before the end, to be sure, he attained a type of self-reliance, higher and more imperturbable. But this was not the fruit of a steadfast unfolding. Rather, he was like a tree with its alternating periods of growth and pause, now richly in leaf, now dormant. Equally applicable is the other familiar image of the successive waves.

The clue seems to have been, in part at least, a matter of vitality. Just as Douglas emanated vitality—so much so that his aura filled the whole Senate chamber and forced an unwilling response in the gifted but hostile woman who watched him from the gallery—Lincoln, conversely, made no such overpowering impression. His observers, however much they have to say about his humor, his seasons of Shakespearian mirth, never forget their impression that at heart he is sad. His fondness for poetry in the minor key has become a byword, especially the line "Oh, why should the spirit of mortal be proud."

It is impossible to discover any law governing the succession of his lapses in self-reliance. But they may be related very plausibly to his sense of failure or at least to his sense of futility. He was one of those intensely sensitive natures to whom the futilities of this world are its most discouraging feature. Whenever such ideas were brought home to him his energy flagged; his vitality, never high, sank. He was prone to turn away from the outward life to lose himself in the inner. All this is part of the phenomena which Herndon perceived more clearly than he comprehended it, which led him to call Lincoln a fatalist.

A humbler but perhaps more accurate explanation is the reminder that he was son to Thomas the unstable. What happened in Lincoln's mind when he returned defeated from Washington, that ghost-like rising of the impulses of old Thomas, recurred more than once thereafter. In fact there is a period well-defined, a span of thirteen years terminating suddenly on a day in 1862, during which the ghost of old Thomas is a thing to be reckoned with in his son's life. It came and went, most of the time fortunately far on the horizon. But now and then it drew near. Always it was lurking somewhere, waiting to seize upon him in those moments when his vitality sank, when his energies were in the ebb, when his thoughts were possessed by a sense of futility.

The year 1859 was one of his ebb tides. In the previous year the rising tide, which had mounted high during his success on the circuit, reached its crest The memory of his failure at Washington was effaced. At Freeport he was a more powerful genius, a more dominant personality, than he had ever been. Gradually, in the months following, the high wave subsided. During 1859 he gave most of his attention to his practice. Though political speech-making continued, and though he did not impair his reputation, he did nothing of a remarkable sort. The one literary fragment of any value is a letter to a Boston committee that had invited him to attend a "festival" in Boston on Jefferson's birthday. He avowed himself a thoroughgoing disciple of Jefferson and pronounced the principles of Jefferson "the definitions and axioms of free society." Without conditions he identified his own cause with the cause of Jefferson, "the man who in the concrete pressure of a struggle for national independence by a single people, had the coolness, forecast and capacity to introduce into a merely revolutionary document, an abstract truth, applicable to all men and all times, and so to embalm it there that today and in all coming days, it shall be a rebuke and a stumbling-block to the very harbingers of reappearing tyranny and oppression."(1)

While the Boston committee were turning their eyes toward this great new phrase-maker of the West, several politicians in Illinois had formed a bold resolve. They would try to make him President. The movement had two sources — the personal loyalty of his devoted friends of the circuit, the shrewdness of the political managers who saw that his duel with Douglas had made him a national figure. As one of them said to him, "Douglas being so widely known, you are getting a national reputation through him." Lincoln replied that he did not lack the ambition but lacked altogether the confidence in the possibility of success.(2)

This was his attitude during most of 1859. The glow, the enthusiasm, of the previous year was gone. "I must in candor say that I do not think myself fit for the Presidency," he wrote to a newspaper editor in April. He used the same words to another correspondent in July. As late as November first, he wrote, "For my single self, I have enlisted for the permanent success of the Republican cause, and for this object I shall labor faithfully in the ranks, unless, as I think not probable, the judgment of the party shall assign me a different position."(3)

Meanwhile, both groups of supporters had labored unceasingly, regardless of his approval. In his personal following, the companionableness of twenty years had deepened into an almost romantic loyalty. The leaders of this enthusiastic attachment, most of them lawyers, had no superiors for influence in Illinois. The man who had such a following was a power in politics whether he would or no. This the mere politicians saw. They also saw that the next Republican nomination would rest on a delicate calculation of probabilities. There were other Republicans more conspicuous than Lincoln — Seward in New York, Sumner in Massachusetts, Chase in Ohio — but all these had inveterate enemies. Despite their importance would it be safe to nominate them? Would not the party be compelled to take some relatively minor figure, some essentially new man? In a word, what we know as a "dark horse." Believing that this would happen, they built hopefully on their faith in Lincoln.

Toward the end of the year he was at last persuaded to take his candidacy seriously. The local campaign for his nomination had gone so far that a failure to go further would have the look of being discarded as the local Republican leader. This argument decided him. Before the year's end he had agreed to become a candidate before the convention. In his own words, "I am not in a position where it would hurt much for me to not be nominated on the national ticket; but I am where it would hurt some for me to not get the Illinois delegates."(4)

It was shortly after this momentous decision that he went to New York by invitation and made his most celebrated, though not in any respect his greatest, oration.(5) A large audience filled Cooper Union, February 27, 1860. William Cullen Bryant presided. David Dudley Field escorted Lincoln to the platform. Horace Greeley was in the audience. Again, the performance was purely literary. No formulation of new policies, no appeal for any new departure. It was a masterly restatement of his position; of the essence of the debates with Douglas. It cleansed the Republican platform of all accidental accretions, as if a ship's hull were being scraped of barnacles preparatory to a voyage; it gave the underlying issues such inflexible definition that they could not be juggled with. Again he showed a power of lucid statement not possessed by any of his rivals. An incident of the speech was his unsparing condemnation of John Brown whose raid and death were on every tongue. "You charge that we stir up insurrections among your slaves," said he, apostrophizing the slave-holders. "We deny it, and what is your proof? 'Harper's Ferry; John Brown!' John Brown was no Republican; and you have failed to implicate a single Republican in this Harper's Ferry enterprise. . .

"John Brown's effort was peculiar. It was not a slave insurrection. It was an attempt by white men to get up a revolt among slaves, in which the slaves refused to participate. In fact, it was so absurd that the slaves with all their ignorance saw plainly enough that it could not succeed. That affair in its philosophy corresponds with the many attempts related in history at the assassination of kings and emperors. An enthusiast broods over the oppression of the people until he fancies himself commissioned by heaven to liberate them. He ventures the attempt which ends in little else than his own execution. Orsini's attempt on Louis Napoleon, and John Brown's attempt at Harper's Ferry were, in their philosophy, precisely the same. The eagerness to cast blame on old England in the one case and on New England in the other, does not disprove the sameness of the two things."

The Cooper Union speech received extravagant praise from all the Republican newspapers. Lincoln's ardent partisans assert that it took New York "by storm." Rather too violent a way of putting it! But there can be no doubt that the speech made a deep impression. Thereafter, many of the Eastern managers were willing to consider Lincoln as a candidate, should factional jealousies prove uncompromising. Any port in a storm, you know. Obviously, there could be ports far more dangerous than this "favorite son" of Illinois.

Many national conventions in the United States have decided upon a compromise candidate, "a dark horse," through just such reasoning. The most noted instance is the Republican Convention of 1860. When it assembled at Chicago in June, the most imposing candidate was the brilliant leader of the New York Republicans, Seward. But no man in the country had more bitter enemies. Horace Greeley whose paper The Tribune was by far the most influential Republican organ, went to Chicago obsessed by one purpose: because of irreconcilable personal quarrels he would have revenge upon Seward. Others who did not hate Seward were afraid of what Greeley symbolized. And all of them knew that whatever else happened, the West must be secured.

The Lincoln managers played upon the Eastern jealousies and the Eastern fears with great skill. There was little sleep among the delegates the night previous to the balloting. At just the right moment, the Lincoln managers, though their chief had forbidden them to do so, offered promises with regard to Cabinet appointments.(6) And they succeeded in packing the galleries of the Convention Hall with a perfectly organized claque—"rooters," the modern American would say.

The result on the third ballot was a rush to Lincoln of all the enemies of Seward, and Lincoln's nomination amid a roaring frenzy of applause.

XI
SECESSION

After twenty-three years of successive defeats, Lincoln, almost fortuitously, was at the center of the political maelstrom. The clue to what follows is in the way he had developed during that long discouraging apprenticeship to greatness. Mentally, he had always been in isolation. Socially, he had lived in a near horizon. The real tragedy of his failure at Washington was in the closing against him of the opportunity to know his country as a whole. Had it been Lincoln instead of Douglas to whom destiny had given a residence at Washington during the 'fifties, it is conceivable that things might have been different in the 'sixties. On the other hand, America would have lost its greatest example of the artist in politics.

And without that artist, without his extraordinary literary gift, his party might not have consolidated in 1860. A very curious party it was. It had sprung to life as a denial, as a device for halting Douglas. Lincoln's doctrine of the golden mean, became for once a political power. Men of the most diverse views on other issues accepted in their need the axiom: "Stand with anybody so long as he stands right." And standing right, for that moment in the minds of them all, meant keeping slavery and the money power from devouring the territories.

The artist of the movement expressed them all in his declaration that the nation needed the Territories to give home and opportunity to free white people. Even the Abolitionists, who hitherto had refused to make common cause with any other faction, entered the negative coalition of the new party. So did Whigs, and anti-slavery Democrats, as well as other factions then obscure which we should now label Socialists and Labormen.

However, this coalition, which in origin was purely negative, revealed, the moment it coalesced, two positive features. To the man of the near horizon in 1860 neither of these features seemed of first importance. To the man outside that horizon, seeing them in perspective as related to the sum total of American life, they had a significance he did not entirely appreciate.

The first of these was the temper of the Abolitionists. Lincoln ignored it. He was content with his ringing assertion of the golden mean. But there spoke the man of letters rather than the statesman. Of temper in politics as an abstract idea, he had been keenly conscious from the first; but his lack of familiarity with political organizations kept him from assigning full value to the temper of any one factor as affecting the joint temper of the whole group. It was appointed for him to learn this in a supremely hard way and to apply the lesson with wonderful audacity. But in 1860 that stern experience still slept in the future. He had no suspicion as yet that he might find it difficult to carry out his own promise to stand with the Abolitionists in excluding slavery from the Territories, and to stand against them in enforcing the Fugitive Slave Law. He did not yet see why any one should doubt the validity of this promise; why any one should be afraid to go along with him, afraid that the temper of one element would infect the whole coalition.

But this fear that Lincoln did not allow for, possessed already a great many minds. Thousands of Southerners, of the sort whom Lincoln credited with good intentions about slavery, feared the Abolitionists Not because the Abolitionists wanted to destroy slavery, but because they wanted to do so fiercely, cruelly. Like Lincoln, these Southerners who were liberals in thought and moderates in action, did not know what to do about slavery. Like Lincoln, they had but one fixed idea with regard to it, — slavery must not be terminated violently. Lincoln, despite his near horizon, sensed them correctly as not being at one with the great plutocrats who wished to exploit slavery. But when the Abolitionist poured out the same fury of vituperation on every sort of slave-holder; when he promised his soul that it should yet have the joy of exulting in the ruin of all such, the moderate Southerners became as flint. When the Abolitionists proclaimed their affiliation with the new party, the first step was taken toward a general Southern coalition to stop the Republican advance.

There was another positive element blended into the negative coalition. In 1857, the Republicans overruling the traditions of those members who had once been Democrats, set their faces toward protection. To most of the Northerners the fatefulness of the step was not obvious. Twenty years had passed since a serious tariff controversy had shaken the North. Financial difficulties in the 'fifties were more prevalent in the North than in the South. Business was in a quandary. Labor was demanding better opportunities. Protection as a solution, or at least as a palliative, seemed to the mass of the Republican coalition, even to the former Democrats for all their free trade traditions, not outrageous. To the Southerners it was an alarm bell. The Southern world was agricultural; its staple was cotton; the bulk of its market was in England. Ever since 1828, the Southern mind had been constantly on guard with regard to tariff, unceasingly fearful that protection would be imposed on it by Northern and Western votes. To have to sell its cotton in England at free trade values, but at the same time to have to buy its commodities at protected values fixed by Northern manufacturers—what did that mean but the despotism of one section over another? When the Republicans took up protection as part of their creed, a general Southern coalition was rendered almost inevitable.

This, Lincoln {Missing text}. Again it is to be accounted for in part by his near horizon. Had he lived at Washington, had he met, frequently, Southern men; had he passed those crucial years of the 'fifties in debates with political leaders rather than in story-telling tournaments on the circuit; perhaps all this would have been otherwise. But one can not be quite sure. Finance never appealed to him. A wide application may be given to Herndon's remark that "he had no money sense." All the rest of the Republican doctrine finds its best statement in Lincoln. On the one subject of its economic policy he is silent. Apparently it is to be classified with the routine side of the law. To neither was he ever able to give more than a perfunctory attention. As an artist in politics he had the defect of his qualities.

What his qualities showed him were two things: the alliance of the plutocratic slave power with the plutocratic money power, and the essential rightness in impulse of the bulk of the Southern people. Hence his conclusion which became his party's conclusion: that, in the South, a political-financial ring was dominating a leaderless people, This was not the truth. Lincoln's defects in 1860 limited his vision. Nevertheless, to the solitary distant thinker, shut in by the near horizon of political Springfield, there was every excuse for the error. The palpable evidence all confirmed it. What might have contradicted it was a cloud of witnesses, floating, incidental, casual, tacit. Just what a nature like Lincoln's, if only he could have met them, would have perceived and comprehended; what a nature like Douglas's, no matter how plainly they were presented to him, could neither perceive nor comprehend. It was the irony of fate that an opportunity to fathom his time was squandered upon the unseeing Douglas, while to the seeing Lincoln it was denied. In a word, the Southern reaction against the Republicans, like the Republican movement itself, had both a positive and a negative side. It was the positive side that could be seen and judged at long range. And this was what Lincoln saw, which appeared to him to have created the dominant issue in 1860.

The negative side of the Southern movement he did not see. He was too far away to make out the details of the picture. Though he may have known from the census of 1850 that only one-third of the Southern whites were members of slave-holding families, he could scarcely have known that only a small minority of the Southern families owned as many as five slaves; that those who had fortunes in slaves were a mere handful—just as today those who have fortunes in steel or beef are mere handfuls. But still less did he know how entirely this vast majority which had so little, if any, interest in slavery, had grown to fear and distrust the North. They, like him, were suffering from a near horizon. They, too, were applying the principle "Stand with anybody so long as he stands right" But for them, standing right meant preventing a violent revolution in Southern life. Indifferent as they were to slavery, they were willing to go along with the "slave-barons" in the attempt to consolidate the South in a movement of denial—a denial of the right of the North, either through Abolitionism or through tariff, to dominate the South.

If only Lincoln with his subtle mind could have come into touch with the negative side of the Southern agitation! It was the other side, the positive side, that was vocal. With immense shrewdness the profiteers of slavery saw and developed their opportunity. They organized the South. They preached on all occasions, in all connections, the need of all Southerners to stand together, no matter how great their disagreements, in order to prevent the impoverishment of the South by hostile economic legislation. During the late 'fifties their propaganda for an all-Southern policy, made slow but constant headway. But even in 1859 these ideas were still far from controlling the South.

And then came John Brown. The dread of slave insurrection was laid deep in Southern recollection. Thirty years before, the Nat Turner Rebellion had filled a portion of Virginia with burned plantation houses amid whose ruins lay the dead bodies of white women. A little earlier, a negro conspiracy at Charleston planned the murder of white men and the parceling out of white women among the conspirators. And John Brown had come into Virginia at the head of a band of strangers calling upon the slaves to rise and arm.

Here was a supreme opportunity. The positive Southern force, the slave profiteers, seized at once the attitude of champions of the South. It was easy enough to enlist the negative force in a shocked and outraged denunciation of everything Northern. And the Northern extremists did all that was in their power to add fuel to the flame. Emerson called Brown "this new saint who had made the gallows glorious as the cross." The Southerners, hearing that, thought of the conspiracy to parcel out the white women of Charleston. Early in 1860 it seemed as if the whole South had but one idea-to part company with the North.

No wonder Lincoln threw all his influence into the scale to discredit the memory of Brown. No wonder the Republicans in their platform carefully repudiated him. They could not undo the impression made on the Southern mind by two facts: the men who lauded Brown as a new saint were voting the Republican ticket; the Republicans had committed themselves to the anti-Southern policy of protection.

And yet, in spite of all the labors of pro-slavery extremists, the movement for a breach with the North lost ground during 1860. When the election came, the vote for President revealed a singular and unforeseen situation. Four candidates were in the field. The Democrats, split into two by the issue of slavery expansion, formed two parties. The slave profiteers secured the nomination by one faction of John C. Breckinridge. The moderate Democrats who would neither fight nor favor slavery, nominated Douglas. The most peculiar group was the fourth. They included all those who would not join the Republicans for fear of the temper of the Abolition-members, but who were not promoters of slavery, and who distrusted Douglas. They had no program but to restore the condition of things that existed before the Nebraska Bill. About four million five hundred thousand votes were cast. Lincoln had less than two million, and all but about twenty-four thousand of these were in the Free States. However, the disposition of Lincoln's vote gave him the electoral college. He was chosen President by the votes of a minority of the nation. But there was another minority vote which as events turned out, proved equally significant. Breckinridge, the symbol of the slave profiteers, and of all those whom they had persuaded to follow them, had not been able to carry the popular vote of the South. They were definitely in the minority in their own section. The majority of the Southerners had so far reacted from the wild alarms of the beginning of the year that they refused to go along with the candidates of the extremists. They were for giving the Union another trial. The South itself had repudiated the slave profiteers.

This was the immensely significant fact of November, 1860. It made a great impression on the whole country. For the moment it made the fierce talk of the Southern extremists inconsequential. Buoyant Northerners, such as Seward, felt that the crisis was over; that the South had voted for a reconciliation; that only tact was needed to make everybody happy. When, a few weeks after the election, Seward said that all would be merry again inside of ninety days, his illusion had for its foundation the Southern rejection of the slave profiteers.

Unfortunately, Seward did not understand the precise significance of the thought of the moderate South. He did not understand that while the South had voted to send Breckinridge and his sort about their business, it was still deeply alarmed, deeply fearful that after all it might at any minute be forced to call them back, to make common cause with them against what it regarded as an alien and destructive political power, the Republicans. This was the Southern reservation, the unspoken condition of the vote which Seward—and for that matter, Lincoln, also,—failed to comprehend. Because of these cross-purposes, because the Southern alarm was based on another thing than the standing or falling of slavery, the situation called for much more than tact, for profound psychological statesmanship.

And now emerges out of the complexities of the Southern situation a powerful personality whose ideas and point of view Lincoln did not understand. Robert Barnwell Rhett had once been a man of might in politics. Twice he had very nearly rent the Union asunder. In 1844, again in 1851, he had come to the very edge of persuading South Carolina to secede. In each case he sought to organize the general discontent of the South,—its dread of a tariff, and of Northern domination. After his second failure, his haughty nature took offense at fortune. He resigned his seat in the Senate and withdrew to private life. But he was too large and too bold a character to attain obscurity. Nor would his restless genius permit him to rust in ease. During the troubled 'fifties, he watched from a distance, but with ever increasing interest, that negative Southern force which he, in the midst of it, comprehended, while it drifted under the wing of the extremists. As he did so, the old arguments, the old ambitions, the old hopes revived. In 1851 his cry to the South was to assert itself as a Separate nation—not for any one reason, but for many reasons—and to lead its own life apart from the North. It was an age of brilliant though ill-fated revolutionary movements in Europe. Kossuth and the gallant Hungarian attempt at independence had captivated the American imagination. Rhett dreamed of seeing the South do what Hungary had failed to do. He thought of the problem as a medieval knight would have thought, in terms of individual prowess, with the modern factors, economics and all their sort, left on one side. "Smaller nations (than South Carolina)," he said in 1851, "have striven for freedom against greater odds."

In 1860 he had concluded that his third chance had come. He would try once more to bring about secession. To split the Union, he would play into the hands of the slave-barons. He would aim to combine with their movement the negative Southern movement and use the resulting coalition to crown with success his third attempt. Issuing from his seclusion, he became at once the overshadowing figure in South Carolina. Around him all the elements of revolution crystallized. He was sixty years old; seasoned and uncompromising in the pursuit of his one ideal, the independence of the South. His arguments were the same which he had used in 1844, in 1851: the North would impoverish the South; it threatens to impose a crushing tribute in the shape of protection; it seeks to destroy slavery; it aims to bring about economic collapse; in the wreck thus produced, everything that is beautiful, charming, distinctive in Southern life will be lost; let us fight! With such a leader, the forces of discontent were quickly, effectively, organized. Even before the election of Lincoln, the revolutionary leaders in South Carolina were corresponding with men of like mind in other Southern States, especially Alabama, where was another leader, Yancey, only second in intensity to Rhett.

The word from these Alabama revolutionists to South Carolina was to dare all, to risk seceding alone, confident that the other States of the South would follow. Rhett and his new associates took this perilous advice. The election was followed by the call of a convention of delegates of the people of South Carolina. This convention, on the twentieth of December, 1860, repealed the laws which united South Carolina with the other States and proclaimed their own independent.

XII
THE CRISIS

Though Seward and other buoyant natures felt that the crisis had passed with the election, less volatile people held the opposite view. Men who had never before taken seriously the Southern threats of disunion had waked suddenly to a terrified consciousness that they were in for it. In their blindness to realities earlier in the year, they were like that brilliant host of camp followers which, as Thackeray puts it, led the army of Wellington dancing and feasting to the very brink of Waterloo. And now the day of reckoning had come. An emotional reaction carried them from one extreme to the other; from self-sufficient disregard of their adversaries to an almost self-abasing regard.

The very type of these people and of their reaction was Horace Greeley. He was destined many times to make plain that he lived mainly in his sensibilities; that, in his kaleidoscopic vision, the pattern of the world could be red and yellow and green today, and orange and purple and blue tomorrow. To descend from a pinnacle of self-complacency into a desolating abyss of panic, was as easy for Greeley as it is — in the vulgar but pointed American phrase — to roll off a log. A few days after the election, Greeley had rolled off his log. He was wallowing in panic. He began to scream editorially. The Southern extremists were terribly in earnest; if they wanted to go, go they would, and go they should. But foolish Northerners would be sure to talk war and the retaining of the South in the Union by force: it must not be; what was the Union compared with bloodshed? There must be no war — no war. Such was Greeley's terrified — appeal to the North. A few weeks after the election he printed his famous editorial denouncing the idea of a Union pinned together by bayonets. He followed up with another startling concession to his fears: the South had as good cause for leaving the Union as the colonies had for leaving the British Empire. A little later, he formulated his ultimate conclusion, — which like many of his ultimates proved to be transitory, — and declared that if any group of Southern States "choose to form an independent nation, they have a clear moral right to do so," and pledging himself and his followers to do "our best to forward their views."

Greeley wielded through The Tribune more influence, perhaps, than was possessed by any other Republican with the single exception of Lincoln. His newspaper constituency was enormous, and the relation between the leader and the led was unusually close. He was both oracle and barometer. As a symptom of the Republican panic, as a cause increasing that panic, he was of first importance.

Meanwhile Congress had met. And at once, the most characteristic peculiarity of the moment was again made emphatic. The popular majorities and the political machines did not coincide. Both in the North and in the South a minority held the situation in the hollow of its hand. The Breckinridge Democrats, despite their repudiation in the presidential vote, included so many of the Southern politicians, they were so well organized, they had scored such a menacing victory with the aid of Rhett in South Carolina, they had played so skilfully on the fears of the South at large, their leaders were such skilled managers, that they were able to continue for the moment the recognized spokesmen of the South at Washington. They lost no time defining their position. If the Union were not to be sundered, the Republicans must pledge themselves to a new and extensive compromise; it must be far different from those historic compromises that had preceded it. Three features must characterize any new agreement: The South must be dealt with as a unit; it must be given a "sphere of influence" — to use our modern term — which would fully satisfy all its impulses of expansion; and in that sphere, every question of slavery must be left entirely, forever, to local action. In a word, they demanded for the South what today would be described as a "dominion" status. Therefore, they insisted that the party which had captured the Northern political machine should formulate its reply to these demands. They gave notice that they would not discuss individual schemes, but only such as the victorious Republicans might officially present. Thus the national crisis became a party crisis. What could the Republicans among themselves agree to propose?

The central figure of the crisis seemed at first to be the brilliant Republican Senator from New York. Seward thought he understood the

South, and what was still more important, human nature. Though he echoed Greeley's cry for peace—translating his passionate hysteria into the polished cynicism of a diplomat who had been known to deny that he was ever entirely serious—he scoffed at Greeley's fears. If the South had not voted lack of confidence in the Breckinridge crowd, what had it voted? If the Breckinridge leaders weren't maneuvering to save their faces, what could they be accused of doing? If Seward, the Republican man of genius, couldn't see through all that, couldn't devise a way to help them save their faces, what was the use in being a brilliant politician?

Jauntily self-complacent, as confident of himself as if Rome were burning and he the garlanded fiddler, Seward braced himself for the task of recreating the Union.

But there was an obstacle in his path. It was Lincoln. Of course, it was folly to propose a scheme which the incoming President would not sustain. Lincoln and Seward must come to an understanding. To bring that about Seward despatched a personal legate to Springfield. Thurlow Weed, editor, man of the world, political wire-puller beyond compare, Seward's devoted henchman, was the legate. One of the great events of American history was the conversation between Weed and Lincoln in December, 1860. By a rare propriety of dramatic effect, it occurred probably, on the very day South Carolina brought to an end its campaign of menace and adopted its Ordinance of Secession, December twentieth.(1)

Weed had brought to Springfield a definite proposal. The Crittenden compromise was being hotly discussed in Congress and throughout the country. All the Northern advocates of conciliation were eager to put it through. There was some ground to believe that the Southern machine at Washington would accept it. If Lincoln would agree, Seward would make it the basis of his policy.

This Compromise would have restored the old line of the Missouri Compromise and would have placed it under the protection of a constitutional amendment. This, together with a guarantee against congressional interference with slavery in the States where it existed, a guarantee the Republicans had already offered, seemed to Seward, to Weed, to Greeley, to the bulk of the party, a satisfactory means of preserving the Union. What was it but a falling back on the original policy of the party, the undoing of those measures of 1854 which had called the party into being? Was it conceivable that Lincoln would balk the wishes of the party by obstructing such a natural mode of extrication? But that was what Lincoln did. His views had advanced since 1854. Then, he was merely for restoring the old duality of the country, the two "dominions," Northern and Southern, each with its own social order. He had advanced to the belief that this duality could not permanently continue. Just how far Lincoln realized what he was doing in refusing to compromise will never be known. Three months afterward, he took a course which seems to imply that his vision during the interim had expanded, had opened before him a new revelation of the nature of his problem. At the earlier date Lincoln and the Southern people — not the Southern machine — were looking at the one problem from opposite points of view, and were locating the significance of the problem in different features. To Lincoln, the heart of the matter was slavery. To the Southerners, including the men who had voted lack of confidence in Breckinridge, the heart of the matter was the sphere of influence. What the Southern majority wanted was not the policy of the slave profiteers but a secure future for expansion, a guarantee that Southern life, social, economic, cultural, would not be merged with the life of the opposite section: in a word, preservation of "dominion" status. In Lincoln's mind, slavery being the main issue, this "dominion" issue was incidental — a mere outgrowth of slavery that should begin to pass away with slavery's restriction. In the Southern mind, a community consciousness, the determination to be a people by themselves, nation within the nation, was the issue, and slavery was the incident. To repeat, it is impossible to say what Lincoln would have done had he comprehended the Southern attitude. His near horizon which had kept him all along from grasping the negative side of the Southern movement prevented his perception of this tragic instance of cross-purposes.

Lacking this perception, his thoughts had centered themselves on a recent activity of the slave profiteers. They had clamored for the annexation of new territory to the south of us. Various attempts had been made to create an international crisis looking toward the seizure of Cuba. Then, too, bold adventurers had staked their heads, seeking to found slave-holding communities in Central America. Why might not such attempts succeed? Why might not new Slave States be created outside the Union, eventually to be drawn in? Why not? said the slave profiteer, and gave money and assistance to the filibusters in Nicaragua. Why not? said Lincoln, also. What protection against such an extension of boundaries? Was the limitation of slave area to be on one side only, the Northern side? And here at last, for Lincoln, was what appeared to be the true issue of the moment. To dualize the Union, assuming its boundaries to be fixed, was one thing. To dualize the Union in the face of a movement for extension of boundaries was another. Hence it was now vital, as Lincoln reasoned, to give slavery a fixed boundary on all sides. Silently, while others fulminated, or rhapsodized, or wailed, he had moved inexorably to a new position which was nothing but a logical development of the old. The old position was—no extension of slave territory; the new position was—no more Slave States.(2) Because Crittenden's Compromise left it possible to have a new Slave State in Cuba, a new Slave State in Nicaragua, perhaps a dozen such new States, Lincoln refused to compromise.(3)

It was a terrible decision, carrying within it the possibility of civil war. But Lincoln could not be moved. This was the first acquaintance of the established political leaders with his inflexible side. In the recesses of his own thoughts the decision had been reached. It was useless to argue with him. Weed carried back his ultimatum. Seward abandoned Crittenden's scheme. The only chance for compromise passed away. The Southern leaders set about their plans for organizing a Southern Confederacy.

XIII
ECLIPSE

Lincoln's ultimatum of December twentieth contained three proposals that might be made to the Southern leaders:

That the enforcement of the Fugitive Slave Law which hitherto had been left to State authorities should be taken over by Congress and supported by the Republicans.

That the Republicans to the extent of their power should work for the repeal of all those "Personal Liberty Laws" which had been established in certain Northern States to defeat the operation of the Fugitive Slave Law.

That the Federal Union must be preserved.(1)

In presenting these proposals along with a refusal to consider the Crittenden Compromise, Seward tampered with their clear-cut form. Fearful of the effect on the extremists of the Republican group, he withheld Lincoln's unconditional promise to maintain the Fugitive Slave Law and instead of pledging his party to the repeal of Personal Liberty Laws he promised only to have Congress request the States to repeal them. He suppressed altogether the assertion that the Union must be preserved.(2) About the same time, in a public speech, he said he was not going to be "humbugged" by the bogy of secession, and gave his fatuous promise that all the trouble would be ended inside ninety days. For all his brilliancy of a sort, he was spiritually obtuse. On him, as on Douglas, Fate had lavished opportunities to see life as it is, to understand the motives of men; but it could not make him use them. He was incorrigibly cynical. He could not divest himself of the idea that all this confusion was hubbub, was but an ordinary political game, that his only cue was to assist his adversaries in saving their faces. In spite of his rich experience, — in spite of being an accomplished man of the world, — at least in his own estimation — he was as blind to the real motives of that Southern majority which had rejected Breckinridge as was the inexperienced Lincoln. The coolness with which he modified Lincoln's proposals was evidence that he considered himself the great Republican and Lincoln an accident. He was to do the same again — to his own regret.

When Lincoln issued his ultimatum, he was approaching the summit, if not at the very summit, of another of his successive waves of vitality, of self-confidence. That depression which came upon him about the end of 1858, which kept him undecided, in a mood of excessive caution during most of 1859, had passed away. The presidential campaign with its thrilling tension, its excitement, had charged him anew with confidence. Although one more eclipse was in store for him—the darkest eclipse of all—he was very nearly the definitive Lincoln of history. At least, he had the courage which that Lincoln was to show.

He was now the target for a besieging army of politicians clamoring for "spoils" in the shape of promises of preferment. It was a miserable and disgraceful assault which profoundly offended him.(3) To his mind this was not the same thing as the simple-hearted personal politics of his younger days—friends standing together and helping one another along—but a gross and monstrous rapacity. It was the first chill shadow that followed the election day.

There were difficult intrigues over the Cabinet. Promises made by his managers at Chicago were presented for redemption. Rival candidates bidding for his favor, tried to cut each other's throats. For example, there was the intrigue of the War Department. The Lincoln managers had promised a Cabinet appointment to Pennsylvania; the followers of Simon Cameron were a power; it had been necessary to win them over in order to nominate Lincoln; they insisted that their leader was now entitled to the Pennsylvania seat in the Cabinet; but there was an anti-Cameron faction almost as potent in Pennsylvania as the Cameron faction. Both sent their agents to Springfield to lay siege to Lincoln. In this duel, the Cameron forces won the first round. Lincoln offered him the Secretaryship. Subsequently, his enemies made so good a case that Lincoln was convinced of the unwisdom of his decision and withdrew the offer. But Cameron had not kept the offer confidential. The withdrawal would discredit him politically and put a trump card into the hands of his enemies. A long dispute followed. Not until Lincoln had reached Washington, immediately before the inauguration, was the dispute ended, the withdrawal withdrawn, and Cameron appointed.(4)

It was a dreary winter for the President-elect. It was also a brand-new experience. For the first time he was a dispenser of favor on a grand scale. Innumerable men showed their meanest side, either to advance themselves or to injure others. As the weeks passed and the spectacle grew in shamelessness, his friends became more and more conscious of his peculiar melancholy. The elation of the campaign subsided into a deep unhappiness over the vanity of this world. Other phases of the shadowy side of his character also asserted themselves. Conspicuous was a certain trend in his thinking that was part of Herndon's warrant for calling him a fatalist. Lincoln's mysticism very early had taken a turn toward predestination, coupled with a belief in dreams.(5) He did not in any way believe in magic; he never had any faith in divinations, in the occult, in any secret mode of alluring the unseen powers to take one's side. Nevertheless, he made no bones about being superstitious. And he thought that coming events cast their shadows before, that something, at least, of the future was sometimes revealed through dreams. "Nature," he would say, "is the workshop of the Almighty, and we form but links in the chain of intellectual and material life."(6) Byron's Dream was one of his favorite poems. He pondered those ancient, historical tales which make free use of portents. There was a fascination for him in the story of Caracalla—how his murder of Geta was foretold, how he was upbraided by the ghosts of his father and brother. This dream-faith of his was as real as was a similar faith held by the authors of the Old Testament. He had his theory of the interpretation of dreams. Because they were a universal experience—as he believed, the universal mode of communication between the unseen and the seen—his beloved "plain people," the "children of Nature," the most universal types of humanity, were their best interpreters. He also believed in presentiment. As faithfully as the simplest of the brood of the forest—those recreated primitives who regulated their farming by the brightness or the darkness of the moon, who planted corn or slaughtered hogs as Artemis directed—he trusted a presentiment if once it really took possession of him. A presentiment which had been formed before this time, we know not when, was clothed with authority by a dream, or rather a vision, that came to him in the days of melancholy disillusion during the last winter at Springfield. Looking into a mirror, he saw two Lincolns,—one alive, the other dead. It was this vision which clenched his pre-sentiment that he was born to a great career and to a tragic end. He interpreted the vision that his administration would be successful, but that it would close with his death.(7)

The record of his inner life during the last winter at Springfield is very dim. But there can be no doubt that a desolating change attacked his spirit. As late as the day of his ultimatum he was still in comparative sunshine, or, at least his clouds were not close about him. His will was steel, that day. Nevertheless, a friend who visited him in January, to talk over their days together, found not only that "the old-time zest" was lacking, but that it was replaced by "gloom and despondency."(8) The ghosts that hovered so frequently at the back of his mind, the brooding tendencies which fed upon his melancholy and made him at times irresolute, were issuing from the shadows, trooping forward, to encompass him roundabout.

In the midst of this spiritual reaction, he was further depressed by the stern news from the South and from Washington. His refusal to compromise was beginning to bear fruit. The Gulf States seceded. A Southern Confederacy was formed. There is no evidence that he lost faith in his course, but abundant evidence that he was terribly unhappy. He was preyed upon by his sense of helplessness, while Buchanan through his weakness and vacillation was "giving away the case." "Secession is being fostered," said he, "rather than repressed, and if the doctrine meets with general acceptance in the Border States, it will be a great blow to the government."(9) He did not deceive himself upon the possible effect of his ultimatum, and sent word to General Scott to be prepared to hold or to "retake" the forts garrisoned by Federal troops in the Southern States.(10)

All the while his premonition of the approach of doom grew more darkly oppressive. The trail of the artist is discernible across his thoughts. In his troubled imagination he identified his own situation with that of the protagonist in tragedies on the theme of fate. He did not withhold his thoughts from the supreme instance. That same friend who found him possessed of gloom preserved these words of his: "I have read on my knees the story of Gethsemane, when the Son of God prayed in vain that the cup of bitterness might pass from him. I am in the Garden of Gethsemane now and my cup of bitterness is full and overflowing now."(11)

"Like some strong seer in a trance,

Seeing all his own mischance,

With a glassy countenance,"

he faced toward Washington, toward the glorious terror promised him by his superstitions.

The last days before the departure were days of mingled gloom, desperation, and the attempt to recover hope. He visited his old stepmother and made a pilgrimage to his father's grave. His thoughts fondly renewed the details of his past life, lingered upon this and that, as if fearful that it was all slipping away from him forever. And then he roused himself as if in sudden revolt against the Fates. The day before he left Springfield forever Lincoln met his partner for the last time at their law office to wind up the last of their unsettled business. "After those things were all disposed of," says Herndon, "he crossed to the opposite side of the room and threw himself down on the old office sofa. . . . He lay there for some moments his face to the ceiling without either of us speaking. Presently, he inquired: 'Billy' — he always called me by that name — 'how long have we been together?' 'Over sixteen years,' I answered. 'We've never had a cross word during all that time, have we?' . . . He gathered a bundle of papers and books he wished to take with him and started to go, but before leaving, he made the strange request that the sign board which swung on its rusty hinges at the foot of the stairway would remain. 'Let it hang there undisturbed,' he said, with a significant lowering of the voice. 'Give our clients to understand that the election of a President makes no change in the firm of Lincoln & Herndon. If I live, I am coming back some time, and then we'll go right on practising law as if nothing had happened.' He lingered for a moment as if to take a last look at the old quarters, and then passed through the door into the narrow hallway."(12)

On a dreary day with a cold rain falling, he set forth. The railway station was packed with friends. He made his way through the crowd slowly, shaking hands. "Having finally reached the train, he ascended the rear platform, and, facing about to the throng which had closed about him, drew himself up to his full height, removed his hat and stood for several seconds in profound silence. His eyes roved sadly over that sea of upturned faces. . . There was an unusual quiver on his lips and a still more unusual tear on his shriveled cheek. His solemn manner, his long silence, were as full of melancholy eloquence as any words he could have uttered."(13) At length, he spoke: "My friends, no one not in my situation can appreciate my feeling of sadness at this parting. To this place and the kindness of these people, I owe everything. Here I have lived a quarter of a century, and have passed from a young to an old man. Here my children have been born and one is buried. I now leave, not knowing when or whether ever, I may return, with a task before me greater than that which rested upon Washington. Without the assistance of that Divine Being who ever attended him, I can not succeed. With that assistance, I can not fail. Trusting in Him who can go with me and remain with you, and be everywhere for good, let us confidently hope that all will yet be well. To His care commending you, as I hope in your prayers you will commend me, I bid you an affectionate farewell."(14)

XIV
THE STRANGE NEW MAN

There is a period of sixteen months—from February, 1861, to a day in June, 1862,—when Lincoln is the most singular, the most problematic of statesmen. Out of this period he issues with apparent abruptness, the final Lincoln, with a place among the few consummate masters of state-craft. During the sixteen months, his genius comes and goes. His confidence, whether in himself or in others, is an uncertain quantity. At times he is bold, even rash; at others, irresolute. The constant factor in his mood all this while is his amazing humility. He seems to have forgotten his own existence. As a person with likes and dislikes, with personal hopes and fears, he has vanished. He is but an afflicted and perplexed mind, struggling desperately to save his country. A selfless man, he may be truly called through months of torment which made him over from a theoretical to a practical statesman. He entered this period a literary man who had been elevated almost by accident to the position of a leader in politics. After many blunders, after doubt, hesitation and pain, he came forth from this stern ordeal a powerful man of action.

The impression which he made on the country at the opening of this period was unfortunate. The very power that had hitherto been the making of him—the literary power, revealing to men in wonderfully convincing form the ideas which they felt within them but could not utter—this had deserted him. Explain the psychology of it any way you will, there is the fact! The speeches Lincoln made on the way to Washington during the latter part of February were appallingly unlike himself. His mind had suddenly fallen dumb. He had nothing to say. The gloom, the desolation that had penetrated his soul, somehow, for the moment, made him commonplace. When he talked—as convention required him to do at all his stopping places—his words were but faint echoes of the great political exponent he once had been. His utterances were fatuous; mere exhortations to the country not to worry. "There is no crisis but an artificial one," he said.(1) And the country stood aghast! Amazement, bewilderment, indignation, was the course of the reaction in many minds of his own party. Their verdict was expressed in the angry language of Samuel Bowles, "Lincoln is a Simple Susan."(2)

In private talk, Lincoln admitted that he was "more troubled about the outlook than he thought it discreet to show." This remark was made to a "Public Man," whose diary has been published but whose identity is still secret. Though keenly alert for any touch of weakness or absurdity in the new President, calling him "the most ill-favored son of Adam I ever saw," the Public Man found him "crafty and sensible." In conversation, the old Lincoln, the matchless phrase-maker, could still express himself. At New York he was told of a wild scheme that was on foot to separate the city from the North, form a city state such as Hamburg then was, and set up a commercial alliance with the Confederacy. "As to the free city business," said Lincoln, "well, I reckon it will be some time before the front door sets up bookkeeping on its own account."(3) The formal round of entertainment on his way to Washington wearied Lincoln intensely. Harassed and preoccupied, he was generally ill at ease. And he was totally unused to sumptuous living. Failures in social usage were inevitable. New York was convulsed with amusement because at the opera he wore a pair of huge black kid gloves which attracted the attention of the whole house, "hanging as they did over the red velvet box front." At an informal reception, between acts in the director's room, he looked terribly bored and sat on the sofa at the end of the room with his hat pushed back on his head. Caricatures filled the opposition papers. He was spoken of as the "Illinois ape" and the "gorilla." Every rash remark, every "break" in social form, every gaucherie was seized upon and ridiculed with-out mercy.

There is no denying that the oddities of Lincoln's manner though quickly dismissed from thought by men of genius, seriously troubled even generous men who lacked the intuitions of genius. And he never overcame these oddities. During the period of his novitiate as a ruler, the critical sixteen months, they were carried awkwardly, with embarrassment. Later when he had found himself as a ruler, when his self-confidence had reached its ultimate form and he knew what he really was, he forgot their existence. None the less, they were always a part of him, his indelible envelope. At the height of his power, he received visitors with his feet in leather slippers. (4) He discussed great affairs of state with one of those slippered feet flung up on to a corner of his desk. A favorite attitude, even when debating vital matters with the great ones of the nation, is described by his secretaries as "sitting on his shoulders" — he would slide far down into his chair and stick up both slippers so high above his head that they could rest with ease upon his mantelpiece.(5) No wonder that his enemies made unlimited fun. And they professed to believe that there was an issue here. When the elegant McClellan was moving heaven and earth, as he fancied, to get the army out of its shirt-sleeves, the President's manner was a cause of endless irritation. Still more serious was the effect of his manner on many men who agreed with him otherwise. Such a high-minded leader as Governor Andrew of Massachusetts never got over the feeling that Lincoln was a rowdy. How could a rowdy be the salvation of the country? In the dark days of 1864, when a rebellion against his leadership was attempted, this merely accidental side of him was an element of danger. The barrier it had created between himself and the more formal types, made it hard for the men who finally saved him to overcome their prejudice and nail his colors to the mast. Andrew's biographer shows himself a shrewd observer when he insists on the unexpressed but inexorable scale by which Andrew and his following measured Lincoln. They had grown up in the faith that you could tell a statesman by certain external signs, chiefly by a grandiose and commanding aspect such as made overpowering the presence of Webster. And this idea was not confined to any one locality. Everywhere, more or less, the conservative portion in every party held this view. It was the view of Washington in 1848 when Washington had failed to see the real Lincoln through his surface peculiarities. It was again the view of Washington when Lincoln returned to it.

Furthermore, his free way of talking, the broad stories he continued to tell, were made counts in his indictment. One of the bequests of Puritanism in America is the ideal, at least, of extreme scrupulousness in talk. To many sincere men Lincoln's choice of fables was often a deadly offense. Charles Francis Adams never got over the shock of their first interview. Lincoln clenched a point with a broad story. Many professional politicians who had no objection to such talk in itself, glared and sneered when the President used it—because forsooth, it might estrange a vote.

Then, too, Lincoln had none of the social finesse that might have adapted his manner to various classes. He was always incorrigibly the democrat pure and simple. He would have laughed uproariously over that undergraduate humor, the joy of a famous American University, supposedly strong on Democracy:

"Where God speaks to Jones, in the very same tones,
That he uses to Hadley and Dwight."

Though Lincoln's queer aplomb, his good-humored familiarity on first acquaintance, delighted most of his visitors, it offended many. It was lacking in tact. Often it was a clumsy attempt to be jovial too soon, as when he addressed Greeley by the name of "Horace" almost on first sight. His devices for putting men on the familiar footing lacked originality. The frequency with which he called upon a tall visitor to measure up against him reveals the poverty of his social invention. He applied this device with equal thoughtlessness to the stately Sumner, who protested, and to a nobody who grinned and was delighted.

It was this mere envelope of the genius that was deplorably evident on the journey from Springfield to Washington. There was one detail of the journey that gave his enemies a more definite ground for sneering. By the irony of fate, the first clear instance of Lincoln's humility, his reluctance to set up his own judgment against his advisers, was also his first serious mistake. There is a distinction here that is vital. Lincoln was entering on a new role, the role of the man of action. Hitherto all the great decisions of his life had been speculative; they had developed from within; they dealt with ideas. The inflexible side of him was intellectual. Now, without any adequate apprenticeship, he was called upon to make practical decisions, to decide on courses of action, at one step to pass from the dream of statecraft to its application. Inevitably, for a considerable time, he was two people; he passed back and forth from one to the other; only by degrees did he bring the two together. Meanwhile, he appeared contradictory. Inwardly, as a thinker, his development was unbroken; he was still cool, inflexible, drawing all his conclusions out of the depths of himself. Outwardly, in action, he was learning the new task, hesitatingly, with vacillation, with excessive regard to the advisers whom he treated as experts in action. It was no slight matter for an extraordinarily sensitive man to take up a new role at fifty-two.

This first official mistake of Lincoln's was in giving way to the fears of his retinue for his safety. The time had become hysterical. The wildest sort of stories filled the air. Even before he left Springfield there were rumors of plots to assassinate him.(6) On his arrival at Philadelphia information was submitted to his companions which convinced them that his life was in danger—an attempt would be made to kill him as he passed through Baltimore. Seward at Washington had heard the same story and had sent his son to Philadelphia to advise caution. Lincoln's friends insisted that he leave his special train and proceed to Washington with only one companion, on an ordinary night train. Railway officials were called in. Elaborate precautions were arranged. The telegraph lines were all to be disconnected for a number of hours so that even if the conspirators—assuming there were any—should discover his change of plan, they would be unable to communicate with Baltimore. The one soldier in the party, Colonel Sumner, vehemently protested that these changes were all "a damned piece of cowardice." But

Lincoln acquiesced in the views of the majority of his advisers. He passed through Baltimore virtually in disguise; nothing happened; no certain evidence of a conspiracy was discovered. And all his enemies took up the cry of cowardice and rang the changes upon it.(7)

Meanwhile, despite all this semblance of indecision, of feebleness, there were signs that the real inner Lincoln, however clouded, was still alive. By way of offset to his fatuous utterances, there might have been set, had the Country been in a mood to weigh with care, several strong and clear pronouncements. And these were not merely telling phrases like that characteristic one about the bookkeeping of the front door. His mind was struggling out of its shadow. And the mode of its reappearance was significant. His reasoning upon the true meaning of the struggle he was about to enter, reached a significant stage in the speech he made at Harrisburg.(8)

"I have often inquired of myself," he said, "what great principle or idea it was that kept this Confederacy (the United States) so long together. It was not the mere matter of the separation of the colonies from the motherland, but that sentiment in the Declaration of Independence which gave liberty not alone to the people of the country but hope to all the world for all future time. It was that which gave promise that in due time the weights would be lifted from the shoulders of all men and that all should have an equal chance. This is the sentiment embodied in the Declaration of Independence. Now, my friends, can this country be saved on that basis? If it can, I will consider myself one of the happiest men in the world, if I can help to save it. If it can not be saved upon that principle, it will be truly awful. But if this country can not be saved without giving up that principle, I was about to say I would rather be assassinated on this spot than surrender it. Now, in my view of the present aspect of affairs, there is no need of bloodshed and war. There is no necessity for it I am not in favor of such a course, and I may say in advance that there will be no bloodshed unless it is forced upon the government. The government will not use force unless force is used against it."

The two ideas underlying this utterance had grown in his thought steadily, consistently, ever since their first appearance in the Protest twenty-four years previous. The great issue to which all else — slavery, "dominion status," everything — was subservient, was the preservation of democratic institutions; the means to that end was the preservation of the Federal government. Now, as in 1852, his paramount object was not to "disappoint the Liberal party throughout the world," to prove that Democracy, when applied on a great scale, had yet sufficient coherence to remain intact, no matter how powerful, nor how plausible, were the forces of disintegration.

Dominated by this purpose he came to Washington. There he met Seward. It was the stroke of fate for both men. Seward, indeed, did not know that it was. He was still firmly based in the delusion that he, not Lincoln, was the genius of the hour. And he had this excuse, that it was also the country's delusion. There was pretty general belief both among friends and foes that Lincoln would be ruled by his Cabinet. In a council that was certain to include leaders of accepted influence—Seward, Chase, Cameron—what chance for this untried newcomer, whose prestige had been reared not on managing men, but on uttering words? In Seward's thoughts the answer was as inevitable as the table of addition. Equally mathematical was the conclusion that only one unit gave value to the combination. And, of course, the leader of the Republicans in the Senate was the unit. A severe experience had to be lived through before Seward made his peace with destiny. Lincoln was the quicker to perceive when they came together that something had happened. Almost from the minute of their meeting, he began to lean upon Seward; but only in a certain way. This was not the same thing as that yielding to the practical advisers which began at Philadelphia, which was subsequently to be the cause of so much confusion. His response to Seward was intellectual. It was of the inner man and revealed itself in his style of writing.

Hitherto, Lincoln's progress in literature had been marked by the development of two characteristics and by the lack of a third. The two that he possessed were taste and rhythm. At the start he was free from the prevalent vice of his time, rhetoricality. His "Address to the Voters of Sangamon County" which was his first state paper, was as direct, as free from bombast, as the greatest of his later achievements. Almost any other youth who had as much of the sense of language as was there exhibited, would have been led astray by the standards of the hour, would have mounted the spread-eagle and flapped its wings in rhetorical clamor. But Lincoln was not precocious. In art, as in everything else, he progressed slowly; the literary part of him worked its way into the matter-of-fact part of him with the gradualness of the daylight through a shadowy wood. It was not constant in its development. For many years it was little more than an irregular deepening of his two original characteristics, taste and rhythm. His taste, fed on Blackstone, Shakespeare, and the Bible, led him more and more exactingly to say just what he meant, to eschew the wiles of decoration, to be utterly non-rhetorical. His sense of rhythm, beginning simply, no more at first than a good ear for the sound of words, deepened into keen perception of the character of the word-march, of that extra significance which is added to an idea by the way it conducts itself, moving grandly or feebly as the case may be, from the unknown into the known, and thence across a perilous horizon, into memory. On the basis of these two characteristics he had acquired a style that was a rich blend of simplicity, directness, candor, joined with a clearness beyond praise, with a delightful cadence, having always a splendidly ordered march of ideas.

But there was the third thing in which the earlier style of Lincoln's was wanting. Marvelously apt for the purpose of the moment, his writings previous to 1861 are vanishing from the world's memory. The more notable writings of his later years have become classics. And the difference does not turn on subject-matter. All the ideas of his late writings had been formulated in the earlier. The difference is purely literary. The earlier writings were keen, powerful, full of character, melodious, impressive. The later writings have all these qualities, and in addition, that constant power to awaken the imagination, to carry an idea beyond its own horizon into a boundless world of imperishable literary significance, which power in argumentative prose is beauty. And how did Lincoln attain this? That he had been maturing from within the power to do this, one is compelled by the analogy of his other mental experiences to believe. At the same time, there can be no doubt who taught him the trick, who touched the secret spring and opened the new door to his mind. It was Seward. Long since it had been agreed between them that Seward was to be Secretary of State.(9) Lincoln asked him to criticize his inaugural. Seward did so, and Lincoln, in the main, accepted his criticism. But Seward went further. He proposed a new paragraph. He was not a great writer and yet he had something of that third thing which Lincoln hitherto had not exhibited. However, in pursuing beauty of statement, he often came dangerously near to mere rhetoric; his taste was never sure; his sense of rhythm was inferior; the defects of his qualities were evident. None the less, Lincoln saw at a glance that if he could infuse into Seward's words his own more robust qualities, the result—'would be a richer product than had ever issued from his own qualities as hitherto he had known them. He effected this transmutation and in doing so raised his style to a new range of effectiveness. The great Lincoln of literature appeared in the first inaugural and particularly in that noble passage which was the work of Lincoln and Seward together. In a way it said only what Lincoln had already said—especially in the speech at Harrisburg—but with what a difference!

"In your hands, my dissatisfied fellow countrymen, and not in mine, is the momentous issue of civil war. The government will not assail you. You can have no conflict without being yourselves the aggressors. You have no oath registered in Heaven to destroy the government, while I shall have the most solemn one to preserve, protect and defend it.

"I am loath to close. We are not enemies but friends. Though passion may have strained, it must not break our bonds of affection. The mystic chords of memory stretching from every battle-field and patriot grave, to every living heart and hearthstone all over this broad land, will yet swell the chorus of the Union when again touched as surely they will be, by the better angels of our nature."*

*Lincoln VI, 184; N. & H., III, 343. Seward advised the omission of part of the original draft of the first of these two paragraphs. After "defend it," Lincoln had written, "You can forbear the assault upon it. I can not shrink from the defense of it. With you and not with me is the solemn question 'Shall it be peace or a sword?'" Having struck this out, he accepted Seward's advice to add "some words of affection — some of calm and cheerful confidence."

The original version of the concluding paragraph was prepared by Seward and read as follows: "I close. We are not, we must not he aliens or enemies, but fellow-countrymen and brethren. Although passion has strained our bonds of affection too hardly, they must not, I am sure, they will not, be broken. The mystic chords which, proceeding from so many battlefields and so many patriot graves, pass through all the hearts and all hearths in this broad continent of ours, will yet again harmonize in their ancient music when breathed upon by the guardian angel of the nation."

These words, now so famous, were spoken in the east portico of the Capitol on "one of our disagreeable, clear, windy, Washington spring days."(10) Most of the participants were agitated; many were alarmed. Chief Justice Taney who administered the oath could hardly speak, so near to uncontrollable was his emotion. General Scott anxiously kept his eye upon the crowd which was commanded by cannon. Cavalry were in readiness to clear the streets in case of riot. Lincoln's carriage on the way to the Capitol had been closely guarded. He made his way to the portico between files of soldiers. So intent — overintent — were his guardians upon his safety that they had been careless of the smaller matter of his comfort. There was insufficient room for the large company that had been invited to attend. The new President stood beside a rickety little table and saw no place on which to put his hat. Senator Douglas stepped forward and relieved him of the burden. Lincoln was "pale and very nervous," and toward the close of his speech, visibly affected. Observers differ point-blank as to the way the inaugural was received. The "Public Man" says that there was little enthusiasm. The opposite version makes the event an oratorical triumph, with the crowd, at the close, completely under his spell.(11)

On the whole, the inauguration and the festivities that followed appear to have formed a dismal event. While Lincoln spoke, the topmost peak of the Capitol, far above his head, was an idle derrick; the present dome was in process of construction; work on it had been arrested, and who could say when, if ever, the work would be resumed? The day closed with an inaugural ball that was anything but brilliant. "The great tawdry ballroom . . . not half full—and such an assemblage of strange costumes, male and female. Very few people of any consideration were there. The President looked exhausted and uncomfortable, and most ungainly in his dress; and Mrs. Lincoln all in blue, with a feather in her hair and a highly flushed face."(12)

XV
PRESIDENT AND PREMIER

The brilliant Secretary, who so promptly began to influence the President had very sure foundations for that influence. He was inured to the role of great man; he had a rich experience of public life; while Lincoln, painfully conscious of his inexperience, was perhaps the humblest-minded ruler that ever took the helm of a ship of state in perilous times. Furthermore, Seward had some priceless qualities which, for Lincoln, were still to seek. First of all, he had audacity—personally, artistically, politically. Seward's instantaneous gift to Lincoln was by way of throwing wide the door of his gathering literary audacity. There is every reason to think that Seward's personal audacity went to Lincoln's heart at once. To be sure, he was not yet capable of going along with it. The basal contrast of the first month of his administration lies between the President's caution and the boldness of the Secretary. Nevertheless, to a sensitive mind, seeking guidance, surrounded by less original types of politicians, the splendid fearlessness of Seward, whether wise or foolish, must have rung like a trumpet peal soaring over the heads of a crowd whose teeth were chattering. While the rest of the Cabinet pressed their ears to the ground, Seward thought out a policy, made a forecast of the future, and offered to stake his head on the correctness of his reasoning. This may have been rashness; it may have been folly; but, intellectually at least, it was valor. Among Lincoln's other advisers, valor at that moment was lacking. Contrast, however, was not the sole, nor the surest basis of Seward's appeal to Lincoln. Their characters had a common factor. For all their immeasurable difference in externals, both at bottom were void of malice. It was this characteristic above all others that gave them spiritually common ground. In Seward, this quality had been under fire for a long while. The political furies of "that iron time" had failed to rouse echoes in his serene and smiling soul. Therefore, many men who accepted him as leader because, indeed, they could not do without him—because none other in their camp had his genius for management, for the glorification of political intrigue—these same men followed him doubtfully, with bad grace, willing to shift to some other leader whenever he might arise. The clue to their distrust was Seward's amusement at the furious.

Could a man who laughed when you preached on the beauty of the hewing of Agag, could such a man be sincere? And that Seward in some respects was not sincere, history generally admits. He loved to poke fun at his opponents by appearing to sneer at himself, by ridiculing the idea that he was ever serious. His scale of political values was different from that of most of his followers. Nineteen times out of twenty, he would treat what they termed "principles" as mere political counters, as legitimate subjects of bargain. If by any deal he could trade off any or all of these nineteen in order to secure the twentieth, which for him was the only vital one, he never scrupled to do so. Against a lurid background of political ferocity, this amused, ironic figure came to be rated by the extremists, both in his own and in the enemy camp as Mephistopheles.

No quality could have endeared him more certainly to Lincoln than the very one which the bigots misunderstood. From his earliest youth Lincoln had been governed by this same quality. With his non-censorious mind, which accepted so much of life as he found it, which was forever stripping principles of their accretions, what could be more inevitable than his warming to the one great man at Washington who like him held that such a point of view was the only rational one. Seward's ironic peacefulness in the midst of the storm gained in luster because all about him raged a tempest of ferocity, mitigated, at least so far as the distracted President could see, only by self-interest or pacifism.

As Lincoln came into office, he could see and hear many signs of a rising fierceness of sectional hatred. His secretary records with disgust a proposal to conquer the Gulf States, expel their white population, and reduce the region to a gigantic state preserve, where negroes should grow cotton under national supervision.(1) "We of the North," said Senator Baker of Oregon, "are a majority of the Union, and we will govern our Union in our own way."(2) At the other extreme was the hysterical pacifism of the Abolitionists. Part of Lincoln's abiding quarrel with the Abolitionists was their lack of national feeling. Their peculiar form of introspection had injected into politics the idea of personal sin. Their personal responsibility for slavery—they being part of a country that tolerated it—was their basal inspiration. Consequently, the most distinctive Abolitionists welcomed this opportunity to cast off their responsibility. If war had been proposed as a crusade to abolish slavery, their attitude might have been different But in March, 1860, no one but the few ultra-extremists, whom scarcely anybody heeded, dreamed of such a war. A war to restore the Union was the only sort that was considered seriously. Such a war, the Abolitionists bitterly condemned. They seized upon pacifism as their defense. Said Whittier of the Seceding States:

They break the links of Union: shall we light
The fires of hell to weld anew the chain,
On that red anvil where each blow is pain?

The fury and the fear offended Lincoln in equal measure. After long years opposing the political temper of the extremists, he was not the man now to change front. To one who believed himself marked out for a tragic end, the cowardice at the heart of the pacifism of his time was revolting. It was fortunate for his own peace of mind that he could here count on the Secretary of State. No argument based on fear of pain would meet in Seward with anything but derision. "They tell us," he had once said, and the words expressed his constant attitude, "that we are to encounter opposition. Why, bless my soul, did anybody ever expect to reach a fortune, or fame, or happiness on earth or a crown in heaven, without encountering resistance and opposition? What are we made men for but to encounter and overcome opposition arrayed against us in the line of our duty?"(3)

But if the ferocity and the cowardice were offensive and disheartening, there was something else that was beneath contempt. Never was self-interest more shockingly displayed. It was revealed in many ways, but impinged upon the new President in only one. A horde of office-seekers besieged him in the White House. The parallel to this amazing picture can hardly be found in history. It was taken for granted that the new party would make a clean sweep of the whole civil list, that every government employee down to the humblest messenger boy too young to have political ideas was to bear the label of the victorious party. Every Congressman who had made promises to his constituents, every politician of every grade who thought he had the party in his debt, every adventurer who on any pretext could make a showing of party service rendered, poured into Washington. It was a motley horde.

"Hark, hark, the dogs do bark,
The beggars are coming to town."

They converted the White House into a leaguer. They swarmed into the corridors and even the private passages. So dense was the swarm that it was difficult to make one's way either in or out. Lincoln described himself by the image of a man renting rooms at one end of his house while the other end was on fire.(4) And all this while the existence of the Republic was at stake! It did not occur to him that it was safe to defy the horde, to send it about its business. Here again, the figure of Seward stood out in brilliant light against the somber background. One of Seward's faculties was his power to form devoted lieutenants. He had that sure and nimble judgment which enables some men to inspire their lieutenants rather than categorically to instruct them. All the sordid side of his political games he managed in this way. He did not appear himself as the bargainer. In the shameful eagerness of most of the politicians to find offices for their retainers, Seward was conspicuous by contrast. Even the Cabinet was not free from this vice of catering to the thirsty horde.(5) Alone, at this juncture, Seward detached himself from the petty affairs of the hour and gave his whole attention to statecraft.

He had a definite policy. Another point of contact with Lincoln was the attitude of both toward the Union, supplemented as it was by their views of the place of slavery in the problem they confronted. Both were nationalists ready to make any sacrifices for the national idea. Both regarded slavery as an issue of second importance. Both were prepared for great concessions if convinced that, ultimately, their concessions would strengthen the trend of American life toward a general exaltation of nationality.

On the other hand, their differences —

Seward approached the problem in the same temper, with the same assumptions, that were his in the previous December. He still believed that his main purpose was to enable a group of politicians to save their faces by effecting a strategic retreat. Imputing to the Southern leaders an attitude of pure self-interest, he believed that if allowed to play the game as they desired, they would mark time until circumstances revealed to them whether there was more profit for them in the Union or out; he also believed that if sufficient time could be given, and if no armed clash took place, it would be demonstrated first, that they did not have so strong a hold on the South as they had thought they had; and second, that on the whole, it was to their interests to patch up the quarrel and come back into the Union. But he also saw that they had a serious problem of leadership, which, if rudely handled, might make it impossible for them to stand still. They had inflamed the sentiment of state-patriotism. In South Carolina, particularly, the popular demand was for independence. With this went the demand that Fort Sumter in Charleston Harbor, garrisoned by Federal troops, should be surrendered, or if not surrendered, taken forcibly from the United States. A few cannon shots at Sumter would mean war. An article in Seward's creed of statecraft asserted that the populace will always go wild over a war. To prevent a war fever in the North was the first condition of his policy at home. Therefore, in order to prevent it, the first step in saving his enemies' faces was to safeguard them against the same danger in their own calm. He must help them to prevent a war fever in the South. He saw but one way to do this. The conclusion which became the bed rock of his policy was inevitable. Sumter must be evacuated.

Even before the inauguration, he had broached this idea to Lincoln. He had tried to keep Lincoln from inserting in the inaugural the words,

"The power confided to me will be used to hold, occupy and possess the property and places belonging to the government." He had proposed instead, "The power confided in me shall be used indeed with efficacy, but also with discretion, in every case and exigency, according to the circumstances actually existing, and with a view and a hope of a peaceful solution of the national troubles, and the restoration of fraternal sympathies and affections."(6) With the rejection of Seward's proffered revision, a difference between them in policy began to develop. Lincoln, says one of his secretaries, accepted Seward's main purpose but did not share his "optimism."(7) It would be truer to say that in this stage of his development, he was lacking in audacity. In his eager search for advice, he had to strike a balance between the daring Seward who at this moment built entirely on his own power of political devination, and the cautious remainder of the Cabinet who had their ears to the ground trying their best to catch the note of authority in the rumblings of vox populi. For his own part, Lincoln began with two resolves: to go very cautiously, — and not give something for nothing. Far from him, as yet, was that plunging mood which in Seward pushed audacity to the verge of a gamble. However, just previous to the inauguration, he took a cautious step in Seward's direction. Virginia, like all the other States of the upper South, was torn by the question which side to take. There was a "Union" party in Virginia, and a "Secession" party. A committee of leading Unionists conferred with Lincoln. They saw the immediate problem very much as Seward did. They believed that if time were allowed, the crisis could be tided over and the Union restored; but the first breath of war would wreck their hopes. The condition of bringing about an adjustment was the evacuation of Sumter. Lincoln told them that if Virginia could be kept in the Union by the evacuation of Sumter, he would not hesitate to recall the garrison.(8) A few days later, despite what he had said in the inaugural, he repeated this offer. A convention was then sitting at Richmond in debate upon the relations of Virginia to the Union. If it would drop the matter and dissolve — so Lincoln told another committee — he would evacuate Sumter and trust the recovery of the lower South to negotiation.(9) No results, so far as is known, came of either of those offers.

During the first half of March, the Washington government marked time. The office-seekers continued to besiege the President. South Carolina continued to clamor for possession of Sumter. The Confederacy sent commissioners to Washington whom Lincoln refused to recognize. The Virginia Convention swayed this way and that.

Seward went serenely about his business, confident that everything was certain to come his way soon or late. He went so far as to advise an intermediary to tell the Confederate Commissioners that all they had to do to get possession of Sumter was to wait. The rest of the Cabinet pressed their ears more tightly than ever to the ground. The rumblings of vox populi were hard to interpret. The North appeared to be in two minds. This was revealed the day following the inauguration, when a Republican Club in New York held a high debate upon the condition of the country. One faction wanted Lincoln to declare for a war-policy; another wished the Club to content itself with a vote of confidence in the Administration. Each faction put its views into a resolution and as a happy device for maintaining harmony, both resolutions were passed.(10) The fragmentary, miscellaneous evidence of newspapers, political meetings, the talk of leaders, local elections, formed a confused clamor which each listener interpreted according to his predisposition. The members of the Cabinet in their relative isolation at Washington found it exceedingly difficult to make up their minds what the people were really saying. Of but one thing they were certain, and that was that they represented a minority party. Before committing themselves any way, it was life and death to know what portion of the North would stand by them.(11)

At this point began a perplexity that was to torment the President almost to the verge of distraction. How far could he trust his military advisers? Old General Scott was at the head of the army. He had once been a striking, if not a great figure. Should his military advice be accepted as final? Scott informed Lincoln that Sumter was short of food and that any attempt to relieve it would call for a much larger force than the government could muster. Scott urged him to withdraw the garrison. Lincoln submitted the matter to the Cabinet. He asked for their opinions in writing.(12) Five advised taking Scott at his word and giving up all thought of relieving Sumter. There were two dissenters. The Secretary of the Treasury, Salmon Portland Chase, struck the key-note of his later political career by an elaborate argument on expediency. If relieving Sumter would lead to civil war, Chase was not in favor of relief; but on the whole he did not think that civil war would result, and therefore, on the whole, he favored a relief expedition. One member of the Cabinet, Montgomery Blair, the Postmaster General, an impetuous, fierce man, was vehement for relief at all costs. Lincoln wanted to agree with Chase and Blair. He reasoned that if the fort was given up, the necessity under which it was done would not be fully understood; that by many it would be construed as part of a voluntary policy, that at home it would discourage the friends of the Union, embolden its adversaries, and go far to insure to the matter a recognition abroad.

Nevertheless, with the Cabinet five to two against him, with his military adviser against him, Lincoln put aside his own views. The government went on marking time and considering the credentials of applicants for country post-offices.

By this time, Lincoln had thrown off the overpowering gloom which possessed him in the latter days at Springfield. It is possible he had reacted to a mood in which there was something of levity. His oscillation of mood from a gloom that nothing penetrated to a sort of desperate mirth, has been noted by various observers. And in 1861 he had not reached his final poise, that firm holding of the middle way,—-which afterward fused his moods and made of him, at least in action, a sustained personality.

About the middle of the month he had a famous interview with Colonel W. T. Sherman who had been President of the University of Louisiana and had recently resigned. Senator John Sherman called at the White House with regard to "some minor appointments in Ohio." The Colonel went with him. When Colonel Sherman spoke of the seriousness of the Secession movement, Lincoln replied, "Oh, we'll manage to keep house." The Colonel was so offended by what seemed to him the flippancy of the President that he abandoned his intention to resume the military life and withdrew from Washington in disgust.(13)

Not yet had Lincoln attained a true appreciation of the real difficulty before him. He had not got rid of the idea that a dispute over slavery had widened accidentally into a needless sectional quarrel, and that as soon as the South had time to think things over, it would see that it did not really want the quarrel. He had a queer idea that meanwhile he could hold a few points on the margin of the Seceded States, open custom houses on ships at the mouths of harbors, but leave vacant all Federal appointments within the Seceded States and ignore the absence of their representatives from Washington.(14) This marginal policy did not seem to him a policy of coercion; and though he was beginning to see that the situation from the Southern point of view turned on the right of a State to resist coercion, he was yet to learn that idealistic elements of emotion and of political dogma were the larger part of his difficulty.

Meanwhile, the upper South had been proclaiming its idealism. Its attitude was creating a problem for the lower South as well as for the North. The pro-slavery leaders had been startled out of a dream. The belief in a Southern economic solidarity so complete that the secession of any one Slave State would compel the secession of all the others, that belief had been proved fallacious. It had been made plain that on the economic issue, even as on the issue of sectional distrust, the upper South would not follow the lower South into secession. When delegates from the Georgia Secessionists visited the legislature of North Carolina, every courtesy was shown to them; the Speaker of the House assured them of North Carolina's sympathy and of her enduring friendliness; but he was careful not to suggest an intention to secede, unless (the condition that was destiny!) an attempt should be made to violate the sovereignty of the State by marching troops across her soil to attack the Confederates. Then, on the one issue of State sovereignty, North Carolina would leave the Union.(15) The Unionists in Virginia took similar ground. They wished to stay in the Union, and they were determined not to go out on the issue of slavery. Therefore they laid their heads together to get that issue out of the way. Their problem was to devise a compromise that would do three things: lay the Southern dread of an inundation of sectional Northern influence; silence the slave profiteers; meet the objections that had induced Lincoln to wreck the Crittenden Compromise. They felt that the first and second objectives would be reached easily enough by reviving the line of the Missouri Compromise. But something more was needed, or again, Lincoln would refuse to negotiate. They met their crucial difficulty by boldly appealing to the South to be satisfied with the conservation of its present life and renounce the dream of unlimited Southern expansion. Their Compromise proposed a death blow to the filibuster and all he stood for. It provided that no new territory other than naval stations should be acquired by the United States on either side the Missouri Line without consent of a majority of the Senators from the States on the opposite side of that line.(16)

As a solution of the sectional quarrel, to the extent that it had been definitely put into words, what could have been more astute? Lincoln himself had said in the inaugural, "One section of our country believes slavery is right and ought to be extended; while the other believes it is wrong and ought not to be extended. That is the only substantial dispute." In the same inaugural, he had pledged himself not to "interfere with the institution of slavery in the States where it now exists;" and also had urged a vigorous enforcement of the Fugitive Slave Law. He never had approved of any sort of emancipation other than purchase or the gradual operation of economic conditions. It was well known that slavery could flourish only on fresh land amid prodigal agricultural methods suited to the most ignorant labor. The Virginia Compromise, by giving to slavery a fixed area and abolishing its hopes of continual extensions into fresh land, was the virtual fulfillment of Lincoln's demand.

The failure of the Virginia Compromise is one more proof that a great deal of vital history never gets into words until after it is over. During the second half of March, Unionists and Secessionists in the Virginia Convention debated with deep emotion this searching new proposal. The Unionists had a fatal weakness in their position. This was the feature of the situation that had not hitherto been put into words. Lincoln had not been accurate when he said that the slavery question was "the only substantial dispute." He had taken for granted that the Southern opposition to nationalism was not a real thing, — a mere device of the politicians to work up excitement. All the compromises he was ready to offer were addressed to that part of the South which was seeking to make an issue on slavery. They had little meaning for that other and more numerous part in whose thinking slavery was an incident. For this other South, the ideas which Lincoln as late as the middle of March did not bring into play were the whole story. Lincoln, willing to give all sorts of guarantees for the noninterference with slavery, would not give a single guarantee supporting the idea of State sovereignty against the idea of the sovereign power of the national Union. The Virginians, willing to go great lengths in making concessions with regard to slavery, would not go one inch in the way of admitting that their State was not a sovereign power included in the American Union of its own free will, and not the legitimate subject of any sort of coercion.

The Virginia Compromise was really a profound new complication. The very care with which it divided the issue of nationality from the issue of slavery was a storm signal. For a thoroughgoing nationalist like Lincoln, deep perplexities lay hidden in this full disclosure of the issue that was vital to the moderate South. Lincoln's shifting of his mental ground, his perception that hitherto he had been oblivious of his most formidable opponent, the one with whom compromise was impossible, occurred in the second half of the month.

As always, Lincoln kept his own counsel upon the maturing of a purpose in his own mind. He listened to every adviser — opening his office doors without reserve to all sorts and conditions — and silently, anxiously, struggled with himself for a decision. He watched Virginia; he watched the North; he listened — and waited. General Scott continued hopeless, though minor military men gave encouragement. And whom should the President trust-the tired old General who disagreed with him, or the eager young men who held views he would like to hold? Many a time he was to ask himself that question during the years to come.

On March twenty-ninth, he again consulted the Cabinet.(17) A great deal of water had run under the mill since they gave their opinions on March sixteenth. The voice of the people was still a bewildering roar, but out of that roar most of the Cabinet seemed to hear definite words. They were convinced that the North was veering toward a warlike mood. The phrase "masterly inactivity," which had been applied to the government's course admiringly a few weeks before, was now being applied satirically. Republican extremists were demanding action. A subtle barometer was the Secretary of the Treasury. Now, as on the sixteenth, he craftily said something without saying it. After juggling the word "if," he assumed his "if" to be a fact and concluded, "If war is to be the result, I perceive no reason why it may not best be begun in consequence of military resistance to the efforts of the Administration to sustain troops of the Union, stationed under authority of the government in a fort of the Union, in the ordinary course of service."

This elaborate equivocation, which had all the force of an assertion, was Chase all over! Three other ministers agreed with him except that they did not equivocate. One evaded. Of all those who had stood with Seward on the sixteenth, only one was still in favor of evacuation. Seward stood fast. This reversal of the Cabinet's position, jumping as it did with Lincoln's desires, encouraged him to prepare for action. But just as he was about to act his diffidence asserted itself. He authorized the preparation of a relief expedition but withheld sailing orders until further notice.(18) Oh, for Seward's audacity; for the ability to do one thing or another and take the consequences!

Seward had not foreseen this turn of events. He had little respect for the rest of the Cabinet, and had still to discover that the President, for all his semblance of vacillation, was a great man. Seward was undeniably vain. That the President with such a Secretary of State should judge the strength of a Cabinet vote by counting noses—preposterous! But that was just what this curiously simple-minded President had done. If he went on in his weak, amiable way listening to the time-servers who were listening to the bigots, what would become of the country? And of the Secretary of State and his deep policies? The President must be pulled up short—brought to his senses—taught a lesson or two.

Seward saw that new difficulties had arisen in the course of that fateful March which those colleagues of his in the Cabinet—well-meaning, inferior men, to be sure—had not the subtlety to comprehend. Of course the matter of evacuation remained what it always had been, the plain open road to an ultimate diplomatic triumph. Who but a president out of the West, or a minor member of the Cabinet, would fail to see that! But there were two other considerations which, also, his well-meaning colleagues were failing to allow for. While all this talk about the Virginia Unionists had been going on, while Washington and Richmond had been trying to negotiate, neither really had any control of its own game. They were card players with all the trumps out of their hands. Montgomery, the Confederate Congress, held the trumps. At any minute it could terminate all this make-believe of diplomatic independence, both at Washington and at Richmond. A few cannon shots aimed at Sumter, the cry for revenge in the North, the inevitable protest against coercion in Virginia, the convention blown into the air, and there you are—War!

And after all that, who knows what next? And yet, Blair and Chase and the rest would not consent to slip Montgomery's trumps out of her hands — the easiest thing in the world to do! — by throwing Sumter into her lap and thus destroying the pretext for the cannon shots. More than ever before, Seward would insist firmly on the evacuation of Sumter.

But there was the other consideration, the really new turn of events. Suppose Sumter is evacuated; suppose Montgomery has lost her chance to force Virginia into war by precipitating the issue of coercion, what follows? All along Seward had advocated a national convention to readjust all the matters "in dispute between the sections." But what would such a convention discuss? In his inaugural, Lincoln had advised an amendment to the Constitution "to the effect that the Federal government shall never interfere with the domestic institutions of the State, including that of persons held to service." Very good! The convention might be expected to accept this, and after this, of course, there would come up the Virginia Compromise. Was it a practical scheme? Did it form a basis for drawing back into the Union the lower South?

Seward's whole thought upon this subject has never been disclosed. It must be inferred from the conclusion which he reached, which he put into a paper entitled, Thoughts for the President's Consideration, and submitted to Lincoln, April first.

The Thoughts outlined a scheme of policy, the most startling feature of which was an instant, predatory, foreign war. There are two clues to this astounding proposal. One was a political maxim in which Seward had unwavering faith. "A fundamental principle of politics," he said, "is always to be on the side of your country in a war. It kills any party to oppose a war. When Mr. Buchanan got up his Mormon War, our people, Wade and Fremont, and The Tribune, led off furiously against it. I supported it to the immense disgust of enemies and friends. If you want to sicken your opponents with their own war, go in for it till they give it up."(19) He was not alone among the politicians of his time, and some other times, in these cynical views. Lincoln has a story of a politician who was asked to oppose the Mexican War, and who replied, "I opposed one war; that was enough for me. I am now perpetually in favor of war, pestilence and famine."

The second clue to Seward's new policy of international brigandage was the need, as he conceived it, to propitiate those Southern expansionists who in the lower South at least formed so large a part of the political machine, who must somehow be lured back into the Union; to whom the Virginia Compromise, as well as every other scheme of readjustment yet suggested, offered no allurement. Like Lincoln defeating the Crittenden Compromise, like the Virginians planning the last compromise, Seward remembered the filibusters and the dreams of the expansionists, annexation of Cuba, annexation of Nicaragua and all the rest, and he looked about for a way to reach them along that line. Chance had played into his hands. Already Napoleon III had begun his ill-fated interference with the affairs of Mexico. A rebellion had just taken place in San Domingo and Spain was supposed to have designs on the island. Here, for any one who believed in predatory war as an infallible last recourse to rouse the patriotism of a country, were pretexts enough. Along with these would go a raging assertion of the Monroe Doctrine and a bellicose attitude toward other European powers on less substantial grounds. And amid it all, between the lines of it all, could not any one glimpse a scheme for the expansion of the United States southward? War with Spain over San Domingo! And who, pray, held the Island of Cuba! And what might not a defeated Spain be willing to do with Cuba? And if France were driven out of Mexico by our conquering arms, did not the shadows of the future veil but dimly a grateful Mexico where American capital should find great opportunities? And would not Southern capital in the nature of things, have a large share in all that was to come? Surely, granting Seward's political creed, remembering the problem he wished to solve, there is nothing to be wondered at in his proposal to Lincoln: "I would demand explanations from Spain and France, categorically, at once." . . . And if satisfactory explanations were not received from Spain and France, "would convene Congress and declare war against them."

His purpose, he said, was to change the question before the public, from one upon slavery, or about slavery, for a question upon Union or Disunion. Sumter was to be evacuated "as a safe means for changing the issue," but at the same time, preparations were to be made for a blockade of the Southern coast.(20) This extraordinary document administered mild but firm correction to the President. He was told that he had no policy, although under the circumstances, this was "not culpable"; that there must be a single head to the government; that the President, if not equal to the task, should devolve it upon some member of the Cabinet. The Thoughts closed with these words, "I neither seek to evade nor assume responsibility."

Like Seward's previous move, when he sent Weed to Springfield, this other brought Lincoln to a point of crisis. For the second time he must render a decision that would turn the scale, that would have for his country the force of destiny. In one respect he did not hesitate. The most essential part of the Thoughts was the predatory spirit. This clashed with Lincoln's character. Serene unscrupulousness met unwavering integrity. Here was one of those subjects on which Lincoln was not asking advice. As to ways and means, he was pliable to a degree in the hands of richer and wider experience; as to principles, he was a rock. Seward's whole scheme of aggrandizement, his magnificent piracy, was calmly waved aside as a thing of no concern. The most striking characteristic of Lincoln's reply was its dignity. He did not, indeed, lay bare his purposes. He was content to point out certain inconsistencies in Seward's argument; to protest that whatever action might be taken with regard to the single fortress, Sumter, the question before the public could not be changed by that one event; and to say that while he expected advice from all his Cabinet, he was none the less President, and in last resort he would himself direct the policy of the government.(21)

Only a strong man could have put up with the patronizing condescension of the Thoughts and betrayed no irritation. Not a word in Lincoln's reply gives the least hint that condescension had been displayed. He is wholly unruffled, distant, objective. There is also a quiet tone of finality, almost the tone one might use in gently but firmly correcting a child. The Olympian impertinence of the Thoughts had struck out of Lincoln the first flash of that approaching masterfulness by means of which he was to ride out successfully such furious storms. Seward was too much the man of the world not to see what had happened. He never touched upon the Thoughts again. Nor did Lincoln. The incident was secret until Lincoln's secretaries twenty-five years afterward published it to the world.

But Lincoln's lofty dignity on the first of April was of a moment only. When the Secretary of the Navy, Gideon Welles, that same day called on him in his offices, he was the easy-going, jovial Lincoln who was always ready half-humorously to take reproof from subordinates—as was evinced by his greeting to the Secretary. Looking up from his writing, he said cheerfully, "What have I done wrong?"(22) Gideon Welles was a pugnacious man, and at that moment an angry man. There can be little doubt that his lips were tightly shut, that a stern frown darkened his brows. Grimly conscientious was Gideon Welles, likewise prosaic; a masterpiece of literalness, the very opposite in almost every respect of the Secretary of State whom he cordially detested. That he had already found occasion to protest against the President's careless mode of conducting business may be guessed—correctly—from the way he was received. Doubtless the very cordiality, the whimsical admission of loose methods, irritated the austere Secretary. Welles had in his hand a communication dated that same day and signed by the President, making radical changes in the program of the Navy Department. He had come to protest.

"The President," said Welles, "expressed as much surprise as I felt, that he had sent me such a document. He said that Mr. Seward with two or three young men had been there during the day on a subject which he (Seward) had in hand and which he had been some time maturing; that it was Seward's specialty, to which he, the President, had yielded, but as it involved considerable details, he had left Mr. Seward to prepare the necessary papers. These papers he had signed, many of them without reading, for he had not time, and if he could not trust the Secretary of State, he knew not whom he could trust. I asked who were associated with Mr. Seward. 'No one,' said the President, 'but these young men who were here as clerks to write down his plans and orders.' Most of the work was done, he said, in the other room.

"The President reiterated that they (the changes in the Navy) were not his instructions, though signed by him; that the paper was an improper one; that he wished me to give it no more consideration than I thought proper; to treat it as cancelled, or as if it had never been written. I could get no satisfactory explanation from the President of the origin of this strange interference which mystified him and which he censured and condemned more severely than myself. . . . Although very much disturbed by the disclosure, he was anxious to avoid difficulty, and to shield Mr. Seward, took to himself the whole blame."

Thus Lincoln began a role that he never afterward abandoned. It was the role of scapegoat Whatever went wrong anywhere could always be loaded upon the President. He appeared to consider it a part of his duty to be the scapegoat for the whole Administration. It was his way of maintaining trust, courage, efficiency, among his subordinates.

Of those papers which he had signed without reading on April first, Lincoln was to hear again in still more surprising fashion six days thereafter.

He was now at the very edge of his second crucial decision. Though the naval expedition was in preparation, he still hesitated over issuing orders to sail. The reply to the Thoughts had not committed him to any specific line of conduct. What was it that kept him wavering at this eleventh hour? Again, that impenetrable taciturnity which always shrouded his progress toward a conclusion, forbids dogmatic assertion. But two things are obvious: his position as a minority president, of which he was perhaps unduly conscious, caused him to delay, and to delay again and again, seeking definite evidence how much support he could command in the North; the change in his comprehension of the problem before him-his perception that it was not an "artificial crisis" involving slavery alone, but an irreconcilable clash of social-political idealism — this disturbed his spirit, distressed, even appalled him. Having a truer insight into human nature than Seward had, he saw that here was an issue immeasurably less susceptible of compromise than was slavery. Whether, the moment he perceived this, he at once lost hope of any peaceable solution, we do not know. Just what he thought about the Virginia Compromise is still to seek. However, the nature of his mind, the way it went straight to the human element in a problem once his eyes were opened to the problem's reality, forbid us to conclude that he took hope from Virginia. He now saw what, had it not been for his near horizon, he would have seen so long before, that, in vulgar parlance, he had been "barking up the wrong tree." Now that he had located the right tree, had the knowledge come too late?

It is known that Seward, possibly at Lincoln's request, made an attempt to bring together the Virginia Unionists and the Administration. He sent a special representative to Richmond urging the despatch of a committee to confer with the President.

The strength of the party in the Convention was shown on April fourth when a proposed Ordinance of Secession was voted down, eighty-nine to forty-five. On the same day, the Convention by a still larger majority formally denied the right of the Federal government to coerce a State. Two days later, John B. Baldwin, representing the Virginia Unionists, had a confidential talk with Lincoln. Only fragments of their talk, drawn forth out of memory long afterward — some of the reporting being at second hand, the recollections of the recollections of the participants — are known to exist. The one fact clearly discernible is that Baldwin stated fully the Virginia position: that her Unionists were not nationalists; that the coercion of any State, by impugning the sovereignty of all, would automatically drive Virginia out of the Union.(23)

Lincoln had now reached his decision. The fear that had dogged him all along — the fear that in evacuating Sumter he would be giving something for nothing, that "it would discourage the friends of the Union, embolden its adversaries" — was in possession of his will. One may hazard the guess that this fear would have determined Lincoln sooner than it did, except for the fact that the Secretary of State, despite his faults, was so incomparably the strongest personality in the Cabinet. We have Lincoln's own word for the moment and the detail that formed the very end of his period of vacillation. All along he had intended to relieve and hold Fort Pickens, off the coast of Florida. To this, Seward saw no objection. In fact, he urged the relief of Pickens, hoping, as compensation, to get his way about Sumter. Assuming as he did that the Southern leaders were opportunists, he believed that they would not make an issue over Pickens, merely because it had not in the public eye become a political symbol. Orders had been sent to a squadron in Southern waters to relieve Pickens. Early in April news was received at Washington that the attempt had failed due to misunderstandings among the Federal commanders. Fearful that Pickens was about to fall, reasoning that whatever happened he dared not lose both forts, Lincoln became peremptory on the subject of the Sumter expedition. This was on April sixth.

On the night of April sixth, Lincoln's signatures to the unread despatches of the first of April, came home to roost. And at last, Welles found out what Seward was doing on the day of All Fools.(24)

While the Sumter expedition was being got ready, still without sailing orders, a supplemental expedition was also preparing for the relief of Pickens. This was the business that Seward was contriving, that Lincoln would not explain, on April first. The order interfering with the Navy Department was designed to checkmate the titular head of the department. Furthermore, Seward had had the amazing coolness to assume that Lincoln would certainly accept his Thoughts and that the simple President need not hereinafter be consulted about details. He aimed to circumvent Welles and to make sure that the Sumter expedition, whether sailing orders were issued or not, should be rendered innocuous. The warship Powhatan, which was being got ready for sea at the Brooklyn Navy Yard, was intended by Welles for the Sumter expedition. One of those unread despatches signed by Lincoln, assigned it to the Pickens expedition. When the sailing orders from Welles were received, the commander of the Sumter fleet claimed the Powhatan. The Pickens commander refused to give it up. The latter telegraphed Seward that his expedition was "being retarded and embarrassed" by "conflicting" orders from Welles. The result was a stormy conference between Seward and Welles which was adjourned to the White House and became a conference with Lincoln. And then the whole story came out. Lincoln played the scapegoat, "took the whole blame upon himself, said it was carelessness, heedlessness on his part; he ought to have been more careful and attentive." But he insisted on immediate correction of his error, on the restoration of the Powhatan to the Sumter fleet. Seward struggled hard for his plan. Lincoln was inflexible. As Seward had directed the preparation of the Pickens expedition, Lincoln required him to telegraph to Brooklyn the change in orders. Seward, beaten by his enemy Welles, was deeply chagrined. In his agitation he forgot to be formal, forgot that the previous order had gone out in the President's name, and wired curtly, "Give up the Powhatan. Seward."

This despatch was received just as the Pickens expedition was sailing. The commander of the Powhatan had now before him, three orders. Naturally, he held that the one signed by the President took precedence over the others. He went on his way, with his great warship, to Florida. The Sumter expedition sailed without any powerful ship of war. In this strange fashion, chance executed Seward's design.

Lincoln had previously informed the Governor of South Carolina that due notice would be given, should he decide to relieve Sumter. Word was now sent that "an attempt will be made to supply Fort Sumter with provisions only; and that if such attempt be not resisted, no effort to throw in men, arms or ammunition will be made without further notice, or in case of an attack upon the fort."(25) Though the fleet was not intended to offer battle, it was supposed to be strong enough to force its way into the harbor, should the relief of Sumter be opposed. But the power to do so was wholly conditioned on the presence in its midst of the Powhatan. And the Powhatan was far out to sea on its way to Florida.

And now it was the turn of the Confederate government to confront a crisis. It, no less than Washington, had passed through a period of disillusion. The assumption upon which its chief politicians had built so confidently had collapsed. The South was not really a unit. It was not true that the secession of any one State, on any sort of issue, would compel automatically the secession of all the Southern States. North Carolina had exploded this illusion. Virginia had exploded it. The South could not be united on the issue of slavery; it could not be united on the issue of sectional dread. It could be united on but one issue-State sovereignty, the denial of the right of the Federal Government to coerce a State. The time had come to decide whether the cannon at Charleston should fire. As Seward had foreseen, Montgomery held the trumps; but had Montgomery the courage to play them? There was a momentous debate in the Confederate Cabinet. Robert Toombs, the Secretary of State, whose rapid growth in comprehension since December formed a parallel to Lincoln's growth, threw his influence on the side of further delay. He would not invoke that "final argument of kings," the shotted cannon. "Mr. President," he exclaimed, "at this time, it is suicide, murder, and will lose us every friend at the North. You will instantly strike a hornet's nest which extends from mountain to ocean, and legions now quiet will swarm out and sting us to death. It is unnecessary; it puts us in the wrong; it is fatal." But Toombs stood alone in the Cabinet. Orders were sent to Charleston to reduce Fort Sumter. Before dawn, April twelfth, the first shot was fired. The flag of the United States was hauled down on the afternoon of the thirteenth. Meanwhile the relieving fleet had arrived — without the Powhatan. Bereft of its great ship, it could not pass the harbor batteries and assist the fort. Its only service was to take off the garrison which by the terms of surrender was allowed to withdraw. On the fourteenth, Sumter was evacuated and the inglorious fleet sailed back to the northward.

Lincoln at once accepted the gage of battle. On the fifteenth appeared his proclamation calling for an army of seventy-five thousand volunteers. Automatically, the upper South fulfilled its unhappy destiny. Challenged at last, on the irreconcilable issue, Virginia, North Carolina, Tennessee, Arkansas, seceded. The final argument of kings was the only one remaining.

XVI
"ON TO RICHMOND!"

It has been truly said that the Americans are an unmilitary but an intensely warlike nation. Seward's belief that a war fury would sweep the country at the first cannon shot was amply justified. Both North and South appeared to rise as one man, crying fiercely to be led to battle.

The immediate effect on Washington had not been foreseen. That historic clash at Baltimore between the city's mob and the Sixth Massachusetts en route to the capital, was followed by an outburst of secession feeling in Maryland; by an attempt to isolate Washington from the North. Railway tracks were torn up; telegraph wires were cut. During several days Lincoln was entirely ignorant of what the North was doing. Was there an efficient general response to his call for troops? Or was precious time being squandered in preparation? Was it conceivable that the war fury was only talk? Looking forth from the White House, he was a prisoner of the horizon; an impenetrable mystery, it shut the capital in a ring of silence all but intolerable. Washington assumed the air of a beleaguered city. General Scott hastily drew in the small forces which the government had maintained in Maryland and Virginia. Government employees and loyal Washingtonians were armed and began to drill. The White House became a barracks. "Jim Lane," writes delightful John Hay in his diary, which is always cool, rippling, sunny, no matter how acute the crisis, "Jim Lane marshalled his Kansas warriors today at Williard's; tonight (they are in) the East Room."(1) Hay's humor brightens the tragic hour. He felt it his duty to report to Lincoln a "yarn" that had been told to him by some charming women who had insisted on an interview; they had heard from "a dashing Virginian" that inside forty-eight hours something would happen which would ring through the world. The ladies thought this meant the capture or assassination of the President. "Lincoln quietly grinned." But Hay who plainly enjoyed the episode, charming women and all, had got himself into trouble. He had to do "some very dexterous lying to calm the awakened fears of Mrs. Lincoln in regard to the assassination suspicion." Militia were quartered in the Capitol, and Pennsylvania Avenue was a drill ground. At the President's reception, the distinguished politician C. C. Clay, "wore with a sublimely unconscious air three pistols and an 'Arkansas toothpick,' and looked like an admirable vignette to twenty-five cents' worth of yellow covered romance."

But Hay's levity was all of the surface. Beneath it was intense anxiety. General Scott reported that the Virginia militia, concentrating about Washington, were a formidable menace, though he thought he was strong enough to hold out until relief should come. As the days passed and nothing appeared upon that inscrutable horizon while the telegraph remained silent, Lincoln became moodily distressed. One afternoon, "the business of the day being over, the executive office deserted, after walking the floor alone in silent thought for nearly a half-hour, he stopped and gazed long and wistfully out of the window down the Potomac in the direction of the expected ships (bringing soldiers from New York); and unconscious of other presence in the room, at length broke out with irrepressible anguish in the repeated exclamation, 'Why don't they come! Why don't they come!'"(2)

His unhappiness flashed into words while he was visiting those Massachusetts soldiers who had been wounded on their way to Washington. "I don't believe there is any North. . . " he exclaimed. "You are the only Northern realities."(3) But even then relief was at hand. The Seventh New York, which had marched down Broadway amid such an ovation as never before was given any regiment in America, had come by sea to Annapolis. At noon on April twenty-fifth, it reached Washington bringing, along with the welcome sight of its own bayonets, the news that the North had risen, that thousands more were on the march.

Hay who met them at the depot went at once to report to Lincoln. Already the President had reacted to a "pleasant, hopeful mood." He began outlining a tentative plan of action: blockade, maintenance of the safety of Washington, holding Fortress Monroe, and then to "go down to Charleston and pay her the little debt we are owing there."(4) But this was an undigested plan. It had little resemblance to any of his later plans. And immediately the chief difficulties that were to embarrass all his plans appeared. He was a minority President; and he was the Executive of a democracy. Many things were to happen; many mistakes were to be made; many times the piper was to be paid, ere Lincoln felt sufficiently sure of his support to enforce a policy of his own, defiant of opposition. Throughout the spring of 1861 his imperative need was to secure the favor of the Northern mass, to shape his policy with that end in view. At least, in his own mind, this seemed to be his paramount obligation. And so it was in the minds of his advisers. Lincoln was still in the pliable mood which was his when he entered office, which continued to be in evidence, except for sudden momentary disappearances when a different Lincoln flashed an instant into view, until another year and more had gone by. Still he felt himself the apprentice hand painfully learning the trade of man of action. Still he was deeply sensitive to advice.

And what advice did the country give him? There was one roaring shout dinning into his ears all round the Northern horizon-"On to Richmond!" Following Virginia's secession, Richmond had become the Confederate capital. It was expected that a session of the Confederate Congress would open at Richmond in July. "On to Richmond! Forward to Richmond!" screamed The Tribune. "The Rebel Congress must not be allowed to meet there on the 20th of July. By that date the place must be held by the national army." The Times advised the resignation of the Cabinet; it warned the President that if he did not give prompt satisfaction he would be superseded. Though Lincoln laughed at the threat of The Times to "depose" him, he took very seriously all the swiftly accumulating evidence that the North was becoming rashly impatient Newspaper correspondents at Washington talked to his secretaries "impertinently."(5) Members of Congress, either carried away by the excitement of the hour or with slavish regard to the hysteria of their constituents, thronged to Washington clamoring for action. On purely political grounds, if on no other, they demanded an immediate advance into Virginia. Military men looked with irritation, if not with contempt, on all this intemperate popular fury. That grim Sherman, who had been offended by Lincoln's tone the month previous, put their feeling into words. Declining the offer of a position in the War Department, he wrote that he wished "the Administration all success in its almost impossible task of governing this distracted and anarchial people."(6)

In the President's councils, General Scott urged delay, and the gathering of the volunteers into camps of instruction, their deliberate transformation into a genuine army. So inadequate were the resources of the government; so loose and uncertain were the militia organizations which were attempting to combine into an army; such discrepancies appeared between the nominal and actual strength of commands, between the places where men were supposed to be and the places where they actually were; that Lincoln in his droll way compared the process of mobilization to shoveling a bushel of fleas across a barn floor.(7) From the military point of view it was no time to attempt an advance. Against the military argument, three political arguments loomed dark in the minds of the Cabinet; there was the clamor of the Northern majority; there were the threats of the politicians who were to assemble in Congress, July fourth; there was the term of service of the volunteers which had been limited by the proclamation to three months. Late in June, the Cabinet decided upon the political course, overruled the military advisers, and gave its voice for an immediate advance into Virginia. Lincoln accepted this rash advice. Scott yielded. General Irwin McDowell was ordered to strike a Confederate force that had assembled at Manassas. (8) On the fourth of July, the day Congress met, the government made use of a coup de theatre. It held a review of what was then considered a "grand army" of twenty-five thousand men. A few days later, the sensibilities of the Congressmen were further exploited. Impressionable members were "deeply moved," when the same host in marching order passed again through the city and wheeled southward toward Virginia. Confident of victory, the Congressmen spent these days in high debate upon anything that took their fancy. When, a fortnight later, it was known that a battle was imminent, many of them treated the Occasion as a picnic. They took horses, or hired vehicles, and away they went southward for a jolly outing on the day the Confederacy was to collapse. In the mind of the unfortunate General who commanded the expedition a different mood prevailed. In depression, he said to a friend, "This is not an army. It will take a long time to make an army. But his duty as a soldier forbade him to oppose his superiors; the poor fellow could not proclaim his distrust of his army in public." (9) Thoughtful observers at Washington felt danger in the air, both military and political.

Sunday, July twenty-first, dawned clear. It was the day of the expected battle. A noted Englishman, setting out for the front as war correspondent of the London Times, observed "the calmness and silence of the streets of Washington, this early morning." After crossing the Potomac, he felt that "the promise of a lovely day given by the early dawn was likely to be realized to the fullest"; and "the placid beauty of the scenery as we drove through the woods below Arlington" delighted him. And then about nine o'clock his thoughts abandoned the scenery. Through those beautiful Virginia woods came the distant roar of cannon.

At the White House that day there was little if any alarm. Reports received at various times were construed by military men as favorable. These, with the rooted preconception that the army had to be successful, established confidence in a victory before nightfall. Late in the afternoon, the President relieved his tension by taking a drive. He had not returned when, about six o'clock, Seward appeared and asked hoarsely where he was. The secretaries told him. He begged them to find the President as quickly as possible. "Tell no one," said he, "but the battle is lost. The army is in full retreat."

The news of the rout at Bull Run did not spread through Washington until close to midnight. It caused an instantaneous panic. In the small hours, the space before the Treasury was "a moving mass of humanity. Every man seemed to be asking every man he met for the latest news, while all sorts of rumors filled the air. A feeling of mingled horror and despair appeared to possess everybody. . . . Our soldiers came straggling into the city covered with dust and many of them wounded, while the panic that led to the disaster spread like a contagion through all classes." The President did not share the panic. He "received the news quietly and without any visible sign of perturbation or excitement"'(10) Now appeared in him the quality which led Herndon to call him a fatalist. All night long he sat unruffled in his office, while refugees from the stricken field—especially those overconfident Senators and Representatives who had gone out to watch the overthrow of the Confederates—poured into his ears their various and conflicting accounts of the catastrophe. During that long night Lincoln said almost nothing. Meanwhile, fragments of the routed army continued to stream into the city. At dawn the next day Washington was possessed by a swarm of demoralized soldiers while a dreary rain settled over it.

The silent man in the White House had forgotten for the moment his dependence upon his advisers. While the runaway Senators were talking themselves out, while the rain was sheeting up the city, he had reached two conclusions. Early in the morning, he formulated both. One conclusion was a general outline for the conduct of a long war in which the first move should be a call for volunteers to serve three years.(11) The other conclusion was the choice of a conducting general. Scott was too old. McDowell had failed. But there was a young officer, a West Pointer, who had been put in command of the Ohio militia, who had entered the Virginia mountains from the West, had engaged a small force there, and had won several small but rather showy victories. Young as he was, he had served in the Mexican War and was supposed to be highly accomplished. On the day following Bull Run, Lincoln ordered McClellan to Washington to take command.(12)

XVII
DEFINING THE ISSUE

While these startling events were taking place in the months between Sumter and Bull Run, Lincoln passed through a searching intellectual experience. The reconception of his problem, which took place in March, necessitated a readjustment of his political attitude. He had prepared his arsenal for the use of a strategy now obviously beside the mark. The vital part of the first inaugural was its attempt to cut the ground from under the slave profiteers. Its assertion that nothing else was important, the idea that the crisis was "artificial," was sincere. Two discoveries had revolutionized Lincoln's thought. The discovery that what the South was in earnest about was not slavery but State sovereignty; the discovery that the North was far from a unit upon nationalism. To meet the one, to organize the other, was the double task precipitated by the fall of Sumter. Not only as a line of attack, but also as a means of defense, Lincoln had to raise to its highest power the argument for the sovereign reality of the national government. The effort to do this formed the silent inner experience behind the surging external events in the stormy months between April and July. It was governed by a firmness not paralleled in his outward course. As always, Lincoln the thinker asked no advice. It was Lincoln the administrator, painfully learning a new trade, who was timid, wavering, pliable in council. Behind the apprentice in statecraft, the lonely thinker stood apart, inflexible as ever, impervious to fear. The thinking which he formulated in the late spring and early summer of 1861 obeyed his invariable law of mental gradualness. It arose out of the deep places of his own past. He built up his new conclusion by drawing together conclusions he had long held, by charging them with his later experience, by giving to them a new turn, a new significance.

Lincoln's was one of those natures in which ideas have to become latent before they can be precipitated by outward circumstance into definite form. Always with him the idea that was to become powerful at a crisis was one that he had long held in solution, that had permeated him without his formulating it, that had entwined itself with his heartstrings; never was it merely a conscious act of the logical faculty. His characteristics as a lawyer—preoccupation with basal ideas, with ethical significance, with those emotions which form the ultimates of life—these always determined his thought. His idea of nationalism was a typical case. He had always believed in the reality of the national government as a sovereign fact. But he had thought little about it; rather he had taken it for granted. It was so close to his desire that he could not without an effort acknowledge the sincerity of disbelief in it. That was why he was so slow in forming a true comprehension of the real force opposing him. Disunion had appeared to him a mere device of party strategy. That it was grounded upon a genuine, a passionate conception of government, one irreconcilable with his own, struck him, when at last he grasped it, as a deep offense. The literary statesman sprang again to life. He threw all the strength of his mind, the peculiar strength that had made him president, into a statement of the case for nationalism.

His vehicle for publishing his case was the first message to Congress. (1) It forms an amazing contrast with the first inaugural. The argument over slavery that underlies the whole of the inaugural has vanished. The message does not mention slavery. From the first word to the last, it is an argument for the right of the central government to exercise sovereign power, and for the duty of the American people—to give their lives for the Union. No hint of compromise; nought of the cautious and conciliatory tone of the inaugural. It is the blast of a trumpet—a war trumpet. It is the voice of a stern mind confronting an adversary that arouses in him no sympathy, no tolerance even, much less any thought of concession. Needless to insist that this adversary is an idea. Toward every human adversary, Lincoln was always unbelievably tender. Though little of a theologian, he appreciated intuitively some metaphysical ideas; he projected into politics the philosopher's distinction between sin and the sinner. For all his hatred of the ideas which he held to be treason, he never had a vindictive impulse directed toward the men who accepted those ideas. Destruction for the idea, infinite clemency for the person—such was his attitude.

It was the idea of disunion, involving as he believed, a misconception of the American government, and by implication, a misconception of the true function of all governments everywhere, against which he declared a war without recourse.

The basis of his argument reaches back to his oration on Clay, to his assertion that Clay loved his country, partly because it was his country, even more because it was a free country. This idea ran through Lincoln's thinking to the end. There was in him a suggestion of internationalism. At the full height of his power, in his complete maturity as a political thinker, he said that the most sacred bond in life should be the brotherhood of the workers of all nations. No words of his are more significant than his remarks to passing soldiers in 1863, such as, "There is more involved in this contest than is realized by every one. There is involved in this struggle the question whether your children and my children shall enjoy the privileges we have enjoyed." And again, "I happen temporarily to occupy this White House. I am a living witness that any one of your children may look to come here as my father's child has."(2)

This idea, the idea that the "plain people" are the chief concern of government was the bed rock of all his political thinking. The mature, historic Lincoln is first of all a leader of the plain people—of the mass—as truly as was Cleon, or Robespierre, or Andrew Jackson. His gentleness does not remove him from that stern category. The latent fanaticism that is in every man, or almost every man, was grounded in Lincoln, on his faith—so whimsically expressed—that God must have loved the plain people because he had made so many of them.(3) The basal appeal of the first message was in the words:

"This is essentially a people's contest. On the side of the Union it is a struggle for maintaining in the world that form and substance of government whose leading object is to elevate the condition of men; to lift artificial weights from all shoulders; to clear the paths of laudable pursuit for all; to afford all an unfettered start and a fair chance in the race of life."(4) Not a war over slavery, not a war to preserve a constitutional system, but a war to assert and maintain the sovereignty of—"We, the People."

But how was it to be proved that this was, in fact, the true issue of the moment? Here, between the lines of the first message, Lincoln's deepest feelings are to be glimpsed. Out of the discovery that Virginia honestly believed herself a sovereign power, he had developed in himself a deep, slow-burning fervor that probably did much toward fusing him into the great Lincoln of history. But why? What was there in that idea which should strike so deep? Why was it not merely one view in a permissible disagreement over the interpretation of the Constitution? Why did the cause of the people inspire its champion to regard the doctrine of State sovereignty as anti-christ? Lincoln has not revealed himself on these points in so many words. But he has revealed himself plainly enough by implication.

The clue is in that element of internationalism which lay at the back of his mind. There must be no misunderstanding of this element. It was not pointing along the way of the modern "international." Lincoln would have fought Bolshevism to the death. Side by side with his assertion of the sanctity of the international bond of labor, stands his assertion of a sacred right in property and that capital is a necessity.(5) His internationalism was ethical, not opportunistic. It grew, as all his ideas grew, not out of a theorem, not from a constitutional interpretation, but from his overpowering commiseration for the mass of mankind. It was a practical matter. Here were poor people to be assisted, to be enriched in their estate, to be enlarged in spirit. The mode of reaching the result was not the thing. Any mode, all sorts of modes, might be used. What counted was the purpose to work relief, and the willingness to throw overboard whatever it might be that tended to defeat the purpose. His internationalism was but a denial of "my country right or wrong." There can be little doubt that, in last resort, he would have repudiated his country rather than go along with it in opposition to what he regarded as the true purpose of government. And that was, to advance the welfare of the mass of mankind.

He thought upon this subject in the same manner in which he thought as a lawyer, sweeping aside everything but what seemed to him the ethical reality at the heart of the case. For him the "right" of a State to do this or that was a constitutional question only so long as it did not cross that other more universal "right," the paramount "charter of liberty," by which, in his view, all other rights were conditioned. He would impose on all mankind, as their basic moral obligation, the duty to sacrifice all personal likes, personal ambitions, when these in their permanent tendencies ran contrary to the tendency which he rated as paramount. Such had always been, and was always to continue, his own attitude toward slavery. No one ever loathed it more. But he never permitted it to take the first place in his thoughts. If it could be eradicated without in the process creating dangers for popular government he would rejoice. But all the schemes of the Abolitionists, hitherto, he had condemned as dangerous devices because they would strain too severely the fabric of the popular state, would violate agreements which alone made it possible. Therefore, being always relentless toward himself, he required of himself the renunciation of this personal hope whenever, in whatever way, it threatened to make less effective the great democratic state which appeared to him the central fact of the world.

The enlargement of his reasoning led him inevitably to an unsparing condemnation of the Virginian theory. One of his rare flashes of irritation was an exclamation that Virginia loyalty always had an "if."(6) At this point, to make him entirely plain, there is needed another basic assumption which he has never quite formulated. However, it is so obviously latent in his thinking that the main lines are to be made out clearly enough. Building ever on that paramount obligation of all mankind to consider first the welfare of God's plain people, he assumed that whenever by any course of action any congregation of men were thrown together and led to form any political unit, they were never thereafter free to disregard in their attitude toward that unit its value in supporting and advancing the general cause of the welfare of the plain people. A sweeping, and in some contingencies, a terrible doctrine! Certainly, as to individuals, classes, communities even, a doctrine that might easily become destructive. But it formed the basis of all Lincoln's thought about the "majority" in America. Upon it would have rested his reply, had he ever made a reply, to the Virginia contention that while his theory might apply to each individual State, it could not apply to the group of States. He would have treated such a reply, whether fairly or unfairly, as a legal technicality. He would have said in substance: here is a congregation to be benefited, this great mass of all the inhabitants of all the States of the Union; accident, or destiny, or what you will, has brought them together, but here they are; they are moving forward, haltingly, irregularly, but steadily, toward fuller and fuller democracy; they are part of the universal democratic movement; their vast experiment has an international significance; it is the hope of the "Liberal party throughout the world"; to check that experiment, to break it into separate minor experiments; to reduce the imposing promise of its example by making it seem unsuccessful, would be treason to mankind. Therefore, both on South and North, both on the Seceders he meant to fight and on those Northerners of whom he was not entirely sure, he aimed to impose the supreme immediate duty of proving to the world that democracy on a great scale could have sufficient vitality to maintain itself against any sort of attack. Anticipating faintly the Gettysburg oration, the first message contained these words: "And this issue embraces more than the fate of these United States. It presents to the whole family of man the question whether a constitutional republic, or democracy—a government of the people by the same people—can or can not maintain its integrity against its own domestic foes. . . . Must a government of necessity be too strong for the liberties of its people or too weak to maintain its own existence?"(7) He told Hay that "the crucial idea pervading this struggle is the necessity that is upon us to prove that popular government is not an absurdity"; "that the basal issue was whether or no the people could govern themselves."(8)

But all this elaborate reasoning, if it went no further, lacked authority. It was political speculation. To clothe itself with authority it had to discover a foundation in historic fact. The real difficulty was not what ought to have been established in America in the past, but what actually had been. Where was the warrant for those bold proposition—who "we, the people," really were; in what their sovereign power really consisted; what was history's voice in the matter? To state an historic foundation was the final aim of the message. To hit its mark it had to silence those Northerners who denied the obligation to fight for the Union; it had to oppose their "free love" ideas of political unity with the conception of an established historic government, one which could not be overthrown except through the nihilistic process of revolution. So much has been written upon the exact location of sovereignty in the American federal State that it is difficult to escape the legalistic attitude, and to treat the matter purely as history. So various, so conflicting, and at times so tenuous, are the theories, that a flippant person might be forgiven did he turn from the whole discussion saying impatiently it was blind man's buff. But on one thing, at least, we must all agree. Once there was a king over this country, and now there is no king. Once the British Crown was the sovereign, and now the Crown has receded into the distance beyond the deep blue sea. When the Crown renounced its sovereignty in America, what became of it? Did it break into fragments and pass peacemeal to the various revolted colonies? Was it transferred somehow to the group collectively? These are the obvious theories; but there are others. And the others give rise to subtler speculations. Who was it that did the actual revolting against the Crown—colonies, parties, individuals, the whole American people, who?

Troublesome questions these, with which Lincoln and the men of his time did not deal in the spirit of historical science. Their wishes fathered their thoughts. Southerners, practically without exception, held the theory of the disintegration of the Crown's prerogative, its distribution among the States. The great leaders of Northern thought repudiated the idea. Webster and Clay would have none of it. But their own theories were not always consistent; and they differed among themselves. Lincoln did the natural thing. He fastened upon the tendencies in Northern thought that supported his own faith. Chief among these was the idea that sovereignty passed to the general congregation of the inhabitants of the colonies—"we, the people"—because we, the people, were the real power that supported the revolt. He had accepted the idea that the American Revolution was an uprising of the people, that its victory was in a transfer of sovereign rights from an English Crown to an American nation; that a new collective state, the Union, was created by this nation as the first act of the struggle, and that it was to the Union that the Crown succumbed, to the Union that its prerogative passed. To put this idea in its boldest and its simplest terms was the crowning effort of the message.

"The States have their status in the Union and they have no other legal status. If they break from this, they can only do so against law and by revolution. The Union, and not themselves separately, procured their independence and their liberty. By conquest or purchase, the Union gave each of them whatever of independence and liberty it has. The Union is older than any of the States, and in fact, it created them as States. Originally some dependent colonies made the Union, and in turn, the Union threw off this old dependence for them and made them States, such as they are."(9)

This first message completes the evolution of Lincoln as a political thinker. It is his third, his last great landmark. The Peoria speech, which drew to a focus all the implications of his early life, laid the basis of his political significance; the Cooper Union speech, summing up his conflict with Douglas, applied his thinking to the new issue precipitated by John Brown; but in both these he was still predominantly a negative thinker, still the voice of an opposition. With the first message, he became creative; he drew together what was latent in his earlier thought; he discarded the negative; he laid the foundation of all his subsequent policy. The breadth and depth of his thinking is revealed by the fulness with which the message develops the implications of his theory. In so doing, he anticipated the main issues that were to follow: his determination to keep nationalism from being narrowed into mere "Northernism"; his effort to create an all-parties government; his stubborn insistence that he was suppressing an insurrection, not waging external war; his doctrine that the Executive, having been chosen by the entire people, was the one expression of the sovereignty of the people, and therefore, the repository of all these exceptional "war powers" that are dormant in time of peace. Upon each of those issues he was destined to wage fierce battles with the politicians who controlled Congress, who sought to make Congress his master, who thwarted, tormented and almost defeated him. In the light of subsequent history the first message has another aspect besides its significance as political science. In its clear understanding of the implications of his attitude, it attains political second sight. As Lincoln, immovable, gazes far into the future, his power of vision makes him, yet again though in a widely different sense, the "seer in a trance, Seeing all his own mischance."

His troubles with Congress began at once. The message was received on July fourth, politely, but with scant response to its ideas. During two weeks, while Congress in its fatuousness thought that the battle impending in Virginia would settle things, the majority in Congress would not give assent to Lincoln's view of what the war was about. And then came Bull Run. In a flash the situation changed. Fatuousness was puffed out like a candle in a wind. The rankest extremist saw that Congress must cease from its debates and show its hand; must say what the war was about; must inform the nation whether it did or did not agree with the President.

On the day following Bull Run, Crittenden introduced this resolution: "That the present, deplorable civil war has been forced upon the country by the Disunionists of the Southern States, now in arms against the constitutional government, and in arms around the capital; that in this national emergency, Congress, banishing all feelings of mere passion and resentment, will recollect only its duty to the whole country; that this war is not waged on their part in any spirit of oppression or for any purpose of conquest or subjugation, or purpose of overthrowing or interfering with the rights or established institutions of these States, but to defend and maintain the supremacy of the Constitution, and to preserve the Union, with all the dignity, equality, and rights of the several States unimpaired; and that as soon as these objects are accomplished, the war ought to cease." This Crittenden Resolution was passed instantly by both Houses, without debate and almost without opposition. (10)

Paradoxically, Bull Run had saved the day for Lincoln, had enabled him to win his first victory as a statesman.

XVIII
THE JACOBIN CLUB

The keen Englishman who had observed the beauty of the Virginian woods on "Bull Run Sunday," said, after the battle was lost, "I hope Senator Wilson is satisfied." He was sneering at the whole group of intemperate Senators none of whom had ever smelled powder, but who knew it all when it came to war; who had done their great share in driving the President and the generals into a premature advance. Senator Wilson was one of those who went out to Manassas to see the Confederacy overthrown, that fateful Sunday. He was one of the most precipitate among those who fled back to Washington. On the way, driving furiously, amid a press of men and vehicles, he passed a carriage containing four Congressmen who were taking their time. Perhaps irritated by their coolness, he shouted to them to make haste. "If we were in as big a hurry as you are," replied Congressman Riddle, scornfully, "we would."

These four Congressmen played a curiously dramatic part before they got back to Washington. So did a party of Senators with whom they joined forces. This other party, at the start, also numbered four. They had planned a jolly picnic—this day that was to prove them right in hurrying the government into battle!—and being wise men who knew how to take time by the forelock, they had taken their luncheon with them. From what is known of Washington and Senators, then as now, one may risk a good deal that the luncheon was worth while. Part of the tragedy of that day was the accidental break-up of this party with the result amid the confusion of a road crowded by pleasure-seekers, that two Senators went one way carrying off the luncheon, while the other two, making the best of the disaster, continued southward through those beautiful early hours when Russell was admiring the scenery, their luncheon all to seek. The lucky men with the luncheon were the Senators Benjamin Wade and Zachary Chandler. Senator Trumbull and Senator Grimes, both on horseback, were left to their own devices. However, fortune was with them. Several hours later they had succeeded in getting food by the wayside and were resting in a grove of trees some distance beyond the village of Centerville. Suddenly, they suffered an appalling surprise; happening to look up, they beheld emerging out of the distance, a stampede of men and horses which came thundering down the country road, not a hundred yards from where they sat. "We immediately mounted our horses," as Trumbull wrote to his wife the next day, "and galloped to the road, by which time it was crowded, hundreds being in advance on the way to Centerville and two guns of Sherman's battery having already passed in full retreat. We kept on with the crowd, not knowing what else to do. We fed our horses at Centerville and left there at six o'clock.... Came on to Fairfax Court House where we got supper and, leaving there at ten o'clock reached home at half past two this morning. . . . I am dreadfully disappointed and mortified."(1)

Meanwhile, what of those other gay picnickers, Senator Wade and Senator Chandler? They drove in a carriage. Viewing the obligations of the hour much as did C. C. Clay at the President's reception, they were armed. Wade had "his famous rifle" which he had brought with him to Congress, which at times in the fury of debate he had threatened to use, which had become a byword. These Senators seem to have ventured nearer to the front than did Trumbull and Grimes, and were a little later in the retreat At a "choke-up," still on the far side of Centerville, their carriage passed the carriage of the four Congressmen — who, by the way, were also armed, having among them "four of the largest navy revolvers."

All these men, whatever their faults or absurdities, were intrepid. The Congressmen, at least, were in no good humor, for they had driven through a regiment of three months men whose time expired that day and who despite the cannon in the distance were hurrying home.

The race of the fugitives continued. At Centerville, the Congressmen passed Wade. Soon afterward Wade passed them for the second time. About a mile out of Fairfax Court House, "at the foot of a long down grade, the pike on the northerly side was fenced and ran along a farm. On the other side for a considerable distance was a wood, utterly impenetrable for men or animals, larger than cats or squirrels." Here the Wade carriage stopped. The congressional carriage drove up beside it. The two blocked a narrow way where as in the case of Horatius at the bridge, "a thousand might well be stopped by three." And then "bluff Ben Wade" showed the mettle that was in him. The "old Senator, his hat well back on his head," sprang out of his carriage, his rifle in his hand, and called to the others, "Boys, we'll stop this damned runaway." And they did it. Only six of them, but they lined up across that narrow road; presented their weapons and threatened to shoot; seized the bridles of horses and flung the horses back on their haunches; checked a panic-stricken army; held it at bay, until just when it seemed they were about to be overwhelmed, military reserves hurrying out from Fairfax Court House, took command of the road. Cool, unpretentious

Riddle calls the episode "Wade's exploit," and adds "it was much talked of." The newspapers dealt with it extravagantly.(2)

Gallant as the incident was, it was all the military service that "Ben" Wade and "Zach" Chandler—for thus they are known in history-over saw. But one may believe that it had a lasting effect upon their point of view and on that of their friend Lyman Trumbull. Certain it is that none of the three thereafter had any doubts about putting the military men in their place. All the error of their own view previous to Bull Run was forgotten. Wade and Chandler, especially, when military questions were in dispute, felt that no one possibly could know more of the subject than did the men who stopped the rout in the narrow road beyond Fairfax.

Three of those picnickers who missed their guess on Bull Run Sunday, Wade, Chandler and Trumbull, were destined to important parts in the stern years that were to come. Before the close of the year 1861 the three made a second visit to the army; and this time they kept together. To that second visit momentous happenings may be traced. How it came about must be fully understood.

Two of the three, Wade and Chandler, were temperamentally incapable of understanding Lincoln. Both were men of fierce souls; each had but a very limited experience. Wade had been a country lawyer in Ohio; Chandler, a prosperous manufacturer in Michigan. They were party men by instinct, blind to the faults of their own side, blind to the virtues of their enemies. They were rabid for the control of the government by their own organized machine.

Of Chandler, in Michigan, it was said that he "carried the Republican organization in his breeches pocket"; partly through control of the Federal patronage, which Lincoln frankly conceded to him, partly through a "judicious use of money."(3) Chandler's first clash with Lincoln was upon the place that the Republican machine was to hold in the conduct of the war.

From the beginning Lincoln was resolved that the war should not be merely a party struggle. Even before he was inaugurated, he said that he meant to hold the Democrats "close to the Administration on the naked Union issue."(4) He had added, "We must make it easy for them" to support the government "because we can't live through the case without them." This was the foundation of his attempt—so obvious between the lines of the first message—to create an all-parties government. This, Chandler violently opposed. Violence was always Chandler's note, so much so that a scornful opponent once called him "Xantippe in pants."

Lincoln had given Chandler a cause of offense in McClellan's elevation to the head of the army.* McClellan was a Democrat. There can be little doubt that Lincoln took the fact into account in selecting him. Shortly before, Lincoln had aimed to placate the Republicans by showing high honor to their popular hero, Fremont.

Strictly speaking he did not become head of the army until the retirement of Scott in November. Practically, he was supreme almost from the moment of his arrival in Washington.

When the catastrophe occurred at Bull Run, Fremont was a major-general commanding the Western Department with headquarters at St. Louis. He was one of the same violent root-and-branch wing of the Republicans — the Radicals of a latter day — of which Chandler was a leader. The temper of that wing had already been revealed by Senator Baker in his startling pronouncement: "We of the North control the Union, and we are going to govern our own Union in our own way." Chandler was soon to express it still more exactly, saying, "A rebel has sacrificed all his rights. He has no right to life, liberty or the pursuit of happiness."(5) Here was that purpose to narrowing nationalism into Northernism, even to radicalism, and to make the war an outlet for a sectional ferocity, which Lincoln was so firmly determined to prevent. All things considered, the fact that on the day following Bull Run he did not summon the Republican hero to Washington, that he did summon a Democrat, was significant. It opened his long duel with the extremists.

The vindictive Spirit of the extremists had been rebuffed by Lincoln in another way. Shortly after Bull Run, Wade and Chandler appealed to Lincoln to call out negro soldiers. Chandler said that he did not care whether or no this would produce a servile insurrection in the South. Lincoln's refusal made another count in the score of the extremists against him.(6)

During the late summer of 1861, Chandler, Wade, Trumbull, were all busily organizing their forces for an attack on the Administration. Trumbull, indeed, seemed out of place in that terrible company. In time, he found that he was out of place. At a crucial moment he came over to Lincoln. But not until he had done yeoman service with Lincoln's bitterest enemies. The clue to his earlier course was an honest conviction that Lincoln, though well-intentioned, was weak.(7) Was this the nemesis of Lincoln's pliability in action during the first stage of his Presidency? It may be. The firm inner Lincoln, the unyielding thinker of the first message, was not appreciated even by well-meaning men like Trumbull. The inner and the outer Lincoln were still disconnected. And the outer, in his caution, in his willingness to be instructed, in his opposition to extreme measures, made the inevitable impression that temperance makes upon fury, caution upon rashness.

Throughout the late summer, Lincoln was the target of many attacks, chiefly from the Abolitionists. Somehow, in the previous spring, they had got it into their heads that at heart he was one of them, that he waited only for a victory to declare the war a crusade of abolition.(8) When the crisis passed and a Democrat was put at the head of the army, while Fremont was left in the relative obscurity of St. Louis, Abolition bitterness became voluble. The Crittenden Resolution was scoffed at as an "ill-timed revival of the policy of conciliation." Threats against the Administration revived, taking the old form of demands for a wholly new Cabinet The keener-sighted Abolitionists had been alarmed by the first message, by what seemed to them its ominous silence as to slavery. Late in July, Emerson said in conversation, "If the Union is incapable of securing universal freedom, its disruption were as the breaking up of a frog-pond."(9) An outcry was raised because Federal generals did not declare free all the slaves who in any way came into their hands. The Abolitionists found no solace in the First Confiscation Act which provided that an owner should lose his claim to a slave, had the slave been used to assist the Confederate government. They were enraged by an order, early in August, informing generals that it was the President's desire "that all existing rights in all the States be fully respected and maintained; in cases of fugitives from the loyal Slave States, the enforcement of the Fugitive Slave Law by the ordinary forms of judicial proceedings must be respected by the military authorities; in the disloyal States the Confiscation Act of Congress must be your guide."(10) Especially, the Abolitionists were angered because of Lincoln's care for the forms of law in those Slave States that had not seceded. They vented their bitterness in a famous sneer—"The President would like to have God on his side, but he must have Kentucky."

A new temper was forming throughout the land. It was not merely the old Abolitionism. It was a blend of all those elements of violent feeling which war inevitably releases; it was the concentration of all these elements on the issue of Abolition as upon a terrible weapon; it was the resurrection of that primitive blood-lust which lies dormant in every peaceful nation like a sleeping beast. This dreadful power rose out of its sleep and confronted, menacing, the statesman who of all our statesmen was most keenly aware of its evil, most determined to put it under or to perish in the attempt With its appearance, the deepest of all the issues involved, according to Lincoln's way of thinking, was brought to a head. Was the Republic to issue from the war a worthy or an unworthy nation? That was pretty definitely a question of whether Abraham Lincoln or, say, Zachary Chandler, was to control its policy.

A vain, weak man precipitated the inevitable struggle between these two. Fremont had been flattered to the skies. He conceived himself a genius.

He was persuaded that the party of the new temper, the men who may fairly be called the Vindictives, were lords of the ascendent. He mistook their volubility for the voice of the nation. He determined to defy Lincoln. He issued a proclamation freeing the slaves of all who had "taken an active part" with the enemies of the United States in the field. He set up a "bureau of abolition."

Lincoln first heard of Fremont's proclamation through the newspapers. His instant action was taken in his own extraordinarily gentle way. "I think there is great danger," he wrote, "that the closing paragraph (of Fremont's proclamation) in relation to the confiscation of property and the liberating of slaves of traitorous owners, will alarm our Southern Union friends and turn them against us; perhaps ruin our rather fair prospect for Kentucky. Allow me, therefore, to ask that you will, as of your own motion, modify that paragraph so as to conform" to the Confiscation Act. He added, "This letter is written in the Spirit of caution, not of censure."(11)

Fremont was not the man to understand instruction of this sort. He would make no compromise with the President. If Lincoln wished to go over his head and rescind his order let him do so–and take the consequences. Lincoln quietly did so. His battle with the Vindictives was on. For a moment it seemed as if he had destroyed his cause. So loud was the outcry of the voluble people, that any one might have been excused momentarily for thinking that all the North had risen against him. Great meetings of protest were held. Eminent men–even such fine natures as Bryant–condemned his course. In the wake of the incident, when it was impossible to say how significant the outcry really was, Chandler, who was staunch for Fremont, began his active interference with the management of the army. McClellan had insisted on plenty of time in which to drill the new three-year recruits who were pouring into Washington. He did not propose to repeat the experience of General McDowell. On the other hand, Chandler was bent on forcing him into action. He, Wade and Trumbull combined, attempting to bring things to pass in a way to suit themselves and their faction. To these men and their followers, clever young Hay gave the apt name of "The Jacobin Club."

They began their campaign by their second visit to the army. Wade was their chief spokesman. He urged McClellan to advance at once; to risk an unsuccessful battle rather than continue to stand still; the country wanted something done; a defeat could easily be repaired by the swarming recruits (12)

This callous attitude got no response from the Commanding General. The three Senators turned upon Lincoln. "This evening," writes Hay in his diary on October twenty-sixth, "the Jacobin Club represented by Trumbull

Chandler and Wade, came out to worry the Administration into a battle. The agitation of the summer is to be renewed. The President defended McClellan's deliberateness. The next night we went over to Seward's and found Chandler and Wade there." They repeated their reckless talk; a battle must be fought; defeat would be no worse than delay; "and a great deal more trash."

But Lincoln was not to be moved. He and Hay called upon McClellan. The President deprecated this new manifestation of popular impatience, but said it was a reality and should be taken into account. "At the same time, General," said he, "you must not fight until you are ready."(13)

At this moment of extreme tension occurred the famous incident of the seizure of the Confederate envoys, Mason and Slidell, who were passengers on the British merchant ship, the Trent. These men had run the blockade which had now drawn its strangling line along the whole coast of the Confederacy; they had boarded the Trent at Havana, and under the law of nations were safe from capture. But Captain Wilkes of the United States Navy, more zealous than discreet, overhauled the Trent and took off the two Confederates. Every thoughtless Northerner went wild with joy. At last the government had done something. Even the Secretary of the Navy so far forgot himself as to telegraph to Wilkes "Congratulate you on the great public service you have rendered in the capture of the rebel emissaries."(14) Chandler promptly applauded the seizure and when it was suggested that perhaps the envoys should be released he at once arrayed himself in opposition.(15) With the truculent Jacobins ready to close battle should the government do its duty, with the country still echoing to cheers for Fremont and hisses for the President, with nothing to his credit in the way of military success, Lincoln faced a crisis. He was carried through the crisis by two strong men. Sumner, head and front of Abolitionism but also a great lawyer, came at once to his assistance. And what could a thinking Abolitionist say after that! Seward skilfully saved the face of the government by his management of the negotiation. The envoys were released and sent to England.

It was the only thing to do, but Chandler and all his sort had opposed it. The Abolition fury against the government was at fever heat. Wendell Phillips in a speech at New York denounced the Administration as having no definite purpose in the war, and was interrupted by frantic cheers for Fremont. McClellan, patiently drilling his army, was, in the eyes of the Jacobins, doing nothing. Congress had assembled. There was every sign that troubled waters lay just ahead.

XIX
THE JACOBINS BECOME INQUISITORS

The temper animating Hay's "Jacobins" formed a new and really formidable danger which menaced Lincoln at the close of 1861. But had he been anything of an opportunist, it would have offered him an unrivaled opportunity. For a leader who sought personal power, this raging savagery, with its triple alliance of an organized political machine, a devoted fanaticism, and the war fury, was a chance in ten thousand. It led to his door the steed of militarism, shod and bridled, champing upon the bit, and invited him to leap into the saddle. Ten words of acquiescence in the program of the Jacobins, and the dreaded role of the man on horseback was his to command.

The fallacy that politics are primarily intellectual decisions upon stated issues, the going forth of the popular mind to decide between programs presented to it by circumstances, receives a brilliant refutation in the course of the powerful minority that was concentrating around the three great "Jacobins." The subjective side of politics, also the temperamental side, here found expression. Statecraft is an art; creative statesmen are like other artists. Just as the painter or the poet, seizing upon old subjects, uses them as outlets for his particular temper, his particular emotion, and as the temper, the emotion are what counts in his work, so with statesmen, with Lincoln on the one hand, with Chandler at the opposite extreme.

The Jacobins stood first of all for the sudden reaction of bold fierce natures from a long political repression. They had fought their way to leadership as captains of an opposition. They were artists who had been denied an opportunity of expression. By a sudden turn of fortune, it had seemed to come within their grasp. Temperamentally they were fighters. Battle for them was an end in itself. The thought of Conquest sang to them like the morning stars. Had they been literary men, their favorite poetry would have been the sacking of Troy town. Furthermore, they were intensely provincial. Undoubted as was their courage, they had also the valor of ignorance. They had the provincial's disdain for the other side of the horizon, his unbounded confidence in his ability to whip all creation. Chandler, scornfully brushing aside a possible foreign war, typified their mood.

And in quiet veto of all their hopes rose against them the apparently easy-going, the smiling, story-telling, unrevengeful, new man at the White House. It is not to be wondered that they spent the summer laboring to build up a party against him, that they turned eagerly to the new session of Congress, hoping to consolidate a faction opposed to Lincoln.

His second message (1), though without a word of obvious defiance, set him squarely against them on all their vital contentions. The winter of 1861-1862 is the strangest period of Lincoln's career. Although the two phases of him, the outer and the inner, were, in point of fact, moving rapidly toward their point of fusion, apparently they were further away than ever before. Outwardly, his most conspicuous vacillations were in this winter and in the following spring. Never before or after did he allow himself to be overshadowed so darkly by his advisers in all the concerns of action. In amazing contrast, in all the concerns of thought, he was never more entirely himself. The second message, prepared when the country rang with what seemed to be a general frenzy against him, did not give ground one inch. This was all the more notable because his Secretary of War had tried to force his hand. Cameron had the reputation of being about the most astute politician in America. Few people attributed to him the embarrassment of principles. And Cameron, in the late autumn, after closely observing the drift of things, determined that Fremont had hit it off correctly, that the crafty thing to do was to come out for Abolition as a war policy. In a word, he decided to go over to the Jacobins. He put into his annual report a recommendation of Chandler's plan for organizing an army of freed slaves and sending it against the Confederacy. Advanced copies of this report had been sent to the press before Lincoln knew of it. He peremptorily ordered their recall, and the exclusion of this suggestion from the text of the report.(2)

On the heels of this refusal to concede to Chandler one of his cherished schemes, the second message was sent to Congress. The watchful and exasperated Jacobins found abundant offense in its omissions. On the whole great subject of possible emancipation it was blankly silent. The nearest it came to this subject was one suggestion which applied only to those captured slaves who had been forfeited by the disloyal owners through being employed to assist the Confederate government Lincoln advised that after receiving their freedom they be sent out of the country and colonized "at some place, or places, in a climate congenial to them." Beyond this there was nothing bearing on the slavery question except the admonition—so unsatisfactory to Chandler and all his sort—that while "the Union must be preserved, and hence all indispensable means must be employed," Congress should "not be in haste to determine that radical and extreme measures, which may reach the loyal as well as the disloyal, are indispensable."

Lincoln was entirely clear in his own mind that there was but one way to head off the passion of destruction that was rioting in the Jacobin temper. "In considering the policy to be adopted in suppressing the insurrection, I have been anxious and careful that the inevitable conflict for this purpose shall not degenerate into a violent and remorseless revolutionary struggle. I have, therefore, in every case, thought it proper to keep the integrity of the Union prominent as the primary object of the contest on our part, leaving all questions which are not of vital military importance to the more deliberate action of the Legislature." He persisted in regarding the war as an insurrection of the "disloyal portion of the American people," not as an external struggle between the North and the South.

Finally, the culmination of the message was a long elaborate argument upon the significance of the war to the working classes. His aim was to show that the whole trend of the Confederate movement was toward a conclusion which would "place capital on an equal footing with, if not above, labor, in the structure of government." Thus, as so often before, he insisted on his own view of the significance in American politics of all issues involving slavery—their bearing on the condition of the free laborer. In a very striking passage, often overlooked, he ranked himself once more, as first of all, a statesman of "the people," in the limited class sense of the term. "Labor is prior to and independent of capital. Capital is only the fruit of labor and could never have existed if labor had not first existed. Labor is the superior of capital, and deserves much the higher consideration." But so far is he from any revolutionary purpose, that he adds immediately, "Capital has its rights which are as worthy of protection as any other rights." His crowning vision is not communism. His ideal world is one of universal opportunity, with labor freed of every hindrance, with all its deserving members acquiring more and more of the benefits of property.

Such a message had no consolation for Chandler, Wade, or, as he then was, for Trumbull. They looked about for a way to retaliate. And now two things became plain. That "agitation of the summer" to which Hay refers, had borne fruit, but not enough fruit. Many members of Congress who had been swept along by the President's policy in July had been won over in the reaction against him and were ripe for manipulation; but it was not yet certain that they held the balance of power in Congress. To lock horns with the Administration, in December, would have been so rash a move that even such bold men as Chandler and Wade avoided it. Instead, they devised an astute plan of campaign. Trumbull was Chairman of the Senate Judiciary

Committee, and in that important position would bide his time to bring pressure to bear on the President through his influence upon legislation. Wade and Chandler would go in for propaganda. But they would do so in disguise. What more natural than that Congress should take an active interest in the army, should wish to do all in its power to "assist" the President in rendering the army-efficient. For that purpose it was proposed to establish a joint committee of the two Houses having no function but to look into military needs and report to Congress. The proposal was at once accepted and its crafty backers secured a committee dominated entirely by themselves. Chandler was a member; Wade became Chairman.(3) This Committee on the Conduct of the War became at once an inquisition. Though armed with no weapon but publicity, its close connection with congressional intrigue, its hostility to the President, the dramatic effect of any revelations it chose to make or any charges it chose to bring, clothed it indirectly with immense power. Its inner purpose may be stated in the words of one of its members, "A more vigorous prosecution of the war and less tenderness toward slavery."(4) Its mode of procedure was in constant interrogation of generals, in frequent advice to the President, and on occasion in threatening to rouse Congress against him.(5) A session of the Committee was likely to be followed by a call on the President of either Chandler or Wade.

The Committee began immediately summoning generals before it to explain what the army was doing. And every general was made to understand that what the Committee wanted, what Congress wanted, what the country wanted, was an advance—"something doing" as soon as possible.

And now appeared another characteristic of the mood of these furious men. They had become suspicious, honestly suspicious. This suspiciousness grew with their power and was rendered frantic by being crossed. Whoever disagreed with them was instantly an object of distrust; any plan that contradicted their views was at once an evidence of treason.

The earliest display of this eagerness to see traitors in every bush concerned a skirmish that took place at Ball's Bluff in Virginia. It was badly managed and the Federal loss, proportionately, was large. The officer held responsible was General Stone. Unfortunately for him, he was particularly obnoxious to the Abolitionists; he had returned fugitive slaves; and when objection was made by such powerful Abolitionists as Governor Andrew of Massachusetts, Stone gave reign to a sharp tongue. In the early days of the session, Roscoe Conkling told the story of Ball's Bluff for the benefit of Congress in a brilliant, harrowing speech. In a flash the rumor spread that the dead at Ball's Bluff were killed by design, that Stone was a traitor, that—

perhaps! — who could say? — there were bigger traitors higher up. Stone was summoned before the Inquisition.(6)

While Stone was on the rack, metaphorically, while the Committee was showing him every brutality in its power, refusing to acquaint him with the evidence against him, intimating that they were able to convict him of treason, between the fifth and the eleventh of January a crisis arose in the War Office. Cameron had failed to ingratiate himself with the rising powers. Old political enemies in Congress were implacable. Scandals in his Department gave rise to sweeping charges of peculation.

There is scarcely another moment when Lincoln's power was so precarious. In one respect, in their impatience, the Committee reflected faithfully the country at large. And by the irony of fate McClellan at this crucial hour, had fallen ill. After waiting for his recovery during several weeks, Lincoln ventured with much hesitation to call a conference of generals.(7) They were sitting during the Stone investigation, producing no result except a distraction in councils, devising plans that were thrown over the moment the Commanding General arose from his bed. A vote in Congress a few days previous had amounted to a censure of the Administration. It was taken upon the Crittenden Resolution which had been introduced a second time. Of those who had voted for it in July, so many now abandoned the Administration that this resolution, the clear embodiment of Lincoln's policy, was laid on the table, seventy-one to sixty-five.(8) Lincoln's hope for an all-parties government was receiving little encouragement The Democrats were breaking into factions, while the control of their party organization was falling into the hands of a group of inferior politicians who were content to "play politics" in the most unscrupulous fashion. Both the Secretary of War and the Secretary of State had authorized arbitrary arrests. Men in New York and New England had been thrown into prison. The privilege of the writ of habeas corpus had been denied them on the mere belief of the government that they were conspiring with its enemies. Because of these arrests, sharp criticism was being aimed at the Administration both within and without Congress.

For all these reasons, the government at Washington appeared to be tottering. Desperate remedies seemed imperative. Lincoln decided to make every concession he could make without letting go his central purpose. First, he threw over Cameron; he compelled him to resign though he saved his face by appointing him minister to Russia. But who was to take his place? At this critical moment, the choice of a new Secretary of War was a political problem of exacting difficulty. Just why Lincoln chose a sullen, dictatorial lawyer whose experience in no way prepared him for the office, has never been disclosed. Two facts appear to explain it. Edwin M. Stanton was temperamentally just the man to become a good brother to Chandler and Wade. Both of them urged him upon Lincoln as successor to Cameron. (9) Furthermore, Stanton hitherto had been a Democrat. His services in Buchanan's Cabinet as Attorney-General had made him a national figure. Who else linked the Democrats and the Jacobins?

However, for almost any one but Lincoln, there was an objection that it would have been hard to overcome. No one has ever charged Stanton with politeness. A gloomy excitable man, of uncertain health, temperamentally an over-worker, chronically apprehensive, utterly without the saving grace of humor, he was capable of insufferable rudeness—one reason, perhaps, why Chandler liked him. He and Lincoln had met but once. As associate council in a case at Cincinnati, three years before, Lincoln had been treated so contemptuously by Stanton that he had returned home in pained humiliation. Since his inauguration, Stanton had been one of his most vituperative critics. Was this insolent scold to be invited into the Cabinet? Had not Lincoln at this juncture been in the full tide of selflessness, surely some compromise would have been made with the Committee, a secretary found less offensive personally to the President. Lincoln disregarded the personal consideration. The candidate of Chandler and Wade became secretary. It was the beginning of an intimate alliance between the Committee and the War Office. Lincoln had laid up for himself much trouble that he did not foresee.

The day the new Secretary took office, he received from the Committee a report upon General Stone:(10) Subsequently, in the Senate, Wade denied that the Committee had advised the arrest of Stone.(11) Doubtless the statement was technically correct. Nevertheless, there can be no doubt that the inquisitors were wholly in sympathy with the Secretary when, shortly afterward, Stone was seized upon Stanton's order, conveyed to a fortress and imprisoned without trial.

This was the Dreyfus case of the Civil War. Stone was never tried and never vindicated. He was eventually released upon parole and after many tantalizing disappointments permitted to rejoin the army. What gives the event significance is its evidence of the power, at that moment, of the Committee, and of the relative weakness of the President. Lincoln's eagerness to protect condemned soldiers survives in many anecdotes. Hay confides to his diary that he was sometimes "amused at the eagerness with which the President caught at any fact which would justify" clemency. And yet, when Stanton informed him of the arrest of Stone, he gloomily acquiesced. "I hope you have good reasons for it," he said. Later he admitted that he knew very little about the case. But he did not order Stone's release.

Lincoln had his own form of ruthlessness. The selfless man, by dealing with others in the same extraordinary way in which he deals with himself, may easily under the pressure of extreme conditions become impersonal in his thinking upon duty. The morality of such a state of mind is a question for the philosopher. The historian must content himself with pointing out the only condition that redeems it—if anything redeems it The leader who thinks impersonally about others and personally about himself-what need among civilized people to characterize him? Borgia, Louis XIV, Napoleon. If we are ever to pardon impersonal thinking it is only in the cases of men who begin by effacing themselves. The Lincoln who accepted Stanton as a Cabinet officer, who was always more or less overshadowed by the belief that in saving the government he was himself to perish, is explicable, at least, when individual men became for him, as at times they did, impersonal factors in a terrible dream.

There are other considerations in the attempt to give a moral value to his failure to interfere in behalf of Stone. The first four months of 1862 are not only his feeblest period as a ruler, the period when he was barely able to hold his own, but also the period when he was least definite as a personality, when his courage and his vitality seemed ebbing tides. Again, his spirit was in eclipse. Singularly enough, this was the darkness before the dawn. June of 1862 saw the emergence, with a suddenness difficult to explain, of the historic Lincoln. But in January of that year he was facing downward into the mystery of his last eclipse. All the dark places of his heredity must be searched for clues to this strange experience. There are moments, especially under strain of a personal bereavement that fell upon him in February, when his will seemed scarcely a reality; when, as a directing force he may be said momentarily to have vanished; when he is hardly more than a ghost among his advisers. The far-off existence of weak old Thomas cast its parting shadow across his son's career.

However, even our Dreyfus case drew from Lincoln another display of that settled conviction of his that part of his function was to be scapegoat. "I serve," which in a way might be taken as his motto always, was peculiarly his motto, and likewise his redemption, in this period of his weakness. The enemies of the Committee in Congress took the matter up and denounced Stanton. Thereupon, Wade flamed forth, criticizing Lincoln for his leniency, venting his fury on all those who were tender of their enemies, storming that "mercy to traitors is cruelty to loyal men."(12) Lincoln replied neither to Wade nor to his antagonists; but, without explaining the case, without a word upon the relation to it of the Secretary and the Committee, he informed the Senate that the President was alone responsible for the arrest and imprisonment of General Stone.(13)

XX
IS CONGRESS THE PRESIDENT'S MASTER?

The period of Lincoln's last eclipse is a period of relative silence. But his mind was not inactive. He did not cease thinking upon the deep theoretical distinctions that were separating him by a steadily widening chasm from the most powerful faction in Congress. In fact, his mental powers were, if anything, more keen than ever before. Probably, it was the very clearness of the mental vision that enfeebled him when it came to action. He saw his difficulties with such crushing certainty. During this trying period there is in him something of Hamlet.

The reaction to his ideas, to what is either expressed or implied, in the first and second messages, was prompt to appear. The Jacobins did not confine their activities within the scope of the terrible Committee. Wade and Chandler worked assiduously undermining his strength in Congress. Trumbull, though always less extreme than they, was still the victim of his delusion that Lincoln was a poor creature, that the only way to save the country was to go along with those grim men of strength who dominated the Committee. In January, a formidable addition appeared in the ranks of Lincoln's opponents. Thaddeus Stevens made a speech in the House that marks a chapter. It brought to a head a cloud of floating opposition and dearly defined an issue involving the central proposition in Lincoln's theory of the government. The Constitution of the United States, in its detailed provisions, is designed chiefly to meet the exigencies of peace. With regard to the abnormal conditions of war, it is relatively silent. Certain "war powers" are recognized but not clearly defined; nor is it made perfectly plain what branch of the government possesses them. The machinery for their execution is assumed but not described—as when the Constitution provides that the privileges of the writ of habeas corpus are to be suspended only in time of war, but does not specify by whom, or in what way, the suspension is to be effected. Are those undefined "war powers," which are the most sovereign functions of our government, vested in Congress or in the President? Lincoln, from the moment he defined his policy, held tenaciously to the theory that all these extraordinary powers are vested in the President. By implication, at least, this idea is in the first message.

Throughout the latter part of 1861, he put the theory into practice. Whatever seemed to him necessary in a state of war, he did, even to the arresting of suspected persons, refusing them the privilege-of the habeas corpus, and retaining them in prison without trial. During 1861, he left the exercise of this sovereign authority to the discretion of the two Secretaries of War and of State.

Naturally, the Abolitionists, the Jacobins, the Democratic machine, conscientious believers in the congressional theory of the government, every one who for any reason, wanted to hit the Administration, united in a chorus of wrath over arbitrary arrests. The greatest orator of the time, Wendell Phillips, the final voice of Abolition, flayed the government in public speeches for reducing America to an absolute despotism. Trumbull introduced into the Senate a resolution calling upon the President for a statement of the facts as to what he had actually done.(1)

But the subject of arrests was but the prelude to the play. The real issue was the theory of the government. Where in last analysis does the Constitution place the ultimate powers of sovereignty, the war powers? In Congress or in the President? Therefore, in concrete terms, is Congress the President's master, or is it only one branch of the government with a definite but united activity of its own, without that sweeping sovereign authority which in course of time has been acquired by its parent body, the Parliament of Great Britain?

On this point Lincoln never wavered. From first to last, he was determined not to admit that Congress had the powers of Parliament. No sooner had the politicians made out this attitude than their attack on it began. It did not cease until Lincoln's death. It added a second constitutional question to the issues of the war. Not only the issue whether a State had a right to secede, but also the issue of the President's possession of the war powers of the Constitution. Time and again the leaders of disaffection in his own party, to say nothing of the violent Democrats, exhausted their rhetoric denouncing Lincoln's position. They did not deny themselves the delights of the sneer. Senator Grimes spoke of a call on the President as an attempt "to approach the footstool of power enthroned at the other end of the Avenue."(2) Wade expanded the idea: "We ought to have a committee to wait on him whenever we send him a bill, to know what his royal pleasure is with regard to it. . . . We are told that some gentlemen . . . have been to see the President. Some gentlemen are very fortunate in that respect. Nobody can see him, it seems, except some privileged gentlemen who are charged with his constitutional conscience."(3) As Lincoln kept his doors open to all the world, as no one came and went with greater freedom than the Chairman of the Committee, the sneer was-what one might expect of the Committee.

Sumner said: "I claim for Congress all that belongs to any government in the exercise of the rights of war." Disagreement with him, he treated with unspeakable disdain: "Born in ignorance and pernicious in consequence, it ought to be received with hissings of contempt, and just in proportion as it obtains acceptance, with execration."(4) Henry Wilson declared that, come what might, the policy of the Administration would be shaped by the two Houses. "I had rather give a policy to the President of the United States than take a policy from the President of the United States."(5) Trumbull thundered against the President's theory as the last word in despotism.(6)

Such is the mental perspective in which to regard the speech of Stevens of January 22, 1862. With masterly clearness, he put his finger on the heart of the matter: the exceptional problems of a time of war, problems that can not be foreseen and prepared for by anticipatory legislation, may be solved in but one way, by the temporary creation of the dictator; this is as true of modern America as of ancient Rome; so far, most people are agreed; but this extraordinary function must not be vested in the Executive; on the contrary, it must be, it is, vested in the Legislature. Stevens did not hesitate to push his theory to its limit. He was not afraid of making the Legislature in time of war the irresponsible judge of its own acts. Congress, said he, has all possible powers of government, even the dictator's power; it could declare itself a dictator; under certain circumstances he was willing that it should do so.(7)

The intellectual boldness of Lincoln was matched by an equal boldness. Between them, he and Stevens had perfectly defined their issue. Granted that a dictator was needed, which should it be — the President or Congress?

In the hesitancy at the White House during the last eclipse, in the public distress and the personal grief, Lincoln withheld himself from this debate. No great utterances break the gloom of this period. Nevertheless, what may be considered his reply to Stevens is to be found. Buried in the forgotten portions of the Congressional Globe is a speech that surely was inspired-or, if not directly inspired, so close a reflection of the President's thinking that it comes to the same thing at the end.

Its author, or apparent author, was one of the few serene figures in that Thirty-Seventh Congress which was swept so pitilessly by epidemics of passion. When Douglas, after coming out valiantly for the Union and holding up Lincoln's hands at the hour of crisis, suddenly died, the Illinois

Legislature named as his successor in the Senate, Orville Henry Browning. The new Senator was Lincoln's intimate friend. Their points of view, their temperaments were similar. Browning shared Lincoln's magnanimity, his hatred of extremes, his eagerness not to allow the war to degenerate into revolution. In the early part of 1862 he was Lincoln's spokesman in the Senate. Now that the temper of Wade and Chandler, the ruthlessness that dominated the Committee, had drawn unto itself such a cohort of allies; now that all their thinking had been organized by a fearless mind; there was urgent need for a masterly reply. Did Lincoln feel unequal, at the moment, to this great task? Very probably he did. Anyhow, it was Browning who made the reply,(8) a reply so exactly in his friend's vein, that—there you are!

His aim was to explain the nature of those war powers of the government "which lie dormant during time of peace," and therefore he frankly put the question, "Is Congress the government?" Senator Fessenden, echoing Stevens had said, "There is no limit on the powers of Congress; everything must yield to the force of martial law as resolved by Congress." "There, sir," said Browning, "is as broad and deep a foundation for absolute despotism as was ever laid." He rang the changes on the need to "protect minorities from the oppression and tyranny of excited majorities."

He went on to lay the basis of all Lincoln's subsequent defense of the presidential theory as opposed to the congressional theory, by formulating two propositions which reappear in some of Lincoln's most famous papers. Congress is not a safe vessel for extraordinary powers, because in our system we have difficulty in bringing it definitely to an account under any sort of plebiscite. On the other hand the President, if he abuses the war powers "when peace returns, is answerable to the civil power for that abuse."

But Browning was not content to reason on generalities. Asserting that Congress could no more command the army than it could adjudicate a case, he further asserted that the Supreme Court had settled the matter and had lodged the war powers in the President. He cited a decision called forth by the legal question, "Can a Circuit Court of the United States inquire whether a President had acted rightly in calling out the militia of a State to suppress an insurrection?" "The elevated office of the President," said the Court, "chosen as he is by the People of the United States, and the high responsibility he could not fail to feel when acting in a case of such moment, appear to furnish as strong safeguards against the wilful abuse of power as human prudence and foresight could well devise. At all events, it is conferred upon him by the Constitution and the laws of the United States, and therefore, must be respected and enforced in its judicial tribunals."(9)

Whether or not constitutional lawyers would agree with Browning in the conclusion he drew from this decision, it was plainly the bed rock of his thought. He believed that the President—whatever your mere historian might have to say—was in point of fact the exponent of the people as a whole, and therefore the proper vessel for the ultimate rights of a sovereign, rights that only the people possess, that only the people can delegate. And this was Lincoln's theory. Roughly speaking, he-conceived of the presidential office about as if it were the office of Tribune of the People.

There was still another reason why both Lincoln and Browning feared to yield anything to the theory of congressional supremacy. It was, in their minds, not only the general question of all Congresses but immediately of this particular Congress. An assembly in which the temper of Wade and Chandler, of Stevens and Sumner, was entering the ascendent, was an assembly to be feared; its supremacy was to be denied, its power was to be fought.

Browning did not close without a startling passage flung square in the teeth of the apostles of fury. He summed up the opposite temper, Lincoln's temper, in his description of "Our brethren of the South—for I am willing to call them brethren; my heart yet yearns toward them with a fervency of love which even their treason has not all extinguished, which tempts me constantly to say in their behalf, 'Father, forgive them, for they know not what they do.'" He pleaded with the Senate not to consider them "as public enemies but as insurgent citizens only," and advocated an Act of Amnesty restoring all political and property rights "instantly upon their return to allegiance and submission to the authority of the government."

Had this narrowly constitutional issue arisen in quiet times, who can say how slight might have been its significance? But Fate had decreed that it should arise in the stormiest moment of our history. Millions of men and women who cared nothing for constitutional theories, who were governed by that passion to see immediate results which the thoughtless ever confuse with achievement, these were becoming hysterical over delay. Why did not the government do something? Everywhere voices were raised accusing the President of cowardice. The mania of suspicion was not confined to the

Committee. The thoughts of a multitude were expressed by Congressman Hickman in his foolish words, "These are days of irresponsibility and imbecility, and we are required to perform two offices—the office of legislator and the office of President." The better part of a year had passed since the day of Sumter, and still the government had no military success to its credit. An impetuous people that lacked experience of war, that had been accustomed in unusual measure to have its wishes speedily gratified, must somehow be marshalled behind the government, unless the alternative was the capture of power by the Congressional Cabal that was forming against the President.

Entering upon the dark days of the first half of 1862, Lincoln had no delusions about the task immediately before him. He must win battles; otherwise, he saw no way of building up that popular support which alone would enable him to keep the direction of policy in the hands of the Executive, to keep it out of the hands of Congress. In a word, the standing or falling of his power appeared to have been committed to the keeping of the army. What the army would do with it, save his policy or wreck his policy, was to no small degree a question of the character and the abilities of the Commanding General.

XXI
THE STRUGGLE TO CONTROL THE ARMY

George Brinton McClellan, when at the age of thirty-four he was raised suddenly to a dizzying height of fame and power, was generally looked upon as a prodigy. Though he was not that, he had a real claim to distinction. Had destiny been considerate, permitting him to rise gradually and to mature as he rose, he might have earned a stable reputation high among those who are not quite great. He had done well at West Point, and as a very young officer in the Mexican War; he had represented his country as a military observer with the allies in the Crimea; he was a good engineer, and a capable man of business. His winning personality, until he went wrong in the terrible days of 1862, inspired "a remarkable affection and regard in every one from the President to the humblest orderly that waited at his door."(1) He was at home among books; he could write to his wife that Prince Napoleon "speaks English very much as the Frenchmen do in the old English comedies";(2) he was able to converse in "French, Spanish, Italian, German, in two Indian dialects and he knew a little Russian and Turkish." Men like Wade and Chandler probably thought of him as a "highbrow," and doubtless he irritated them by invariably addressing the President as "Your Excellency." He had the impulses as well as the traditions of an elder day. But he had three insidious defects. At the back of his mind there was a vein of theatricality, hitherto unrevealed, that might, under sufficient stimulus, transform him into a poseur. Though physically brave, he had in his heart, unsuspected by himself or others, the dread of responsibility. He was void of humor. These damaging qualities, brought out and exaggerated by too swift a rise to apparent greatness, eventually worked his ruin. As an organizer he was unquestionably efficient. His great achievement which secures him a creditable place in American history was the conversion in the autumn of 1861 of a defeated rabble and a multitude of raw militia into a splendid fighting machine. The very excellence of this achievement was part of his undoing. It was so near to magical that it imposed on himself, gave him a false estimate of himself, hid from him his own limitation. It imposed also on his enemies. Crude, fierce men like the Vindictive leaders of Congress, seeing this miracle take place so astoundingly soon, leaped at once to the conclusion that he could, if he would, follow it by another miracle. Having forged the thunderbolt, why could he not, if he chose, instantly smite and destroy? All these hasty inexperienced zealots labored that winter under the delusion that one great battle might end the war. When McClellan, instead of rushing to the front, entered his second phase—the one which he did not understand himself, which his enemies never understood—when he entered upon his long course of procrastination, the Jacobins, startled, dumfounded, casting about for reasons, could find in their unanalytical vision, but one. When Jove did not strike, it must be because Jove did not wish to strike. McClellan was delaying for a purpose. Almost instantaneous was the whisper, followed quickly by the outcry among the Jacobins, "Treachery! We are betrayed. He is in league with the enemy."

Their distrust was not allayed by the manner in which he conducted himself. His views of life and of the office of commanding general were not those of frontier America. He believed in pomp, in display, in an ordered routine. The fine weather of the autumn of 1861 was utilized at Washington for frequent reviews. The flutter of flags, the glint of marching bayonets, the perfectly ordered rhythm of marching feet, the blare of trumpets, the silvery notes of the bugles, the stormily rolling drums, all these filled with martial splendor the golden autumn air when the woods were falling brown. And everywhere, it seemed, look where one might, a sumptuously uniformed Commanding General, and a numerous and sumptuous staff, were galloping past, mounted on beautiful horses. Plain, blunt men like the Jacobins, caring nothing for this ritual of command, sneered. They exchanged stories of the elaborate dinners he was said to give daily, the several courses, the abundance of wine, the numerous guests; and after these dinners, he and his gorgeous staff, "clattering up and down the public streets" merely to show themselves off. All this sneering was wildly exaggerated. The mania of exaggeration, the mania of suspicion, saturated the mental air breathed by every politician at Washington, that desperate winter, except the great and lonely President and the cynical Secretary of State.

McClellan made no concessions to the temper of the hour. With Lincoln, his relations at first were cordial. Always he was punctiliously respectful to "His Excellency." It is plain that at first Lincoln liked him and that his liking was worn away slowly. It is equally plain that Lincoln did not know how to deal with him. The tendency to pose was so far from anything in Lincoln's make-up that it remained for him, whether in McClellan or another, unintelligible. That humility which was so conspicuous in this first period of his rule, led him to assume with his General a modest, even an appealing tone. The younger man began to ring false by failing to appreciate it. He even complained of it in a letter to his wife. The military ritualist would have liked a more Olympian superior. And there is no denying that his head was getting turned. Perhaps he had excuse. The newspapers printed nonsensical editorials praising "the young Napoleon." His mail was filled with letters urging him to carry things with a high hand; disregard, if necessary, the pusillanimous civil government, and boldly "save the country." He had so little humor that he could take this stuff seriously. Among all the foolish letters which the executors of famous men have permitted to see the light of publicity, few outdo a letter of McClellan's in which he confided to his wife that he was willing to become dictator, should that be the only way out, and then, after saving his country, to perish.(3)

In this lordly mood of the melodramatic, he gradually — probably without knowing it — became inattentive to the President. Lincoln used to go to his house to consult him, generally on foot, clad in very ordinary clothes. He was known to sit in McClellan's library "rather unnoticed" awaiting the General's pleasure.(4)

At last the growing coolness of McClellan went so far that an event occurred which Hay indignantly set down in his diary: "I wish here to record what I consider a portent of evil to come. The President, Governor Seward and I went over to McClellan's house tonight. The servant at the door said the General was at the wedding of Colonel Wheaton at General Buell's and would soon return. We went in and after we had waited about an hour, McClellan came in, and without paying particular attention to the porter who told him the President was waiting to see him, went up-stairs, passing the door of the room where the President and the Secretary of State were seated. They waited about half an hour, and sent once more a servant to tell the General they were there; and the answer came that the General had gone to bed.

"I merely record this unparalleled insolence of epaulettes without comment It is the first indication I have yet seen of the threatened supremacy of the military authorities. Coming home, I spoke to the President about the matter, but he seemed not to have noticed it specially, saying it were better at this time not to be making points of etiquette and personal dignity."(5)

Did ever a subordinate, even a general, administer to a superior a more astounding snub? To Lincoln in his selfless temper, it was Only a detail in his problem of getting the army into action. What room for personal affronts however gross in a mood like his? To be sure he ceased going to McClellan's house, and thereafter summoned McClellan to come to him, but no change appeared in the tone of his intercourse with the General. "I will hold McClellan's horse," said he, "if he will win me victories."(6)

All this while, the two were debating plans of campaign and McClellan was revealing-as we now see, though no one saw it at the time-the deep dread of responsibility that was destined to paralyze him as an active general. He was never ready. Always, there must be more preparation, more men, more this, more that.

In January, 1862, Lincoln, grown desperate because of hope deferred, made the first move of a sort that was to be lamentably frequent the next six months. He went over the head of the Commanding General, and, in order to force a result, evoked a power not recognized in the military scheme of things. By this time the popular adulation of McClellan was giving place to a general imitation of the growling of the Jacobins, now well organized in the terrible Committee and growing each day more and more hostile to the Administration. Lincoln had besought McClellan to take into account the seriousness of this rising tide of opposition.(7) His arguments made no impression. McClellan would not recognize the political side of war. At last, partly to allay the popular clamor, partly to force McClellan into a corner, Lincoln published to the country a military program. He publicly instructed the Commanding General to put all his forces in movement on all fronts, on Washington's birthday.(8)

From this moment the debate between the President and the General with regard to plans of campaign approached the nature of a dispute. McClellan repeated his demand for more time in which to prepare. He objected to the course of advance which the President wished him to pursue. Lincoln, seeing the situation first of all as a political problem, grounded his thought upon two ideas neither of which was shared by McClellan: the idea that the supreme consideration was the safety of Washington; the resultant idea that McClellan should move directly south, keeping his whole army constantly between Washington and the enemy. McClellan wished to treat Washington as but one important detail in his strategy; he had a grandiose scheme for a wide flanking movement, for taking the bulk of his army by sea to the coast of Virginia, and thus to draw the Confederate army homeward for a duel to the death under the walls of Richmond. Lincoln, neither then nor afterward more than an amateur in strategy, was deeply alarmed by this bold mode of procedure. His political instinct told him that if there was any slip and Washington was taken, even briefly, by the Confederates, the game was up. He was still further alarmed when he found that some of the eider generals held views resembling his own.(9) To his modest, still groping mind, this was a trying situation. In the President lay the ultimate responsibility for every move the army should make. And whose advice should he accept as authoritative? The first time he asked himself that question, such peace of mind as had survived the harassing year 1861 left him, not to return for many a day.

At this moment of crises, occurred one of his keenest personal afflictions. His little son Willie sickened and died. Lincoln's relation to his children was very close, very tender. Many anecdotes show this boy frolicking about the White House, a licensed intruder everywhere. Another flood of anecdotes preserve the stupefying grief of his father after the child's death. Of these latter, the most extreme which portray Lincoln toward the close of February so unnerved as to be incapable of public duty, may be dismissed as apocryphal. But there can be no doubt that his unhappiness was too great for the vain measurement of descriptive words; that it intensified the nervous mood which had already possessed him; that anxiety, deepening at times into terrible alarm, became his constant companion.

In his dread and sorrow, his dilemma grew daily more intolerable. McClellan had opposed so stoutly the Washington birthday order that Lincoln had permitted him to ignore it. He was still wavering which advice to take, McClellan's or the elder generals'. To remove McClellan, to try at this critical moment some other general, did not occur to him as a rational possibility. But somehow he felt he must justify himself to himself for yielding to McClellan's views. In his zeal to secure some judgment more authoritative than his own, he took a further step along the dangerous road of going over the Commander's head, of bringing to bear upon him influences not strictly included in the military system. He required McClellan to submit his plan to a council of his general officers. Lincoln attended this council and told the generals "he was not a military man and therefore would be governed by the opinion of a majority."(10) The council decided in McClellan's favor by a vote of eight to four. This was a disappointment to Lincoln. So firm was his addiction to the overland route that he could not rest content with the council's decision. Stanton urged him to disregard it, sneering that the eight who voted against him were McClellan's creatures, his "pets." But Lincoln would not risk going against the majority of the council. "We are civilians," said he, "we should justly be held responsible for any disaster if we set up our opinions against those of experienced military men in the practical management of a campaign."(11)

Nevertheless, from this quandary, in which his reason forced him to do one thing while all his sensibilities protested, he extricated himself in a curious way. Throughout the late winter he had been the object of a concerted attack from Stanton and the Committee. The Committee had tacitly annexed Stanton. He conferred with them confidentially. At each important turn of events, he and they always got together in a secret powwow. As early as

February twentieth, when Lincoln seemed to be breaking down with grief and anxiety, one of those secret conferences of the high conspirators ended in a determination to employ all their forces, direct and indirect, to bring about McClellan's retirement. They were all victims of that mania of suspicion which was the order of the day. "A majority of the Committee," wrote its best member, long afterward when he had come to see things in a different light, "strongly suspected that General McClellan was a traitor." Wade vented his spleen in furious words about "King McClellan." Unrestrained by Lincoln's anguish, the Committee demanded a conference a few days after his son's death and threatened an appeal from President to Congress if he did not quickly force McClellan to advance.(12)

All this while the Committee was airing another grievance. They clamored to have the twelve divisions of the army of the Potomac grouped into corps. They gave as their motive, military efficiency. And perhaps they thought they meant it. But there was a cat in the bag which they carefully tried to conceal. The generals of divisions formed two distinct groups, the elder ones who did not owe their elevation to McClellan and the younger ones who did. The elder generals, it happened, sympathized generally with the Committee in politics, or at least did not sympathize with McClellan. The younger generals reflected the politics of their patron. And McClellan was a Democrat, a hater of the Vindictives, unsympathetic with Abolition. Therefore, the mania of suspicion being in full flood, the Committee would believe no good of McClellan when he opposed advancing the elder generals to the rank of corps commanders. His explanation that he "wished to test them in the field," was poohpoohed. Could not any good Jacobin see through that! Of course, it was but an excuse to hold back the plums until he could drop them into the itching palms of those wicked Democrats, his "pets." Why should not the good men and true, elder and therefore better soldiers, whose righteousness was so well attested by their political leanings, why should not they have the places of power to which their rank entitled them?

Hitherto, however, Lincoln had held out against the Committee's demand and bad refused to compel McClellan to reorganize his army against his will. He now observed that in the council which cast the die against the overland route, the division between the two groups of generals, what we may call the Lincoln generals and the McClellan generals, was sharply evident. The next day he issued a general order which organized the army of the Potomac into corps, and promoted to the rank of corps commanders, those elder generals whose point of view was similar to his own.(13) Thereafter, any reference of crucial matters to a council of general officers, would mean submitting it, not to a dozen commanders of divisions with McClellan men in the majority, but to four or five commanders of corps none of whom was definitely of the McClellan faction. Thus McClellan was virtually put under surveillance of an informal war council scrutinizing his course from the President's point of view. It was this reduced council of the subordinates, as will presently appear, that made the crucial decision of the campaign.

On the same day Lincoln issued another general order accepting McClellan's plan for a flanking movement to the Virginia coast.(14) The Confederate lines at this time ran through Manassas—the point Lincoln wished McClellan to strike. It was to be known later that the Confederate General gave to Lincoln's views the high endorsement of assuming that they were the inevitable views that the Northern Commander, if he knew his business, would act upon. Therefore, he had been quietly preparing to withdraw his army to more defensible positions farther South. By a curious coincidence, his "strategic retreat" occurred immediately after McClellan had been given authority to do what he liked. On the ninth of March it was known at Washington that Manassas had been evacuated. Whereupon, McClellan's fatal lack of humor permitted him to make a great blunder. The man who had refused to go to Manassas while the Confederates were there, marched an army to Manassas the moment he heard that they were gone— and then marched back again. This performance was instantly fixed upon for ridicule as McClellan's "promenade to Manassas."

To Lincoln the news of the promenade seemed both a vindication of his own plan and crushing evidence that if he had insisted on his plan, the Confederate army would have been annihilated, the war in one cataclysm brought to an end. He was ridden, as most men were, by the delusion of one terrific battle that was to end all. In a bitterness of disappointment, his slowly tortured spirit burst into rage. The Committee was delighted. For once, they approved of him. The next act of this man, ordinarily so gentle, seems hardly credible. By a stroke of his pen, he stripped McClellan of the office of Commanding General, reduced him to the rank of mere head of a local army, the army of the Potomac; furthermore, he permitted him to hear of his degradation through the heartless medium of the daily papers. (15) The functions of Commanding General were added to the duties of the Secretary of War. Stanton, now utterly merciless toward McClellan, instantly took possession of his office and seized his papers, for all the world as if he were pouncing upon the effects of a malefactor. That McClellan was not yet wholly spoiled was shown by the way he received this blow. It was the McClellan of the old days, the gallant gentleman of the year 1860, not the poseur of 1861, who wrote at once to Lincoln making no complaint, saying that his services belonged to his country in whatever capacity they might be required.

Again a council of subordinates was invoked to determine the next move. McClellan called together the newly made corps commanders and obtained their approval of a variation of his former plan. He now proposed to use Fortress Monroe as a base, and thence conduct an attack upon Richmond. Again, though with a touch of sullenness very rare in Lincoln, the President acquiesced. But he added a condition to McClellan's plan by issuing positive orders, March thirteenth, that it should not be carried out unless sufficient force was left at Washington to render the city impregnable.

During the next few days the Committee must have been quite satisfied with the President. For him, he was savage. The normal Lincoln, the man of immeasurable mercy, had temporarily vanished. McClellan's blunder had touched the one spring that roused the tiger in Lincoln. By letting slip a chance to terminate the war—as it seemed to that deluded Washington of March, 1862—McClellan had converted Lincoln from a brooding gentleness to an incarnation of the last judgment. He told Hay he thought that in permitting McClellan to retain any command, he had shown him "very great kindness."(16) Apparently, he had no consciousness that he had been harsh in the mode of McClellan's abatement, no thought of the fine manliness of McClellan's reply.

During this period of Lincoln's brief vengefulness, Stanton thought that his time for clearing scores with McClellan had come. He even picked out the man who was to be rushed over other men's heads to the command of the army of the Potomac. General Hitchcock, an accomplished soldier of the regular army, a grandson of Ethan Allen, who had grown old in honorable service, was summoned to Washington, and was "amazed" by having plumped at him the question, would he consent to succeed McClellan? Though General Hitchcock was not without faults—and there is an episode in his later relations with McClellan which his biographer discreetly omits—he was a modest man. He refused to consider Stanton's offer. But he consented to become the confidential adviser of the War Office. This was done after an interview with Lincoln who impressed on Hitchcock his sense of a great responsibility and of the fact that he "had no military knowledge" and that he must have advice.(17) Out of this congested sense of helplessness in Lincoln, joined with the new labors of the Secretary of War as executive head of all the armies, grew quickly another of those ill-omened, extra-constitutional war councils, one more wheel within the wheels, that were all doing their part to make the whole machine unworkable; distributing instead of concentrating power. This new council which came to be known as the Army Board, was made up of the heads of the Bureaus of the War Department with the addition of Hitchcock as "Advising General." Of the temper of the Army Board, composed as it was entirely of the satellites of Stanton, a confession in Hitchcock's diary speaks volumes. On the evening of the first day of their new relation, Stanton poured out to him such a quantity of oral evidence of McClellan's "incompetency" as to make this new recruit for anti-McClellanism "feel positively sick."(18)

By permitting this added source of confusion among his advisers, Lincoln treated himself much as he had already treated McClellan. By going over McClellan's head to take advice from his subordinates he had put the General on a leash; now, by setting Hitchcock and the experts in the seat of judgment, he virtually, for a short while, put himself on a leash. Thus had come into tacit but real power three military councils none of which was recognized as such by law—the Council of the Subordinates behind McClellan; the Council of the Experts behind Lincoln; the Council of the Jacobins, called The Committee, behind them all.

The political pressure on Lincoln now changed its tack. Its unfailing zeal to discredit McClellan assumed the form of insisting that he had a secret purpose in waiting to get his army away from Washington, that he was scheming to leave the city open to the Confederates, to "uncover" it, as the soldiers said. By way of focussing the matter on a definite issue, his enemies demanded that he detach from his army and assign to the defense of Washington, a division which was supposed to be peculiarly efficient General Blenker had recruited a sort of "foreign legion," in which were many daring adventurers who had seen service in European armies. Blenker's was the division demanded. So determined was the pressure that Lincoln yielded. However, his brief anger had blown itself out. To continue vengeful any length of time was for Lincoln impossible. He was again the normal Lincoln, passionless, tender, fearful of doing an injustice, weighed down by the sense of responsibility. He broke the news about Blenker in a personal note to McClellan that was almost apologetic. "I write this to assure you that I did so with great pain, understanding that you would wish it otherwise. If you could know the full pressure of the case, I am confident you would justify it."(19) In conversation, he assured McClellan that no other portion of his army should be taken from him.(20)

The change in Lincoln's mood exasperated Stanton. He called on his pals in the Committee for another of those secret confabulations in which both he and they delighted. Speaking with scorn of Lincoln's return to magnanimity, he told them that the President had "gone back to his first love," the traitor McClellan. Probably all those men who wagged their chins in that conference really believed that McClellan was aiming to betray them. One indeed, Julian, long afterward had the largeness of mind to confess his fault and recant. The rest died in their absurd delusion, maniacs of suspicion to the very end. At the time all of them laid their heads together—for what purpose? Was it to catch McClellan in a trap?

Meanwhile, in obedience to Lincoln's orders of March thirteenth, McClellan drew up a plan for the defense of Washington. As Hitchcock was now in such high feather, McClellan sent his plan to the new favorite of the War Office, for criticism. Hitchcock refused to criticize, and when McClellan's chief of staff pressed for "his opinion, as an old and experienced officer," Hitchcock replied that McClellan had had ample opportunity to know what was needed, and persisted in his refusal.(21) McClellan asked no further advice and made his arrangements to suit himself. On April first he took boat at Alexandria for the front. Part of his army had preceded him. The remainder-except the force he had assigned to the defense of Washington-was speedily to follow.

With McClellan's departure still another devotee of suspicion moves to the front of the stage. This was General Wadsworth. Early in March, Stanton had told McClellan that he wanted Wadsworth as commander of the defenses of Washington. McClellan had protested. Wadsworth was not a military man. He was a politician turned soldier who had tried to be senator from New York and failed; tried to be governor and failed; and was destined to try again to be governor, and again to fail. Why should such a person be singled out to become responsible for the safety of the capital? Stanton's only argument was that the appointment of Wadsworth was desirable for political reasons. He added that it would be made whether McClellan liked it or not. And made it was.(22) Furthermore, Wadsworth, who had previously professed friendship for McClellan, promptly joined the ranks of his enemies. Can any one doubt, Stanton being Stanton, mad with distrust of McClellan, that Wadsworth was fully informed of McClellan's opposition to his advancement?

On the second of April Wadsworth threw a bomb after the vanishing McClellan, then aboard his steamer somewhere between Washington and Fortress Monroe. Wadsworth informed Stanton that McClellan had not carried out the orders of March thirteenth, that the force he had left at Washington was inadequate to its safety, that the capital was "uncovered." Here was a chance for Stanton to bring to bear on Lincoln both those unofficial councils that were meddling so deeply in the control of the army. He threw this firebrand of a report among his satellites of the Army Board and into the midst of the Committee.2(3)

It is needless here to go into the furious disputes that ensued-the accusations, the recriminations, the innuendoes! McClellan stoutly insisted that he had obeyed both the spirit and the letter of March thirteenth; that Washington was amply protected. His enemies shrieked that his statements were based on juggled figures; that even if the number of soldiers was adequate, the quality and equipment were wretched; in a word that he lied. It is a shame-less controversy inconceivable were there not many men in whom politics and prejudice far outweighed patriotism. In all this, Hitchcock was Stanton's trump card. He who had refused to advise McClellan, did not hesitate to denounce him. In response to a request from Stanton, he made a report sustaining Wadsworth. The Committee summoned Wadsworth before it; he read them his report to Stanton; reiterated its charges, and treated them to some innuendoes after their own hearts, plainly hinting that McClellan could have crushed the Confederates at Manassas if he had wished to.(24)

A wave of hysteria swept the Committee and the War Office and beat fiercely upon Lincoln. The Board charged him to save the day by mulcting the army of the Potomac of an entire corps, retaining it at Washington. Lincoln met the Board in a long and troubled conference. His anxious desire to do all he could for McClellan was palpable.(25) But what, under the circumstances, could he do? Here was this new device for the steadying of his judgment, this Council of Experts, singing the same old tune, assuring him that McClellan was not to be trusted. Although in the reaction from his momentary vengefulness he had undoubtedly swung far back toward recovering confidence in McClellan, did he dare—painfully conscious as he was that he "had no military knowledge" — did he dare go against the Board, disregard its warning that McClellan's arrangements made of Washington a dangling plum for Confederate raiders to snatch whenever they pleased. His bewilderment as to what McClellan was really driving at came back upon him in full force. He reached at last the dreary conclusion that there was nothing for it but to let the new wheel within the wheels take its turn at running the machine. Accepting the view that McClellan had not kept faith on the basis of the orders of March thirteenth, Lincoln "after much consideration" set aside his own promise to McClellan and authorized the Secretary of War to detain a full corps.(26)

McClellan never forgave this mutilation of his army and in time fixed upon it as the prime cause of his eventual failure on the Peninsula. It is doubtful whether relations between him and Lincoln were ever again really cordial.

In their rather full correspondence during the tense days of April, May and June, the steady deterioration of McClellan's judgment bore him down into amazing depths of fatuousness. In his own way he was as much appalled by the growth of his responsibility as ever Lincoln had been. He moved with incredible caution.*

*Commenting on one of his moments of hesitation, J.S. Johnston wrote to Lee: "No one but McClellan could have hesitated to attack." 14 O. R., 416.

His despatches were a continual wailing for more men. Whatever went wrong was at once blamed on Washington. His ill-usage had made him bitter. And he could not escape the fact that his actual performance did not come up to expectation; that he was constantly out-generaled. His prevailing temper during these days is shown in a letter to his wife. "I have raised an awful row about McDowell's corps. The President very coolly telegraphed me yesterday that he thought I ought to break the enemy's lines at once. I was much tempted to reply that he had better come and do it himself." A despatch to Stanton, in a moment of disaster, has become notorious: "If I save this army now, I tell you plainly I owe no thanks to you or to any other persons in Washington. You have done your best to sacrifice this army."(27)

Throughout this preposterous correspondence, Lincoln maintained the even tenor of his usual patient stoicism, "his sad lucidity of soul." He explained; he reasoned; he promised, over and over, assistance to the limit of his power; he never scolded; when complaint became too absurd to be reasoned with, he passed it over in silence. Again, he was the selfless man, his sensibilities lost in the purpose he sought to establish.

Once during this period, he acted suddenly, on the spur of the moment, in a swift upflaring of his unconquerable fear for the safety of Washington. Previously, he had consented to push the detained corps, McDowell's, southward by land to cooperate with McClellan, who adapted his plans to this arrangement. Scarcely had he done so, than Lincoln threw his plans into confusion by ordering McDowell back to Washington.(28) Jackson, who had begun his famous campaign of menace, was sweeping like a whirlwind down the Shenandoah Valley, and in the eyes of panic-struck Washington appeared to be a reincarnation of Southey's Napoleon, —

"And the great Few-Faw-Fum, would presently come,

With a hop, skip and jump"

into Pennsylvania Avenue. As Jackson's object was to bring McDowell back to Washington and enable Johnston to deal with McClellan unreinforced, Lincoln had fallen into a trap. But he had much company. Stanton was well-nigh out of his head. Though Jackson's army was less than fifteen thousand and the Union forces in front of him upward of sixty thousand, Stanton telegraphed to Northern governors imploring them to hasten forward militia because "the enemy in great force are marching on Washington."(29)

The moment Jackson had accomplished his purpose, having drawn a great army northwestward away from McClellan, most of which should have been marching southeastward to join McClellan, he slipped away, rushed his own army across the whole width of Virginia, and joined Lee in the terrible fighting of the Seven Days before Richmond.

In the midst of this furious confusion, the men surrounding Lincoln may be excused for not observing a change in him. They have recorded his appearance of indecision, his solicitude over McClellan, his worn and haggard look. The changing light in those smoldering fires of his deeply sunken eyes escaped their notice. Gradually, through profound unhappiness, and as always in silence, Lincoln was working out of his last eclipse. No certain record of his inner life during this transition, the most important of his life, has survived. We can judge of it only by the results. The outstanding fact with regard to it is a certain change of attitude, an access of determination, late in June. What desperate wrestling with the angel had taken place in the months of agony since his son's death, even his private secretaries have not felt able to say. Neither, apparently, did they perceive, until it flashed upon them full-blown, the change that was coming over his resolution. Nor did the Cabinet have any warning that the President was turning a corner, developing a new phase of himself, something sterner, more powerful than anything they had suspected. This was ever his way. His instinctive reticence stood firm until the moment of the new birth. Not only the Cabinet but the country was amazed and startled, when, late in June, the President suddenly left Washington. He made a flying trip to West Point where Scott was living in virtual retirement.(30) What passed between the two, those few hours they spent together, that twenty-fourth of June, 1862, has never been divulged. Did they have any eyes, that day, for the wonderful prospect from the high terrace of the parade ground; for the river so far below, flooring the valley with silver; for the mountains pearl and blue? Did they talk of Stanton, of his waywardness, his furies? Of the terrible Committee? Of the way Lincoln had tied his own hands, brought his will to stalemate, through his recognition of the unofficial councils? Who knows?

Lincoln was back in Washington the next day. Another day, and by a sweeping order he created a new army for the protection of Washington, and placed in command of it, a western general who was credited with a brilliant stroke on the Mississippi.(31) No one will now defend the military genius of John Pope. But when Lincoln sent for him, all the evidence to date appeared to be in his favor. His follies were yet to appear. And it is more than likely that in the development of Lincoln's character, his appointment has a deep significance. It appears to mark the moment when Lincoln broke out of the cocoon of advisement he had spun unintentionally around his will. In the sorrows of the grim year, new forces had been generated. New spiritual powers were coming to his assistance. At last, relatively, he had found peace. Worn and torn as he was, after his long inward struggle, few bore so calmly as he did the distracting news from the front in the closing days of June and the opening days of July, when Lee was driving his whole strength like a superhuman battering-ram, straight at the heart of the wavering McClellan. A visitor at the White House, in the midst of the terrible strain of the Seven Days, found Lincoln "thin and haggard, but cheerful . . . quite as placid as usual . . . his manner was so kindly and so free from the ordinary cocksureness of the politician, and the vanity and self-importance of official position that nothing but good will was inspired by his presence."(32)

His serenity was all the more remarkable as his relations with Congress and the Committee were fast approaching a crisis. If McClellan failed-and by the showing of his own despatches, there was every reason to expect him to fail, so besotted was he upon the idea that no one could prevail with the force allowed him—the Committee who were leaders of the congressional party against the presidential party might be expected promptly to measure strength with the Administration. And McClellan failed. At that moment Chandler, with the consent of the Committee, was making use of its records preparing a Philippic against the government. Lincoln, acting on his own initiative, without asking the Secretary of War to accompany him, went immediately to the front. He passed two days questioning McClellan and his generals.(33) But there was no council of war. It was a different Lincoln from that other who, just four months previous, had called together the general officers and promised them to abide by their decisions. He returned to Washington without telling them what he meant to do.

The next day closed a chapter and opened a chapter in the history of the Federal army. Stanton's brief and inglorious career as head of the national forces came to an end. He fell back into his rightful position, the President's executive officer in military affairs. Lincoln telegraphed another Western general, Halleck, ordering him to Washington as General-in-Chief.(34) He then, for a season, turned his whole attention from the army to politics. Five days after the telegram to Halleck, Chandler in the Senate, loosed his insatiable temper in what ostensibly was a denunciation of McClellan, what in point of fact was a sweeping arraignment of the military efficiency of the government.(35)

XXII
LINCOLN EMERGES

While Lincoln was slowly struggling out of his last eclipse, giving most of his attention to the army, the Congressional Cabal was laboring assiduously to force the issue upon slavery. The keen politicians who composed it saw with unerring vision where, for the moment, lay their opportunity. They could not beat the President on any one issue then before the country. No one faction was strong enough to be their stand-by. Only by a combination of issues and a coalition of factions could they build up an anti-Lincoln party, check-mate the Administration, and get control of the government. They were greatly assisted by the fatuousness of the Democrats. That party was in a peculiar situation. Its most positive characters, naturally, had taken sides for or against the government. The powerful Southerners who had been its chief leaders were mainly in the Confederacy. Such Northerners as Douglas and Stanton, and many more, had gone over to the Republicans. Suddenly the control of the party organization had fallen into the hands of second-rate men. As by the stroke of an enchanter's wand, men of small caliber who, had the old conditions remained, would have lived and died of little consequence saw opening before them the role of leadership. It was too much for their mental poise. Again the subjective element in politics! The Democratic party for the duration of the war became the organization of Little Men. Had they possessed any great leaders, could they have refused to play politics and responded to Lincoln's all-parties policy, history might have been different. But they were not that sort. Neither did they have the courage to go to the other extreme and become a resolute opposition party, wholeheartedly and intelligently against the war. They equivocated, they obstructed, they professed loyalty and they practised-it would be hard to say what! So short-sighted was their political game that its effect continually was to play into the hands of their most relentless enemies, the grim Jacobins.

Though, for a brief time while the enthusiasm after Sumter was still at its height they appeared to go along with the all-parties program, they soon revealed their true course. In the autumn of 1861, Lincoln still had sufficient hold upon all factions to make it seem likely that his all-parties program would be given a chance. The Republicans generally made overtures to the Democratic managers, offering to combine in a coalition party with no platform but the support of the war and the restoration of the Union. Here was the test of the organization of the Little Men. The insignificant new managers, intoxicated by the suddenness of their opportunity, rang false. They rejected the all-parties program and insisted on maintaining their separate party formation.(1) This was a turning point in Lincoln's career. Though nearly two years were to pass before he admitted his defeat, the all-parties program was doomed from that hour. Throughout the winter, the Democrats in Congress, though steadily ambiguous in their statements of principle, were as steadily hostile to Lincoln. If they had any settled policy, it was no more than an attempt to hold the balance of power among the warring factions of the Republicans. By springtime the game they were playing was obvious; also its results. They had prevented the President from building up a strong Administration group wherewith he might have counterbalanced the Jacobins. Thus they had released the Jacobins from the one possible restraint that might have kept them from pursuing their own devices.

The spring of 1862 saw a general realignment of factions. It was then that the Congressional Cabal won its first significant triumph. Hitherto, all the Republican platforms had been programs of denial. A brilliant new member of the Senate, john Sherman, bluntly told his colleagues that the Republican party had always stood on the defensive. That was its weakness. "I do not know any measure on which it has taken an aggressive position."(2) The clue to the psychology of the moment was in the raging demand of the masses for a program of assertion, for aggressive measures. The President was trying to meet this demand with his all-parties program, with his policy of nationalism, exclusive of everything else. And recently he had added that other assertion, his insistence that the executive in certain respects was independent of the legislative. Of his three assertions, one, the all-parties program, was already on the way to defeat Another, nationalism, as the President interpreted it, had alienated the Abolitionists. The third, his argument for himself as tribune, was just what your crafty politician might twist, pervert, load with false meanings to his heart's content. Men less astute than Chandler and Wade could not have failed to see where fortune pointed. Their opportunity lay in a combination of the two issues. Abolition and the resistance to executive "usurpation." Their problem was to create an anti-Lincoln party that should also be a war party. Their coalition of aggressive forces must accept the Abolitionists as its backbone, but it must also include all violent elements of whatever persuasion, and especially all those that could be wrought into fury on the theme of the President as a despot. Above all, their coalition must absorb and then express the furious temper so dear to their own hearts which they fondly believed-mistakenly, they were destined to discover-was the temper of the country.

It can not be said that this was the Republican program. The President's program, fully as positive as that of the Cabal, had as good a right to appropriate the party label—as events were to show, a better right. But the power of the Cabal was very great, and the following it was able to command in the country reached almost the proportions of the terrible. A factional name is needed. For the Jacobins, their allies in Congress, their followers in the country, from the time they acquired a positive program, an accurate label is the Vindictives.

During the remainder of the session, Congress may be thought of as having—what Congress seldom has—three definite groups, Right, Left and Center. The Right was the Vindictives; the Left, the irreconcilable Democrats; the Center was composed chiefly of liberal Republicans but included a few Democrats, those who rebelled against the political chicanery of the Little Men.

The policy of the Vindictives was to force upon the Administration the double issue of emancipation and the supremacy of Congress. Therefore, their aim was to pass a bill freeing the slaves on the sole authority of a congressional act. Many resolutions, many bills, all having this end in view, were introduced. Some were buried in committees; some were remade in committees and subjected to long debate by the Houses; now and then one was passed upon. But the spring wore through and the summer came, and still the Vindictives were not certainly in control of Congress. No bill to free slaves by congressional action secured a majority vote. At the same time it was plain that the strength of the Vindictives was slowly, steadily, growing.

Outside Congress, the Abolitionists took new hope. They had organized a systematic propaganda. At Washington, weekly meetings were held in the Smithsonian Institute, where all their most conspicuous leaders, Phillips, Emerson, Brownson, Garret Smith, made addresses. Every Sunday a service was held in the chamber of the House of Representatives and the sermon was almost always a "terrific arrangement of slavery." Their watch-word was "A Free Union or Disintegration." The treatment of fugitive slaves by commanders in the field produced a clamor. Lincoln insisted on strict obedience to the two laws, the Fugitive Slave Act and the First Confiscation Act. Abolitionists sneered at "all this gabble about the sacredness of the Constitution."(3) But Lincoln was not to be moved. When General Hunter, taking a leaf from the book of Fremont, tried to force his hand, he did not hesitate. Hunter had issued a proclamation by which the slaves in the region where he commanded were "declared forever free."

This was in May when Lincoln's difficulties with McClellan were at their height; when the Committee was zealously watching to catch him in any sort of mistake; when the House was within four votes of a majority for emancipation by act of Congress;(4) when there was no certainty whether the country was with him or with the Vindictives. Perhaps that new courage which definitely revealed itself the next month, may be first glimpsed in the proclamation overruling Hunter:

"I further make known that whether it be competent for me, as Commander-in-Chief of the Army and Navy, to declare the slaves of any State or States free, and whether at any time, in any case, it shall have become a necessity indispensable to the maintenance of the government to exercise such supposed power, are questions which, under my responsibility, I reserve to myself, and which I can not feel justified in leaving to the decision of commanders in the field."(5)

The revocation of Hunter's order infuriated the Abolitionists. It deeply disappointed the growing number who, careless about slavery, wanted emancipation as a war measure, as a blow at the South. Few of either of these groups noticed the implied hint that emancipation might come by executive action. Here was the matter of the war powers in a surprising form. However, it was not unknown to Congress. Attempts had been made to induce Congress to concede the war powers to the President and to ask, not command, him to use them for the liberation of slaves in the Seceded States. Long before, in a strangely different connection, such vehement Abolitionists as Giddings and J. Q. Adams had pictured the freeing of slaves as a natural incident of military occupation.

What induced Lincoln to throw out this hint of a possible surrender on the subject of emancipation? Again, as so often, the silence as to his motives is unbroken. However, there can be no doubt that his thinking on the subject passed through several successive stages. But all his thinking was ruled by one idea. Any policy he might accept, or any refusal of policy, would be judged in his own mind by the degree to which it helped, or hindered, the national cause. Nothing was more absurd than the sneer of the Abolitionists that he was "tender" of slavery. Browning spoke for him faithfully, "If slavery can survive the shock of war and secession, be it so. If in the conflict for liberty, the Constitution and the Union, it must necessarily perish, then let it perish." Browning refused to predict which alternative would develop. His point was that slaves must be treated like other property. But, if need be, he would sacrifice slavery as he would sacrifice anything else, to save the Union. He had no intention to "protect" slavery.(6)

In the first stage of Lincoln's thinking on this thorny subject, his chief anxiety was to avoid scaring off from the national cause those Southern

Unionists who were not prepared to abandon slavery. This was the motive behind his prompt suppression of Fremont. It was this that inspired the Abolitionist sneer about his relative attitude toward God and Kentucky. As a compromise, to cut the ground from under the Vindictives, he had urged the loyal Slave States to endorse a program of compensated emancipation. But these States were as unable to see the handwriting on the wall as were the Little Men. In the same proclamation that overruled Hunter, while hinting at what the Administration might feel driven to do, Lincoln appealed again to the loyal Slave States to accept compensated emancipation. "I do not argue," said he, "I beseech you to make the argument for yourselves. You can not, if you would, be blind to the signs of the times. . . . This proposal makes common cause for a common object, casting no reproaches upon any. It acts not the Pharisee. The change it contemplates would come gently as the dews of heaven, not rending or wrecking anything."(7)

Though Lincoln, at this moment, was anxiously watching the movement in Congress to force his hand, he was not apparently cast down. He was emerging from his eclipse. June was approaching and with it the final dawn. Furthermore, when he issued this proclamation on May nineteenth, he had not lost faith in McClellan. He was still hoping for news of a crushing victory; of McClellan's triumphal entry into Richmond. The next two months embraced both those transformations which together revolutionized his position. He emerged from his last eclipse; and McClellan failed him.

When Lincoln returned to Washington after his two days at the front, he knew that the fortunes of his Administration were at a low ebb. Never had he been derided in Congress with more brazen injustice. The Committee, waiting only for McClellan's failure, would now unmask their guns-as Chandler did, seven days later. The line of Vindictive criticism could easily be foreshadowed: the government had failed; it was responsible for a colossal military catastrophe; but what could you expect of an Administration that would not strike its enemies through emancipation; what a shattering demonstration that the Executive was not a safe repository of the war powers.

Was there any way to forestall or disarm the Vindictives? His silence gives us no clue when or how the answer occurred to him—by separating the two issues; by carrying out the hint in the May proclamation; by yielding on emancipation while, in the very act, pushing the war powers of the President to their limit, declaring slaves free by an executive order.

The importance of preserving the war power of the President had become a fixed condition of Lincoln's thought. Already, he was looking forward not only to victory but to the great task that should come after victory. He was determined, if it were humanly possible, to keep that task in the hands of the President, and out of the hands of Congress. A first step had already been taken. In portions of occupied territory, military governors had been appointed. Simple as this seemed to the careless observer, it focussed the whole issue. The powerful, legal mind of Sumner at once perceived its significance. He denied in the Senate the right of the President to make such appointments; he besought the Senate to demand the cancellation of such appointment. He reasserted the absolute sovereignty of Congress.(8) It would be a far-reaching stroke if Lincoln, in any way, could extort from Congress acquiescence in his use of the war powers on a vast scale. Freeing the slaves by executive order would be such a use.

Another train of thought also pointed to the same result. Lincoln's desire to further the cause of "the Liberal party throughout the world," that desire which dated back to his early life as a politician, had suffered a disappointment. European Liberals, whose political vision was less analytical than his, had failed to understand his policy. The Confederate authorities had been quick to publish in Europe his official pronouncements that the war had been undertaken not to abolish slavery but to preserve the Union. As far back as September, 1861, Carl Schurz wrote from Spain to Seward that the Liberals abroad were disappointed, that "the impression gained ground that the war as waged by the Federal government, far from being a war of principle, was merely a war of policy," and "that from this point of view much might be said for the South."(9) In fact, these hasty Europeans had found a definite ground for complaining that the American war was a reactionary influence. The concentration of American cruisers in the Southern blockade gave the African slave trade its last lease of life. With no American war-ship among the West Indies, the American flag became the safeguard of the slaver. Englishmen complained that "the swift ships crammed with their human cargoes" had only to "hoist the Stars and Stripes and pass under the bows of our cruisers."(10) Though Seward scored a point by his treaty giving British cruisers the right to search any ships carrying the American flag, the distrust of the foreign Liberals was not removed. They inclined to stand aside and to allow the commercial classes of France and England to dictate policy toward the United States. The blockade, by shutting off the European supply of raw cotton, on both sides the channel, was the cause of measureless unemployment, of intolerable misery. There was talk in both countries of intervention. Napoleon, especially, loomed large on the horizon as a possible ally of the Confederacy. And yet, all this while, Lincoln had it in his power at any minute to lay the specter of foreign intervention. A pledge to the "Liberal party throughout the world" that the war would bring about the destruction of slavery, and great political powers both in England and in France would at once cross the paths of their governments should they move toward intervention. Weighty as were all these reasons for a change of policy—turning the flank of the Vindictives on the war powers, committing the Abolitionists to the Administration, winning over the European Liberals—there was a fourth reason which, very probably, weighed upon Lincoln most powerfully of them all. Profound gloom had settled upon the country. There was no enthusiasm for military service. And Stanton, who lacked entirely the psychologic vision of the statesman, had recently committed an astounding blunder. After a few months in power he had concluded that the government had enough soldiers and had closed the recruiting offices.(11) Why Lincoln permitted this singular proceeding has never been satisfactorily explained.* Now he was reaping the fruits. A defeated army, a hopeless country, and no prospect of swift reinforcement! If a shift of ground on the question of emancipation would arouse new enthusiasm, bring in a new stream of recruits, Lincoln was prepared to shift.

Stanton's motive was probably economy. Congress was terrified by the expense of the war. The Committee was deeply alarmed over the political effect of war taxation. They and Stanton were all convinced that McClellan was amply strong enough to crush the Confederacy.

But even in this dire extremity, he would not give way without a last attempt to save his earlier policy. On July twelfth, he called together the Senators and Representatives of the Border States. He read to them a written argument in favor of compensated emancipation, the Federal government to assist the States in providing funds for the purpose.

"Let the States that are in rebellion," said he, "see definitely and certainly that in no event will the States you represent ever join their proposed Confederacy, and they can not much longer maintain the contest. But you can not divest them of their hope to ultimately have you with them so long as you show a determination to perpetuate the institution within your own States. . . . If the war continues long, as it must if the object be not sooner attained, the institution in your States will be extinguished by mere friction and abrasion—by the mere incidents of war. . . . Our common country is in great peril, demanding the loftiest views and boldest action to bring it speedy relief. Once relieved its form of government is saved to the world, its beloved history and cherished memories are vindicated, and its happy future fully assured and rendered inconceivably grand."(12)

He made no impression. They would commit themselves to nothing. Lincoln abandoned his earlier policy.

Of what happened next, he said later, "It had got to be. . . . Things had gone on from bad to worse until I felt that we had reached the end of our rope on the plan of operations we had been pursuing; that we had about played our last card and must change our tactics or lose the game. I now determined upon the adoption of the emancipation policy. . . "(13)

The next day he confided his decision and his reasons to Seward and Welles. Though "this was a new departure for the President," both these Ministers agreed with him that the change of policy had become inevitable. (14)

Lincoln was now entirely himself, astute in action as well as bold in thought. He would not disclose his change of policy while Congress was in session. Should he do so, there was no telling what attempt the Cabal would make to pervert his intention, to twist his course into the semblance of an acceptance of the congressional theory. He laid the matter aside until Congress should be temporarily out of the way, until the long recess between July and December should have begun. In this closing moment of the second session of the Thirty-Seventh Congress, which is also the opening moment of the great period of Lincoln, the feeling against him in Congress was extravagantly bitter. It caught at anything with which to make a point. A disregard of technicalities of procedure was magnified into a serious breach of constitutional privilege. Reviving the question of compensated emancipation, Lincoln had sent a special message to both Houses, submitting the text of a compensation bill which he urged them to consider. His enemies raised an uproar. The President had no right to introduce a bill into Congress! Dictator Lincoln was trying in a new way to put Congress under his thumb.(15)

In the last week of the session, Lincoln's new boldness brought the old relation between himself and Congress to a dramatic close. The Second Confiscation Bill had long been under discussion. Lincoln believed that some of its provisions were inconsistent with the spirit at least of our fundamental law. Though its passage was certain, he prepared a veto message. He then permitted the congressional leaders to know what he intended to do when the bill should reach him. Gall and wormwood are weak terms for the bitterness that may be tasted in the speeches of the Vindictives. When, in order to save the bill, a resolution was appended purging it of the interpretation which Lincoln condemned, Trumbull passionately declared that Congress was being "coerced" by the President. "No one at a distance," is the deliberate conclusion of Julian who was present, "could have formed any adequate conception of the hostility of the Republican members toward Lincoln at the final adjournment, while it was the belief of many that our last session of Congress had been held in Washington. Mr. Wade said the country was going to hell, and that the scenes witnessed in the French Revolution were nothing in comparison with what we should see here."(16)

Lincoln endured the rage of Congress in unwavering serenity. On the last day of the session, Congress surrendered and sent to him both the Confiscation Act and the explanatory resolution. Thereupon, he indulged in what must have seemed to those fierce hysterical enemies of his a wanton stroke of irony. He sent them along with his approval of the bill the text of the veto message he would have sent had they refused to do what he wanted.(17) There could be no concealing the fact that the President had matched his will against the will of Congress, and that the President had had his way.

Out of this strange period of intolerable confusion, a gigantic figure had at last emerged. The outer and the inner Lincoln had fused. He was now a coherent personality, masterful in spite of his gentleness, with his own peculiar fashion of self-reliance, having a policy of his own devising, his colors nailed upon the masthead.

XXIII
THE MYSTICAL STATESMAN

Lincoln's final emergence was a deeper thing than merely the consolidation of a character, the transformation of a dreamer into a man of action. The fusion of the outer and the inner person was the result of a profound interior change. Those elements of mysticism which were in him from the first, which had gleamed darkly through such deep overshadowing, were at last established in their permanent form. The political tension had been matched by a spiritual tension with personal sorrow as the connecting link. In a word, he had found his religion.

Lincoln's instinctive reticence was especially guarded, as any one might expect, in the matter of his belief. Consequently, the precise nature of it has been much discussed. As we have seen, the earliest current report charged him with deism. The devoted Herndon, himself an agnostic, eagerly claims his hero as a member of the noble army of doubters. Elaborate arguments have been devised in rebuttal. The fault on both sides is in the attempt to base an impression on detached remarks and in the further error of treating all these fragments as of one time, or more truly, as of no time, as if his soul were a philosopher of the absolute, speaking oracularly out of a void. It is like the vicious reasoning that tortures systems of theology out of disconnected texts.

Lincoln's religious life reveals the same general divisions that are to be found in his active life: from the beginning to about the time of his election; from the close of 1860 to the middle of 1862; the remainder.

Of his religious experience in the first period, very little is definitely known. What glimpses we have of it both fulfill and contradict the forest religion that was about him in his youth. The superstition, the faith in dreams, the dim sense of another world surrounding this, the belief in communion between the two, these are the parts of him that are based unchangeably in the forest shadows. But those other things, the spiritual passions, the ecstacies, the vague sensing of the terribleness of the creative powers,—to them always he made no response. And the crude philosophizing of the forest theologians, their fiercely simple dualism—God and Satan, thunder and lightning, the eternal war in the heavens, the eternal lake of fire—it meant nothing to him. Like all the furious things of life, evil appeared to him as mere negation, a mysterious foolishness he could not explain. His aim was to forget it. Goodness and pity were the active elements that roused him to think of the other world; especially pity. The burden of men's tears, falling ever in the shadows at the backs of things—this was the spiritual horizon from which he could not escape. Out of the circle of that horizon he had to rise by spiritual apprehension in order to be consoled. And there is no reason to doubt that at times, if not invariably, in his early days, he did rise; he found consolation. But it was all without form. It was a sentiment, a mood,—philosophically bodiless. This indefinite mysticism was the real heart of the forest world, closer than hands or feet, but elusive, incapable of formulation, a presence, not an idea. Before the task of expressing it, the forest mystic stood helpless. Just what it was that he felt impinging upon him from every side he did not know. He was like a sensitive man, neither scientist nor poet, in the midst of a night of stars. The reality of his experience gave him no power either to explain or to state it.

There is little reason to suppose that Lincoln's religious experience previous to 1860 was more than a recurrent visitor in his daily life. He has said as much himself. He told his friend Noah Brooks "he did not remember any precise time when he passed through any special change of purpose, or of heart, but he would say that his own election to office and the crisis immediately following, influentially determined him in what he called 'a process of crystallization' then going on in his mind."(1)

It was the terrible sense of need—the humility, the fear that he might not be equal to the occasion—that searched his soul, that bred in him the craving for a spiritual up-holding which should be constant. And at this crucial moment came the death of his favorite son. "In the lonely grave of the little one lay buried Mr. Lincoln's fondest hopes, and strong as he was in the matter of self-control, he gave way to an overmastering grief which became at length a serious menace to his health."(2) Though firsthand accounts differ as to just how he struggled forth out of this darkness, all agree that the ordeal was very severe. Tradition makes the crisis a visit from the Reverend Francis Vinton, rector of Trinity Church, New York, and his eloquent assertion of the faith in immortality, his appeal to Lincoln to remember the sorrow of Jacob over the loss of Joseph, and to rise by faith out of his own sorrow even as the patriarch rose.(3)

Although Lincoln succeeded in putting his grief behind him, he never forgot it. Long afterward, he called the attention of Colonel Cannon to the lines in King John:

"And Father Cardinal, I have heard you say That we shall see and know our friends in heaven; If that be true, I shall see my boy again."

"Colonel," said he, "did you ever dream of a lost friend, and feel that you were holding sweet communion with that friend, and yet have a sad consciousness that it was not a reality? Just so, I dream of my boy, Willie." And he bent his head and burst into tears.(4)

As he rose in the sphere of statecraft with such apparent suddenness out of the doubt, hesitation, self-distrust of the spring of 1862 and in the summer found himself politically, so at the same time he found himself religiously. During his later life though the evidences are slight, they are convincing. And again, as always, it is not a violent change that takes place, but merely a better harmonization of the outer and less significant part of him with the inner and more significant. His religion continues to resist intellectual formulation. He never accepted any definite creed. To the problems of theology, he applied the same sort of reasoning that he applied to the problems of the law. He made a distinction, satisfactory to himself at least, between the essential and the incidental, and rejected everything that did not seem to him altogether essential.

In another negative way his basal part asserted itself. Just as in all his official relations he was careless of ritual, so in religion he was not drawn to its ritualistic forms. Again, the forest temper surviving, changed, into such different conditions! Real and subtle as is the ritualistic element, not only in religion but in life generally, one may doubt whether it counts for much among those who have been formed mainly by the influences of nature. It implies more distance between the emotion and its source, more need of stimulus to arouse and organize emotion, than the children of the forest are apt to be aware of. To invoke a philosophical distinction, illumination rather than ritualism, the tense but variable concentration on a result, not the ordered mode of an approach, is what distinguishes such characters as Lincoln. It was this that made him careless &f form in all the departments of life. It was one reason why McClellan, born ritualist of the pomp of war, could never overcome a certain dislike, or at least a doubt, of him.

Putting together his habit of thinking only in essentials and his predisposition to neglect form, it is not strange that he said: "I have never united myself to any church because I have found difficulty in giving my assent, without mental reservation, to the long, complicated statements of Christian doctrine which characterize their Articles of Belief and Confessions of Faith. When any church will inscribe over its altar, as its sole qualification for membership, the Savior's condensed statement of the substance of both Law and Gospel, 'Thou shalt love the Lord thy God, with all thy heart and with all thy soul, and with all thy mind, and thy neighbor as thyself,' that church will I join with all my heart and with all my soul."(5)

But it must not be supposed that his religion was mere ethics. It had three cardinal possessions. The sense of God is through all his later life. It appears incidentally in his state papers, clothed with language which, in so deeply sincere a man, must be taken literally. He believed in prayer, in the reality of communion with the Divine. His third article was immortality.

At Washington, Lincoln was a regular attendant, though not a communicant, of the New York Avenue Presbyterian Church. With the Pastor, the Reverend P. D. Gurley, he formed a close friendship. Many hours they passed in intimate talk upon religious subjects, especially upon the question of immortality.(6) To another pious visitor he said earnestly, "I hope I am a Christian."(7) Could anything but the most secure faith have written this "Meditation on the Divine Will" which he set down in the autumn of 1862 for no eye but his own: "The will of God prevails. In great contests each party claims to act in accordance with the will of God. Both may be, and one must be, wrong. God can not be for and against the same thing at the same time. In the present civil war it is quite possible that God's purpose is something different from the purpose of either party; and yet the human instrumentalities, working just as they do, are of the best adaptation to effect His purpose. I am almost ready to say that this is probably true; that God wills this contest, and wills that it shall not end yet. By His mere great power on the minds of the now contestants, He could have either saved or destroyed the Union without a human contest. Yet the contest began. And, having begun, He could give the final victory to either side any day. Yet the contest proceeds."(8)

His religion flowered in his later temper. It did not, to be sure, overcome his melancholy. That was too deeply laid. Furthermore, we fail to discover in the surviving evidences any certainty that it was a glad phase of religion. Neither the ecstatic joy of the wild women, which his mother had; nor the placid joy of the ritualist, which he did not understand; nor those other variants of the joy of faith, were included in his portion. It was a lofty but grave religion that matured in his final stage. Was it due to far-away Puritan ancestors? Had austere, reticent Iron-sides, sure of the Lord, but taking no liberties with their souls, at last found out their descendant? It may be. Cromwell, in some ways, was undeniably his spiritual kinsman. In both, the same aloofness of soul, the same indifference to the judgments of the world, the same courage, the same fatalism, the same encompassment by the shadow of the Most High. Cromwell, in his best mood, had he been gifted with Lincoln's literary power, could have written the Fast Day Proclamation of 1863 which is Lincoln's most distinctive religious fragment.

However, Lincoln's gloom had in it a correcting element which the old Puritan gloom appears to have lacked. It placed no veto upon mirth. Rather, it valued mirth as its only redeemer. And Lincoln's growth in the religious sense was not the cause of any diminution of his surface hilarity. He saved himself from what otherwise would have been intolerable melancholy by seizing, regardless of the connection, anything whatsoever that savored of the comic.

His religious security did not destroy his superstition. He continued to believe that he would die violently at the end of his career as President. But he carried that belief almost with gaiety. He refused to take precautions for his safety. Long lonely rides in the dead of night; night walks with a single companion, were constant anxieties to his intimates. To the President, their fears were childish. Although in the sensibilities he could suffer all he had ever suffered, and more; in the mind he had attained that high serenity in which there can be no flagging of effort because of the conviction that God has decreed one's work; no failure of confidence because of the twin conviction that somehow, somewhere, all things work together for good. "I am glad of this interview," he said in reply to a deputation of visitors, in September, 1862, "and glad to know that I have your sympathy and your prayers. . I happened to be placed, being a humble instrument in the hands of our Heavenly Father, as I am, and as we all are, to work out His great purpose. . . . I have sought His aid; but if after endeavoring to do my best in the light He affords me, I find my efforts fail, I must believe that for some purpose unknown to me He wills it otherwise. If I had my way, this war would never have commenced. If I had been allowed my way, this war would have been ended before this; but it still continues and we must believe that He permits it for some wise purpose of His own, mysterious and unknown to us; and though with our limited understandings we may not be able to comprehend it, yet we can not but believe that He who made the world still governs it."(9)

XXIV
GAMBLING IN GENERALS

On July 22, 1862, there was a meeting of the Cabinet. The sessions of Lincoln's Council were the last word for informality. The President and the Ministers interspersed their great affairs with mere talk, story-telling, gossip. With one exception they were all lovers of their own voices, especially in the telling of tales. Stanton was the exception. Gloomy, often in ill-health, innocent of humor, he glowered when the others laughed. When the President, instead of proceeding at once to business, would pull out of his pocket the latest volume of Artemus Ward, the irate War Minister felt that the overthrow of the nation was impending. But in this respect, the President was incorrigible. He had been known to stop the line of his guests at a public levee, while he talked for some five minutes in a whisper to an important personage; and though all the room thought that jupiter was imparting state secrets, in point of fact, he was making sure of a good story the great man had told him a few days previous.(1) His Cabinet meetings were equally careless of social form. The Reverend Robert Collyer was witness to this fact in a curious way. Strolling through the White House grounds, "his attention was suddenly arrested by the apparition of three pairs of feet resting on the ledge of an open window in one of the apartments of the second story and plainly visible from below." He asked a gardener for an explanation. The brusk reply was: "Why, you old fool, that's the Cabinet that is a-settin', and them thar big feet are ole Abe's."(2)

When the Ministers assembled on July twenty-second they had no intimation that this was to be a record session. Imagine the astonishment when, in his usual casual way, though with none of that hesitancy to which they had grown accustomed, Lincoln announced his new policy, adding that he "wished it understood that the question was settled in his own mind; that he had decreed emancipation in a certain contingency and the responsibility of the measure was his."(3) President and Cabinet talked it over in their customary offhand way, and Seward made a suggestion that instantly riveted Lincoln's attention. Seward thought the moment was ill-chosen. "If the Proclamation were issued now, it would be received and considered as a despairing cry — a shriek from and for the Administration, rather than for freedom."(4) He added the picturesque phrase, "The government stretching forth its hands to Ethiopia, instead of Ethiopia stretching forth her hands to the government." This idea struck Lincoln with very great force. It was an aspect of the case "which he had entirely overlooked."(5) He accepted Seward's advice, laid aside the proclamation he had drafted and turned again with all his energies to the organization of victory.

The next day Halleck arrived at Washington. He was one of Lincoln's mistakes. However, in his new mood, Lincoln was resolved to act on his own opinion of the evidence before him, especially in estimating men. It is just possible that this epoch of his audacities began in a reaction; that after too much self-distrust, he went briefly to the other extreme, indulging in too much self-confidence. Be that as it may, he had formed exaggerated opinions of both these Western generals, Halleck and Pope. Somehow, in the brilliant actions along the Mississippi they had absorbed far more than their fair share of credit. Particularly, Lincoln went astray with regard to Pope. Doubtless a main reason why he accepted the plan of campaign suggested by Halleck was the opportunity which it offered to Pope. Perhaps, too, the fatality in McClellan's character turned the scale. He begged to be left where he was with his base on James River, and to be allowed to renew the attack on Richmond.1 But he did not take the initiative. The government must swiftly hurry up reinforcements, and then—the old, old story! Obviously, it was a question at Washington either of superseding McClellan and leaving the army where it was, or of shifting the army to some other commander without in so many words disgracing McClellan. Halleck's approval of the latter course jumped with two of Lincoln's impulses—his trust in Pope, his reluctance to disgrace McClellan. Orders were issued transferring the bulk of the army of the Potomac to the new army of Virginia lying south of Washington under the command of Pope. McClellan was instructed to withdraw his remaining forces from the Peninsula and retrace his course up the Potomac.(6)

Lincoln had committed one of his worst blunders. Herndon has a curious, rather subtle theory that while Lincoln's judgments of men in the aggregate were uncannily sure, his judgments of men individually were unreliable. It suggests the famous remark of Goethe that his views of women did not derive from experience; that they antedated experience; and that he corrected experience by them. Of the confessed artist this may be true. The literary concept which the artist works with is often, apparently, a more constant, more fundamental, more significant thing, than is the broken, mixed, inconsequential impression out of which it has been wrought. Which seems to explain why some of the writers who understand human nature so well in their books, do not always understand people similarly well in life. And always it is to be remembered that Lincoln was made an artist by nature, and made over into a man of action by circumstance. If Herndon's theory has any value it is in asserting his occasional danger—by no means a constant danger—of forming in his mind images of men that were more significant than it was possible for the men themselves to be. John Pope was perhaps his worst instance. An incompetent general, he was capable of things still less excusable. Just after McClellan had so tragically failed in the Seven Days, when Lincoln was at the front, Pope was busy with the Committee, assuring them virtually that the war had been won in the West, and that only McClellan's bungling had saved the Confederacy from speedy death.(7) But somehow Lincoln trusted him, and continued to trust him even after he had proved his incompetency in the catastrophe at Manassas.

During August, Pope marched gaily southward issuing orders that were shot through with bad rhetoric, mixing up army routine and such irrelevant matters as "the first blush of dawn."

Lincoln was confident of victory. And after victory would come the new policy, the dissipation of the European storm-cloud, the break-up of the vindictive coalition of Jacobins and Abolitionists, the new enthusiasm for the war. But of all this, the incensed Abolitionists received no hint. The country rang with their denunciations of the President. At length, Greeley printed in The Tribune an open letter called "The Prayer of Twenty Millions." It was an arraignment of what Greeley chose to regard as the pro-slavery policy of the Administration. This was on August twentieth. Lincoln, in high hope that a victory was at hand, seized the opportunity both to hint to the country that he was about to change his policy, and to state unconditionally his reason for changing. He replied to Greeley through the newspapers:

"As to the policy I 'seem to be pursuing,' as you say, I have meant to leave no one in doubt.

"I would save the Union. I would save it the shortest way under the Constitution. The sooner the national authority can be restored, the nearer the Union will be 'the Union as it was' If there be those who would not save the Union unless they could at the same time save Slavery, I do not agree with them. If there be those who would not save the Union, unless they could at the same time destroy slavery, I do not agree with them. My paramount object in this struggle is to save the Union, and it is not either to save or destroy slavery. If I could save the Union without freeing any slave, I would do it; and if I could save it by freeing all the slaves, I would do it; and if I could save it by freeing some of the slaves and leaving others alone, I would also do that. What I do about slavery and the colored race, I do because I believe it will help to save the Union; and what I forbear, I forbear because I do not believe it would help to save the Union. I shall do less whenever I shall believe that what I am doing hurts the cause; and I shall do more whenever I believe that doing more will help the cause."(8) The effect of this on the Abolitionists was only to increase their rage. The President was compared to Douglas with his indifference whether slavery was voted "up or down."(9) Lincoln, now so firmly hopeful, turned a deaf ear to these railing accusations. He was intent upon watching the army. It was probably at this time that he reached an unfortunate conclusion with regard to McClellan. The transfer of forces from the James River to northern Virginia had proceeded slowly. It gave rise to a new controversy, a new crop of charges. McClellan was accused of being dilatory on purpose, of aiming to cause the failure of Pope. Lincoln accepted, at last, the worst view of him. He told Hay that "it really seemed that McClellan wanted Pope defeated. . . . The President seemed to think him a little crazy."(10)

But still the confidence in Pope, marching so blithely through "the blush of dawn," stood fast. If ever an Administration was in a fool's paradise, it was Lincoln's, in the last few days of August, while Jackson was stealthily carrying out his great flanking movement getting between Pope and Washington. However, the Suspicious Stanton kept his eyes on McClellan. He decided that troops were being held back from Pope; and he appealed to other members of the Cabinet to join with him in a formal demand upon the President for McClellan's dismissal from the army. While the plan was being discussed, came the appalling news of Pope's downfall.

The meeting of the Cabinet, September second, was another revelation of the new independence of the President. Three full days had passed since Pope had telegraphed that the battle was lost and that he no longer had control of his army. The Ministers, awaiting the arrival of the President, talked excitedly, speculating what would happen next. "It was stated," says Welles in his diary, "that Pope was falling back, intending to retreat within the Washington entrenchments, Blair, who has known him intimately, says he is a braggart and a liar, with some courage, perhaps, but not much capacity. The general conviction is that he is a failure here, and there is a belief . . . that he has not been seconded and sustained as he should have been by McClellan . . ." Stanton entered; terribly agitated. He had news that fell upon the Cabinet like a bombshell. He said "in a suppressed voice, trembling with excitement, he was informed that McClellan had been ordered to take command of the forces in Washington."

Never was there a more tense moment in the Cabinet room than when Lincoln entered that day. And all could see that he was in deep distress. But he confirmed Stanton's information. That very morning he had gone himself to McClellan's house and had asked him to resume command. Lincoln discussed McClellan with the Cabinet quite simply, admitting all his bad qualities, but finding two points in his favor—his power of organization, and his popularity with the men.(11)

He was still more frank with his Secretaries. "'He has acted badly in this matter,' Lincoln said to Hay, 'but we must use what tools we have. There is no man in the army who can man these fortifications and lick these troops of ours into shape half as well as he.' I spoke of the general feeling against McClellan as evinced by the President's mail. He rejoined: 'Unquestionably, he has acted badly toward Pope; he wanted him to fail. That is unpardonable, but he is too useful now to sacrifice.'"(12) At another time, he said: "'If he can't fight himself, he excels in making others ready to fight.'"(13)

McClellan justified Lincoln's confidence. In this case, Herndon's theory of Lincoln's powers of judgment does not apply. Though probably unfair on the one point of McClellan's attitude to Pope, he knew his man otherwise. Lincoln had also discovered that Halleck, the veriest martinet of a general, was of little value at a crisis. During the next two months, McClellan, under the direct oversight of the President, was the organizer of victory.

Toward the middle of September, when Lee and McClellan were gradually converging upon the fated line of Antietam Creek, Lincoln's new firmness was put to the test. The immediate effect of Manassas was another, a still more vehement outcry for an anti-slavery policy. A deputation of Chicago clergymen went to Washington for the purpose of urging him to make an anti-slavery pronouncement. The journey was a continuous ovation. If at any time Lincoln was tempted to forget Seward's worldly wisdom, it was when these influential zealots demanded of him to do the very thing he intended to do. But it was one of the characteristics of this final Lincoln that when once he had fully determined on a course of action, nothing could deflect him. With consummate coolness he gave them no new light on his purpose. Instead, he seized the opportunity to "feel" the country. He played the role of advocate arguing the case against an emancipation policy.(14) They met his argument with great Spirit and resolution. Taking them as an index, there could be little question that the country was ripe for the new policy. At the close of the interview Lincoln allowed himself to jest. One of the clergymen dramatically charged him to give heed to their message as to a direct commission from the Almighty. "Is it not odd," said Lincoln, "that the only channel he could send it was that roundabout route by the awfully wicked city of Chicago?"*

* *Reminiscences, 335. This retort is given by Schuyler Colfax. There are various reports of what Lincoln said. In another version, "I hope it will not be irreverent for me to*

say that if it is probable that God would reveal His will to others on a point so connected with my duty, it might be supposed He would reveal it directly to me." Tarbell, II, 12.

Lincoln's pertinacity, holding fast the program he had accepted, came to its reward. On the seventeenth occurred that furious carnage along the Antietam known as the bloodiest single day of the whole war. Military men have disagreed, calling it sometimes a victory, sometimes a drawn battle. In Lincoln's political strategy the dispute is immaterial. Psychologically, it was a Northern victory. The retreat of Lee was regarded by the North as the turn of the tide. Lincoln's opportunity had arrived.

Again, a unique event occurred in a Cabinet meeting. On the twenty-second of September, with the cannon of Antietam still ringing in their imagination, the Ministers were asked by the President whether they had seen the new volume just published by Artemus Ward. As they had not, he produced it and read aloud with evident relish one of those bits of nonsense which, in the age of Dickens, seemed funny enough. Most of the Cabinet joined in the merriment—Stanton, of course, as always, excepted. Lincoln closed the book, pulled himself together, and became serious.

"Gentlemen," said he, according to the diary of Secretary Chase, "I have, as you are aware, thought a great deal about the relation of this war to slavery; and you all remember that several weeks ago I read you an order I had prepared on this subject, which, on account of objections made by some of you, was not issued. Ever since, my mind has been much occupied with this subject, and I have thought all along that the time for acting on it might probably come. I think the time has come now. I wish it was a better time. I wish that we were in a better condition. The action of the army against the Rebels has not been quite what I should have best liked. But they have been driven out of Maryland; and Pennsylvania is no longer in danger of invasion. When the Rebel army was at Frederick, I determined, as soon as it should be driven out of Maryland, to issue a proclamation of emancipation, such as I thought most likely to be useful. I said nothing to any one, but I made the promise to myself, and (hesitating a little) to my Maker. The Rebel army is now driven out and I am going to fulfill that promise. I have got you together to hear what I have written down. I do not wish your advice about the main matter, for that I have determined for myself. This, I say without intending anything but respect for any one of you. But I already know the views of each on this question. They have been heretofore expressed, and I have considered them as thoroughly and as carefully as I can. What I have written is that which my reflections have determined me to say. . . . I must do the best I can, and bear the responsibility of taking the course which I feel I ought to take."(15) The next day the Proclamation was published.

This famous document (16) is as remarkable for the parts of it that are now forgotten as for the rest. The remembered portion is a warning that on the first of January, one hundred days subsequent to the date of the Proclamation—"all persons held as slaves within any State or designated part of a State, the people whereof shall then be in rebellion against the United States, shall be then, thenceforward, and forever free." The forgotten portions include four other declarations of executive policy. Lincoln promised that "the Executive will in due time recommend that all citizens of the United States who have remained loyal thereto shall be compensated for all losses by acts of the United States, including the loss of slaves." He announced that he would again urge upon Congress "the adoption of a practical measure tendering pecuniary aid" to all the loyal Slave States that would "voluntarily adopt immediate or gradual abolishment of slavery within their limits." He would continue to advise the colonization of free Africans abroad. There is still to be mentioned a detail of the Proclamation which, except for its historical setting in the general perspective of Lincoln's political strategy, would appear inexplicable. One might expect in the opening statement, where the author of the Proclamation boldly assumes dictatorial power, an immediate linking of that assumption with the matter in hand. But this does not happen. The Proclamation begins with the following paragraph:

"I, Abraham Lincoln, President of the United States of America, and Commander-in-Chief of the Army and Navy thereof, do hereby proclaim and declare that hereafter, as heretofore, the war will be prosecuted for the object of practically restoring the constitutional relation between the United States and each of the States and the people thereof in which States that relation is or may be suspended or disturbed."

XXV
A WAR BEHIND THE SCENES

By the autumn of 1862, Lincoln had acquired the same political method that Seward had displayed in the spring of 1861. What a chasm separates the two Lincolns! The cautious, contradictory, almost timid statesman of the Sumter episode; the confident, unified, quietly masterful statesman of the Emancipation Proclamation. Now, in action, he was capable of staking his whole future on the soundness of his own thinking, on his own ability to forecast the inevitable. Without waiting for the results of the Proclamation to appear, but in full confidence that he had driven a wedge between the Jacobins proper and the mere Abolitionists, he threw down the gage of battle on the issue of a constitutional dictatorship. Two days after issuing the Proclamation he virtually proclaimed himself dictator. He did so by means of a proclamation which divested the whole American people of the privileges of the writ of habeas corpus. The occasion was the effort of State governments to establish conscription of their militia. The Proclamation delivered any one impeding that attempt into the hands of the military authorities without trial.

Here was Lincoln's final answer to Stevens; here, his audacious challenge to the Jacobins. And now appeared the wisdom of his political strategy, holding back emancipation until Congress was out of the way. Had Congress been in session what a hubbub would have ensued! Chandler, Wade, Trumbull, Sumner, Stevens, all hurrying to join issue on the dictatorship; to get it before the country ahead of emancipation. Rather, one can not imagine Lincoln daring to play this second card, so soon after the first, except with abundant time for the two issues to disentangle themselves in the public mind ere Congress met. And that was what happened. When the Houses met in December, the Jacobins found their position revolutionized. The men who, in July at the head of the Vindictive coalition, dominated Congress, were now a minority faction biting their nails at the President amid the ruins of their coalition.

There were three reasons for this collapse. First of all, the Abolitionists, for the moment, were a faction by themselves. Six weeks had sufficed to intoxicate them with their opportunity. The significance of the Proclamation had had time to arise towering on their spiritual vision, one of the gates of the New Jerusalem.

Limited as it was in application who could doubt that, with one condition, it doomed slavery everywhere. The condition was a successful prosecution of the war, the restoration of the Union. Consequently, at that moment, nothing that made issue with the President, that threatened any limitation of his efficiency, had the slightest chance of Abolitionist support. The one dread that alarmed the whole Abolitionist group was a possible change in the President's mood, a possible recantation on January first. In order to hold him to his word, they were ready to humor him as one might cajole, or try to cajole, a monster that one was afraid of. No time, this, to talk to Abolitionists about strictly constitutional issues, or about questions of party leadership. Away with all your "gabble" about such small things! The Jacobins saw the moving hand — at least for this moment — in the crumbling wall of the palace of their delusion.

Many men who were not Abolitionists perceived, before Congress met, that Lincoln had made a great stroke internationally. The "Liberal party throughout the world" gave a cry of delight, and rose instantly to his support. John Bright declared that the Emancipation Proclamation "made it impossible for England to intervene for the South" and derided "the silly proposition of the French Emperor looking toward intervention."(1) Bright's closest friend in America was Sumner and Sumner was chairman of the Senate Committee on Foreign Relations. He understood the value of international sentiment, its working importance, as good provincials like Chandler did not. Furthermore, he was always an Abolitionist first and a Jacobin second — if at all. From this time forward, the Jacobins were never able to count on him, not even when they rebuilt the Vindictive Coalition a year and a half later. In December, 1862, how did they dare — true blue politicians that they were — how did they dare raise a constitutional issue involving the right of the President to capture, in the way he had, international security?

The crowning irony in the new situation of the Jacobins was the revelation that they had played unwittingly into the hands of the Democrats. Their short-sighted astuteness in tying up emancipation with the war powers was matched by an equal astuteness equally short-sighted. The organization of the Little Men, when it refused to endorse Lincoln's all-parties program, had found itself in the absurd position of a party without an issue. It contained, to be sure, a large proportion of the Northerners who were opposed to emancipation. But how could it make an issue upon emancipation, as long as the President, the object of its antagonism, also refused to support emancipation? The sole argument in the Cabinet against Lincoln's new policy was that it would give the Democrats an issue. Shrewd Montgomery Blair prophesied that on this issue they could carry the autumn elections for Congress. Lincoln had replied that he would take the risk. He presented them with the issue. They promptly accepted it But they did not stop there. They aimed to take over the whole of the position that had been vacated by the collapse of the Vindictive Coalition. By an adroit bit of political legerdemain they would steal their enemies' thunder, reunite the emancipation issue with the issue of the war powers, reverse the significance of the conjunction, and, armed with this double club, they would advance from a new and unexpected angle and win the leadership of the country by overthrowing the dictator. And this, they came very near doing. On their double issue they rallied enough support to increase their number in Congress by thirty-three. Had not the moment been so tragic, nothing could have been more amusing than the helpless wrath of the Jacobins caught in their own trap, compelled to gnaw their tongues in silence, while the Democrats, paraphrasing their own arguments, hurled defiant at Lincoln.

Men of intellectual courage might have broken their party ranks, daringly applied Lincoln's own maxim "stand with any one who stands right," and momentarily joined the Democrats in their battle against the two proclamations. But in American politics, with a few glorious exceptions, courage of this sort has never been the order of the day. The Jacobins kept their party line; bowed their heads to the storm; and bided their time. In the Senate, an indiscreet resolution commending the Emancipation Proclamation was ordered to be printed, and laid on the table.(2) In the House, party exigencies were more exacting. Despite the Democratic successes, the Republicans still had a majority. When the Democrats made the repudiation of the President a party issue, arguing on those very grounds that had aroused the eloquence of Stevens and the rest—why, what's the Constitution between friends! Or between political enemies? The Democrats forced all the Republicans into one boat by introducing a resolution "That the policy of emancipation as indicated in that Proclamation is an assumption of powers dangerous to the rights of citizens and to the perpetuity of a free people." The resolution was rejected. Among those who voted NO was Stevens.(3) Indeed, the star of the Jacobins was far down on the horizon.

But the Jacobins were not the men to give up the game until they were certainly in the last ditch. Though their issues had been slipped out of their hands; though for the moment at least, it was not good policy to fight the President on a principle; it might still be possible to recover their prestige on some other contention. The first of January was approaching. The final proclamation of emancipation would bring to an end the temporary alliance of the Administration and the Abolitionists. Who could say what new pattern of affairs the political kaleidoscope might not soon reveal? Surely the Jacobin cue was to busy themselves, straightway, making trouble for the President. Principles being unavailable, practices might do. And who was satisfied with the way the war was going? To rouse the party against the Administration on the ground of inefficient practices, of unsatisfactory military progress, might be the first step toward regaining their former dominance.

There was a feather in the wind that gave them hope. The ominous first paragraph of the Emancipation Proclamation was evidence that the President was still stubbornly for his own policy; that he had not surrendered to the opposite view. But this was not their only strategic hope. Lincoln's dealings with the army between September and December might, especially if anything in his course proved to be mistaken, deliver him into their hands.

Following Antietam, Lincoln had urged upon McClellan swift pursuit of Lee. His despatches were strikingly different from those of the preceding spring. That half apologetic tone had disappeared. Though they did not command, they gave advice freely. The tone was at least that of an equal who, while not an authority in this particular matter, is entitled to express his views and to have them taken seriously.

"You remember my speaking to you of what I called your overcautiousness? Are you not over-cautious when you assume that you can not do what the enemy is constantly doing? Should you not claim to be at least his equal in prowess and act upon that claim . . . one of the standard maxims of war, as you know, is to operate upon the enemy's communications as much as possible without exposing your own. You seem to act as if this applies against you, but can not apply in your favor. Change positions with the enemy and think you not he would break your communications with Richmond within the next twenty-four hours. . . .

"If he should move northward, I would follow him closely, holding his communications. If he should prevent your seizing his communications and move toward Richmond; I would press closely to him, fight him if a favorable opportunity should present, and at least try to beat him to Richmond on the inside track. I say 'try'; if we never try we shall never succeed. . . . We should not operate so as to merely drive him away. . . . This letter is in no sense an order."(4)

But once more the destiny that is in character intervened, and McClellan's tragedy reached its climax. His dread of failure hypnotized his will. So cautious were his movements that Lee regained Virginia with his army intact. Lincoln was angry. Military amateur though he was, he had filled his spare time reading books on strategy, Von Clausewitz and the rest, and he had grasped the idea that war's aim is not to win technical victories, nor to take cities, but to destroy armies. He felt that McClellan had thrown away an opportunity of first magnitude. He removed him from command. (5)

This was six weeks after the two proclamations. The country was ringing with Abolition plaudits. The election had given the Democrats a new lease of life. The anti-Lincoln Republicans were silent while their party enemies with their stolen thunder rang the changes on the presidential abuse of the war powers. It was a moment of crisis in party politics. Where did the President stand? What was the outlook for those men who in the words of Senator Wilson "would rather give a policy to the President of the United States than take a policy from the President of the United States."

Lincoln's situation was a close parallel to the situation of July, 1861, when McDowell failed. Just as in choosing a successor to McDowell, he revealed a political attitude, now, he would again make a revelation choosing a successor to McClellan. By passing over Fremont and by elevating a Democrat, he had spoken to the furious politicians in the language they understood. Whatever appointment he now made would be interpreted by those same politicians in the same way. In the atmosphere of that time, there was but one way for Lincoln to rank himself as a strict party man, to recant his earlier heresy of presidential independence, and say to the Jacobins, "I am with you." He must appoint a Republican to succeed McClellan. Let him do that and the Congressional Cabal would forgive him. But he did not do it. He swept political considerations aside and made a purely military appointment Burnside, on whom he fixed, was the friend and admirer of McClellan and might fairly be considered next to him in prestige. He was loved by his troops. In the eyes of the army, his elevation represented "a legitimate succession rather than the usurpation of a successful rival."(6) He was modest. He did not want promotion. Nevertheless, Lincoln forced him to take McClellan's place against his will, in spite of his protest that he had not the ability to command so large an army.(7)

When Congress assembled and the Committee resumed its inquisition, Burnside was moving South on his fated march to Fredericksburg. The Committee watched him like hungry wolves. Woe to Burnside, woe to Lincoln, if the General failed! Had the Little Men possessed any sort of vision they would have seized their opportunity to become the President's supporters. But they, like the Jacobins, were partisans first and patriots second. In the division among the Republicans they saw, not a chance to turn the scale in the President's favor, but a chance to play politics on their own account. A picturesque Ohio politician known as "Sunset" Cox opened the ball of their fatuousness with an elaborate argument in Congress to the effect that the President was in honor bound to regard the recent elections as strictly analogous to an appeal to the country in England; that it was his duty to remodel his policy to suit the Democrats. Between the Democrats and the Jacobins Lincoln was indeed between the devil and the deep blue sea with no one certainly on his side except the volatile Abolitionists whom he did not trust and who did not trust him. A great victory might carry him over. But a great defeat—what might not be the consequence!

On the thirteenth of December, through Burnside's stubborn incompetence, thousands of American soldiers flung away their lives in a holocaust of useless valor at Fredericksburg. Promptly the Jacobins acted. They set up a shriek: the incompetent President, the all-parties dreamer, the man who persists in coquetting with the Democrats, is blundering into destruction! Burnside received the dreaded summons from the Committee. So staggering was the shock of horror that even moderate Republicans were swept away in a new whirlpool of doubt.

But even thus it was scarcely wise, the Abolitionists being still fearful over the emancipation policy, to attack the President direct. Nevertheless, the resourceful Jacobins found a way to begin their new campaign. Seward, the symbol of moderation, the unforgivable enemy of the Jacobins, had recently earned anew the hatred of the Abolitionists. Letters of his to Charles Francis Adams had appeared in print. Some of their expressions had roused a storm. For example: "extreme advocates of African slavery and its most vehement exponents are acting in concert together to precipitate a servile war."(8) To be sure, the date of this letter was long since, before he and Lincoln had changed ground on emancipation, but that did not matter. He had spoken evil of the cause; he should suffer. All along, the large number that were incapable of appreciating his lack of malice had wished him out of the Cabinet. As Lincoln put it: "While they seemed to believe in my honesty, they also appeared to think that when I had in me any good purpose or intention, Seward contrived to suck it out of me unperceived."(9)

The Jacobins were skilful politicians. A caucus of Republican Senators was stampeded by the cry that Seward was the master of the Administration, the chief explanation of failure. It was Seward who had brought them to the verge of despair. A committee was named to demand the reorganization of the Cabinet Thereupon, Seward, informed of this action, resigned. The Committee of the Senators called upon Lincoln. He listened; did not commit himself; asked them to call again; and turned into his own thoughts for a mode of saving the day.

During twenty months, since their clash in April, 1861, Seward and Lincoln had become friends; not merely official associates, but genuine comrades. Seward's earlier condescension had wholly disappeared. Perhaps his new respect for Lincoln grew out of the President's silence after Sumter. A few words revealing the strange meddling of the Secretary of State would have turned upon Seward the full fury of suspicion that destroyed McClellan. But Lincoln never spoke those words. Whatever blame there was for the failure of the Sumter expedition, he quietly accepted as his own. Seward, whatever his faults, was too large a nature, too genuinely a lover of courage, of the nonvindictive temper, not to be struck with admiration. Watching with keen eyes the unfolding of Lincoln, Seward advanced from admiration to regard. After a while he could write, "The President is the best of us." He warmed to him; he gave out the best of himself. Lincoln responded. While the other secretaries were useful, Seward became necessary. Lincoln, in these dark days, found comfort in his society.(10) Lincoln was not going to allow Seward to be driven out of the Cabinet. But how could he prevent it? He could not say. He was in a quandary. For the moment, the Republican leaders were so nearly of one mind in their antagonism to Seward, that it demanded the greatest courage to oppose them. But Lincoln does not appear to have given a thought to surrender. What puzzled him was the mode of resistance.

Now that he was wholly himself, having confidence in whatever mode of procedure his own thought approved, he had begun using methods that the politicians found disconcerting. The second conference with the Senators was an instance. Returning in the same mood in which they had left him, with no suspicion of a surprise in store, the Senators to their amazement were confronted by the Cabinet—or most of it, Seward being absent.(11) The Senators were put out. This simple maneuver by the President was the beginning of their discomfiture. It changed their role from the ambassadors of an ultimatum to the participants in a conference. But even thus, they might have succeeded in dominating the event, though it is hardly conceivable that they could have carried their point; they might have driven Lincoln into a corner; had it not been for the make-up of one man. Again, the destiny that is in character! Lincoln was delivered from a quandary by the course which the Secretary of the Treasury could not keep himself from pursuing.

Chase, previous to this hour, may truly be called an imposing figure. As a leader of the extreme Republicans, he had earned much fame. Lincoln had given him a free hand in the Treasury and all the financial measures of the government were his. Hitherto, Vindictives of all sorts had loved him. He was a critic of the President's mildness, and a severe critic of Seward. But Chase was not candid. Though on the surface he scrupulously avoided any hint of cynicism, any point of resemblance to Seward, he was in fact far more devious, much more capable of self-deception. He had little of Seward's courage, and none of his aplomb. His condemnation of Seward had been confided privately to Vindictive brethren.

When the Cabinet and the Senators met, Chase was placed in a situation of which he had an instinctive horror. His caution, his secretiveness, his adroit confidences, his skilful silences, had created in these two groups of men, two impressions of his character. The Cabinet knew him as the faithful, plausible Minister who found the money for the President. The Senators, or some of them, knew him as the discontented Minister who was their secret ally. For the two groups to compare notes, to check up their impressions, meant that Chase was going to be found out. And it was the central characteristic of Chase that he had a horror of being found out.

The only definite result of the conference was Chase's realization when the Senators departed that mischance was his portion. In the presence of the Cabinet he had not the face to stick to his guns. He feebly defended Seward. The Senators opened their eyes and stared. The ally they had counted on had failed them. Chase bit his lips and was miserable.

The night that followed was one of deep anxiety for Lincoln. He was still unable to see his way out. But all the while the predestination in Chase's character was preparing the way of escape. Chase was desperately trying to discover how to save his face. An element in him that approached the melodramatic at last pointed the way. He would resign. What an admirable mode of recapturing the confidence of his disappointed friends, carrying out their aim to disrupt the Cabinet! But he could not do a bold thing like this in Seward's way — at a stroke, without hesitation. When he called on Lincoln the next day with the resignation in his hand, he wavered. It happened that Welles was in the room.

"Chase said he had been painfully affected," is Welles' account, "by the meeting last evening, which was a surprise, and after some not very explicit remarks as to how he was affected, informed the President he had prepared his resignation of the office of Secretary of the Treasury. 'Where is it,' said the President, quickly, his eye lighting up in a moment. 'I brought it with me,' said Chase, taking the paper from his pocket. 'I wrote it this morning.' 'Let me have it,' said the President, reaching his long arm and fingers toward Chase, who held on seemingly reluctant to part with the letter which was sealed and which he apparently hesitated to surrender. Something further he wished to say, but the President was eager and did not perceive it, but took and hastily opened the letter.

"'This,' said he, looking towards me with a triumphal laugh, 'cuts the Gordian knot.' An air of satisfaction spread over his countenance such as I had not seen for some time. 'I can dispose of this subject now without difficulty,' he added, as he turned in his chair; 'I see my way clear.'"(12) In Lincoln's distress during this episode, there was much besides his anxiety for the fate of a trusted minister. He felt he must not permit himself to be driven into the arms of the Vindictives by disgracing Seward. Seward had a following which Lincoln needed. But to proclaim to the world his confidence in Seward without at the same time offsetting it by some display of confidence, equally significant in the enemies of Seward, this would have amounted to committing himself to Seward's following alone. And that would not do. Should either faction appear to dominate him, Lincoln felt that "the whole government must cave in. It could not stand, could not hold water; the bottom would be out."(13)

The incredible stroke of luck, the sheer good fortune that Chase was Chase and nobody else, — vain, devious, stagey and hypersensitive, — was salvation. Lincoln promptly rejected both resignations and called upon both Ministers to resume their portfolios. They did so. The incident was closed. Neither faction could say that Lincoln had favored the other. He had saved himself, or rather, Chase's character had saved him, by the margin of a hair.

For the moment, a rebuilding of the Vindictive Coalition was impossible. Nevertheless, the Jacobins, again balked of their prey, had it in their power, through the terrible Committee, to do immense mischief. The history of the war contains no other instance of party malice quite so fruitless and therefore so inexcusable as their next move. After severely interrogating Burnside, they published an exoneration of his motives and revealed the fact that Lincoln had forced him into command against his will. The implication was plain.

January came in. The Emancipation Proclamation was confirmed. The jubilation of the Abolitionists became, almost at once, a propaganda for another issue upon slavery. New troubles were gathering close about the President The overwhelming benefit which had been anticipated from the new policy had not clearly arrived. Even army enlistments were not satisfactory. Conscription loomed on the horizon as an eventual necessity. A bank of returning cloud was covering the political horizon, enshrouding the White House in another depth of gloom.

However, out of all this gathering darkness, one clear light solaced Lincoln's gaze. One of his chief purposes had been attained. In contrast to the doubtful and factional response to his policy at home, the response abroad was sweeping and unconditional. He had made himself the hero of the "Liberal party throughout the world." Among the few cheery words that reached him in January, 1863, were New Year greetings of trust and sympathy sent by English working men, who, because of the blockade, were on the verge of starvation. It was in response to one of these letters from the working men of Manchester that Lincoln wrote:

"I have understood well that the duty of self-preservation rests solely with the American people; but I have at the same time been aware that the favor or disfavor of foreign nations might have a material influence in enlarging or prolonging the struggle with disloyal men in which the country is engaged. A fair examination of history has served to authorize a belief that the past actions and influences of the United States were generally regarded as having been beneficial toward mankind. I have therefore reckoned upon the forbearance of nations. Circumstances—to some of which you kindly allude—induce me especially to expect that if justice and good faith should be practised by the United States they would encounter no hostile influence on the part of Great Britain. It is now a pleasant duty to acknowledge the demonstration you have given of your desire that a spirit of amity and peace toward this country may prevail in the councils of your Queen, who is respected and esteemed in your own country only more than she is, by the kindred nation which has its home on this side of the Atlantic.

"I know and deeply deplore the sufferings which the working men at Manchester, and in all Europe, are called on to endure in this crisis. It has been often and studiously represented that the attempt to overthrow this government which was built upon the foundation of human rights, and to substitute for it one which should rest exclusively on the basis of human slavery, was likely to obtain the favor of Europe. Through the action of our disloyal citizens, the working men of Europe have been subjected to severe trials for the purpose of forcing their sanction to that attempt. Under the circumstances, I can not but regard your decisive utterances upon the question as an instance of sublime Christian heroism which has not been surpassed in any age or in any country. It is indeed an energetic and reinspiring assurance of the inherent power of the truth, and of the ultimate and universal triumph of justice, humanity and freedom. I do not doubt that the sentiments you have expressed will be sustained by your great nation; and on the other hand, I have no hesitation in assuring you that they will excite admiration, esteem, and the most reciprocal feelings of friendship among the American people. I hail this interchange of sentiment, therefore, as an augury that whatever else may happen, whatever misfortune may befall your country or my own, the peace and friendship which now exist between the two nations, will be, as it shall be my desire to make them, perpetual."(14)

XXVI
THE DICTATOR, THE MARPLOT
AND THE LITTLE MEN

While the Jacobins were endeavoring to reorganize the Republican antagonism to the President, Lincoln was taking thought how he could offset still more effectually their influence. In taking up the emancipation policy he had not abandoned his other policy of an all-parties Administration, or of something similar to that. By this time it was plain that a complete union of parties was impossible. In the autumn of 1862, a movement of liberal Democrats in Michigan for the purpose of a working agreement with the Republicans was frustrated by the flinty opposition of Chandler. (1) However, it still seemed possible to combine portions of parties in an Administration group that should forswear the savagery of the extreme factions and maintain the war in a merciful temper. The creation of such a group was Lincoln's aim at the close of the year.

The Republicans were not in doubt what he was driving at. Smarting over their losses in the election, there was angry talk that Lincoln and Seward had "slaughtered the Republican party."(2) Even as sane a man as John Sherman, writing to his brother on the causes of the apparent turn of the tide could say "the first is that the Republican organization was voluntarily abandoned by the President and his leading followers, and a no-party union was formed to run against an old, well-drilled party organization."(3) When Julian returned to Washington in December, he found that the menace to the Republican machine was "generally admitted and (his) earnest opposition to it fully justified in the opinion of the Republican members of Congress."(4) How fully they perceived their danger had been shown in their attempt to drive Lincoln into a corner on the issue of a new Cabinet.

Even before that, Lincoln had decided on his next move. As in the emancipation policy he had driven a wedge between the factions of the Republicans, so now he would drive a wedge into the organization of the Democrats. It had two parts which had little to hold them together except their rooted partisan habit.(5) One branch, soon to receive the label "Copperhead," accepted the secession principle and sympathized with the

Confederacy. The other, while rejecting secession and supporting the war, denounced the emancipation policy as usurped authority, and felt personal hostility to Lincoln. It was the latter faction that Lincoln still hoped to win over. Its most important member was Horatio Seymour, who in the autumn of 1862 was elected governor of New York. Lincoln decided to operate on him by one of those astounding moves which to the selfless man seemed natural enough, by which the ordinary politician was always hopelessly mystified. He called in Thurlow Weed and authorized him to make this proposal: if Seymour would bring his following into a composite Union party with no platform but the vigorous prosecution of the war, Lincoln would pledge all his influence to securing for Seymour the presidential nomination in 1864. Weed delivered his message. Seymour was noncommittal and Lincoln had to wait for his answer until the new Governor should show his hand by his official acts. Meanwhile a new crisis had developed in the army. Burnside's character appears to have been shattered by his defeat. Previous to Fredericksburg, he had seemed to be a generous, high-minded man. From Fredericksburg onward, he became more and more an impossible. A reflection of McClellan in his earlier stage, he was somehow transformed eventually into a reflection of vindictivism. His later character began to appear in his first conference with the Committee subsequent to his disaster. They visited him on the field and "his conversation disarmed all criticism." This was because he struck their own note to perfection. "Our soldiers," he said, "were not sufficiently fired by resentment, and he exhorted me (Julian) if I could, to breathe into our people at home the same spirit toward our enemies which inspired them toward us."(6) What a transformation in McClellan's disciple!

But the country was not won over so easily as the Committee. There was loud and general disapproval and of course, the habitual question, "Who next?" The publication by the Committee of its insinuation that once more the stubborn President was the real culprit did not stem the tide. Burnside himself made his case steadily worse. His judgment, such as it was, had collapsed. He seemed to be stubbornly bent on a virtual repetition of his previous folly. Lincoln felt it necessary to command him to make no forward move without consulting the President.(7)

Burnside's subordinates freely criticized their commander. General Hooker was the most outspoken. It was known that a movement was afoot—an intrigue, if you will-to disgrace Burnside and elevate Hooker. Chafing under criticism and restraint, Burnside completely lost his sense of propriety. On the twenty-fourth of January, 1863, when Henry W. Raymond, the powerful editor of the New York Times, was on a visit to the camp, Burnside took him into his tent and read him an order removing

Hooker because of his unfitness "to hold a command in a cause where so much moderation, forbearance, and unselfish patriotism were required." Raymond, aghast, inquired what he would do if Hooker resisted, if he raised his troops in mutiny? "He said he would Swing him before sundown if he attempted such a thing."

Raymond, though more than half in sympathy with Burnside, felt that the situation was startling. He hurried off to Washington. "I immediately," he writes, "called upon Secretary Chase and told him the whole story. He was greatly surprised to hear such reports of Hooker, and said he had looked upon him as the man best fitted to command the army of the Potomac. But no man capable of so much and such unprincipled ambition was fit for so great a trust, and he gave up all thought of him henceforth. He wished me to go with him to his house and accompany him and his daughter to the President's levee. I did so and found a great crowd surrounding President Lincoln. I managed, however, to tell him in brief terms that I had been with the army and that many things were occurring there which he ought to know. I told him of the obstacles thrown in Burnside's way by his subordinates and especially General Hooker's habitual conversation. He put his hand on my shoulder and said in my ear as if desirous of not being overheard, 'That is all true; Hooker talks badly; but the trouble is, he is stronger with the country today than any other man.' I ventured to ask how long he would retain that strength if his real conduct and character should be understood. 'The country,' said he, 'would not believe it; they would say it was all a lie.'"(8)

Whether Chase did what he said he would do and ceased to be Hooker's advocate, may be questioned. Tradition preserves a deal between the Secretary and the General—the Secretary to urge his advancement, the General, if he reached his goal, to content himself with military honors and to assist the Secretary in succeeding to the Presidency. Hooker was a public favorite. The dashing, handsome figure of "Fighting Joe" captivated the popular imagination. The terrible Committee were his friends. Military men thought him full of promise. On the whole, Lincoln, who saw the wisdom of following up his clash over the Cabinet by a concession to the Jacobins, was willing to take his chances with Hooker.

His intimate advisers were not of the same mind. They knew that there was much talk on the theme of a possible dictator-not the constitutional dictator of Lincoln and Stevens, but the old-fashioned dictator of historical melodrama. Hooker was reported to have encouraged such talk. All this greatly alarmed one of Lincoln's most devoted henchmen—Lamon, Marshal of the District of Columbia, who regarded himself as personally responsible for Lincoln's safety. "In conversation with Mr. Lincoln," says Lamon, "one night about the time General Burnside was relieved, I was urging upon him the necessity of looking well to the fact that there was a scheme on foot to depose him, and to appoint a military dictator in his stead. He laughed and said, 'I think, for a man of accredited courage, you are the most panicky person I ever knew; you can see more dangers to me than all the other friends I have. You are all the time exercised about somebody taking my life; murdering me; and now you have discovered a new danger; now you think the people of this great government are likely to turn me out of office. I do not fear this from the people any more than I fear assassination from an individual. Now to show my appreciation of what my French friends would call a coup d'etat, let me read you a letter I have written to General Hooker whom I have just appointed to the command of the army of the Potomac."(9)

Few letters of Lincoln's are better known, few reveal more exactly the tone of his final period, than the remarkable communication he addressed to Hooker two days after that whispered talk with Raymond at the White House levee:

"General, I have placed you at the head of the army of the Potomac. Of course I have done this upon what appear to me to be sufficient reasons, and yet I think it best for you to know that there are some things in regard to which I am not quite satisfied with you. I believe you to be a brave and skilful soldier, which of course I like. I also believe you do not mix politics with your profession, in which you are right. You have confidence in yourself, which is a valuable, if not an indispensable quality. You are ambitious, which within reasonable bounds, does good rather than harm; but I think that during General Burnside's command of the army you have taken counsel of your ambition and thwarted him as much as you could, in which you did a great wrong to the country and to a most meritorious and honorable brother officer. I have heard in such a way as to believe it, of your recently Saying that both the army and the government needed a dictator. Of course it was not for this, but in spite of it, that I have given you the command. Only those generals who gain successes can set up dictators. What I now ask you is military success, and I will risk the dictatorship. The government will support you to the utmost of its ability, which is neither more nor less than it has done and will do for all commanders. I much fear that the spirit which you have aided to infuse into the army, of criticizing their commander and withholding confidence from him, will now turn upon you. I shall assist you as far as I can to put it down. Neither you nor Napoleon, if he were alive again, could get any good out of an army while such a Spirit prevails in it; and now beware of rashness. Beware of rashness, but with energy and sleepless vigilance go forward and give us victories."(10)

The appointment of Hooker had the effect of quieting the Committee for the time. Lincoln turned again to his political scheme, but not until he had made another military appointment from which at the moment no one could have guessed that trouble would ever come. He gave to Burnside what might be called the sinecure position of Commander of the Department of the Ohio with headquarters at Cincinnati.(11)

During the early part of 1863 Lincoln's political scheme received a serious blow. Seymour ranked himself as an irreconcilable enemy of the Administration. The anti-Lincoln Republicans struck at the President in roundabout ways. Heralding a new attack, the best man on the Committee, Julian, ironically urged his associates in Congress to "rescue" the President from his false friends—those mere Unionists who were luring him away from the party that had elected him, enticing him into a vague new party that should include "Democrats." It was said that there were only two Lincoln men in the House.(12) Greeley was coquetting with Rosecrans, trying to induce him to come forward as Republican presidential "timber." The Committee in April published an elaborate report which portrayed the army of the Potomac as an army of heroes tragically afflicted in the past by the incompetence of their commanders. The Democrats continued their abuse of the dictator.

It was a moment of strained pause, everybody waiting upon circumstance. And in Washington, every eye was turned Southward. How soon would they glimpse the first messenger from that glorious victory which "Fighting Joe" had promised them. "The enemy is in my power," said he, "and God Almighty can not deprive me of them."(13)

Something of the difference between Hooker and Lincoln, between all the Vindictives and Lincoln, may be felt by turning from these ribald words to that Fast Day Proclamation which this strange statesman issued to his people, that anxious spring,—that moment of trance as it were—when all things seemed to tremble toward the last judgment:

"And whereas, it is the duty of nations as well as of men to own their dependence upon the overruling power of God; to confess their sins and transgressions in humble sorrow, yet with assured hope that genuine repentance will lead to mercy and pardon; and to recognize the sublime truth announced in the Holy Scriptures and proven by all history, that those nations only are blessed whose God is the Lord:

"And insomuch as we know that by His divine law nations, like individuals, are subjected to punishments and chastisements in this world, may we not justly fear that the awful calamity of civil war which now desolates the land may be but a punishment inflicted upon us for our presumptuous sins, to the needful end of our national reformation as a whole people. We have been the recipients of the choicest bounties of Heaven. We have been preserved, these many years, in peace and prosperity. We have grown in numbers, wealth and power as no other nation has ever grown; but we have forgotten God. We have forgotten the gracious hand which preserved us in peace, and multiplied and enriched and strengthened us; and we have vainly imagined, in the deceitfulness of our hearts, that all these blessings were produced by some superior wisdom and virtue of our own. Intoxicated with unbroken success, we have become too self-sufficient to feel the necessity of redeeming and preserving grace, too proud to pray to God that made us:

"It behooves us then to humble ourselves before the offended Power, to confess our national sins, and to pray for clemency and forgiveness.

"All this being done in sincerity and truth, let us then rest humbly in the hope authorized by the divine teachings, that the united cry of the nation will be heard on high, and answered with blessings no less than the pardon of our national sins and the restoration of our now divided and suffering country to its former happy condition of unity and peace."(14)

Alas, for such men as Hooker! What seemed to him in his vainglory beyond the reach of Omnipotence, was accomplished by Lee and Jackson and a Confederate army at Chancellorsville. Profound gloom fell upon Washington. Welles heard the terrible news from Sumner who came into his room "and raising both hands exclaimed, 'Lost, lost, all is lost!'"(15)

The aftermath of Manassas was repeated. In the case of Pope, no effort had been spared to save the friend of the Committee, to find some one else on whom to load his incompetence. The course was now repeated. Again, the Jacobins raised the cry, "We are betrayed!" Again, the stir to injure the President. Very strange are the ironies of history! At this critical moment, Lincoln's amiable mistake in sending Burnside to Cincinnati demanded expiation. Along with the definite news of Hooker's overthrow, came the news that Burnside had seized the Copperhead leader, Vallandigham, and had cast him into prison; that a hubbub had ensued; that, as the saying goes, the woods were burning in Ohio.

Vallandigham's offense was a public speech of which no accurate report survives. However, the fragments recorded by "plain clothes" men in Burnside's employ, when set in the perspective of Vallandigham's thinking as displayed in Congress, make its tenor plain enough. It was an out-and-out Copperhead harangue. If he was to be treated as hundreds of others had been, the case against him was plain. But the Administration's policy toward agitators had gradually changed. There was not the same fear of them that had existed two years before. Now the tendency of the Administration was to ignore them.

The Cabinet regretted what Burnside had done. Nevertheless, the Ministers felt that it would not do to repudiate him. Lincoln took that view. He wrote to Burnside deploring his action and sustaining his authority.(16) And then, as a sort of grim practical joke, he commuted Vallandigham's sentence from imprisonment to banishment. The agitator was sent across the lines into the Confederacy.

Burnside had effectually played the marplot. Very little chance now of an understanding between Lincoln and either wing of the Democrats. The opportunity to make capital out of the war powers was quite too good to be lost! Vallandigham was nominated for governor by the Ohio Democrats. In all parts of the country Democratic committees resolved in furious protest against the dictator. And yet, on the whole, perhaps, the incident played into Lincoln's hands. At least, it silenced the Jacobins. With the Democrats ringing the changes on the former doctrine of the supple politicians, how certain that their only course for the moment was to lie low. A time came, to be sure, when they thought it safe to resume their own creed; but that was not yet.

The hubbub over Vallandigham called forth two letters addressed to protesting committees, that have their place among Lincoln's most important statements of political science. His argument is based on the proposition which Browning developed a year before. The core of it is:

"You ask in substance whether I really claim that I may override all guaranteed rights of individuals on the plea of conserving the public safety, whenever I may choose to say the public safety requires it. This question, divested of the phraseology calculated to represent me as struggling for an arbitrary personal prerogative, is either simply a question who shall decide, or an affirmation that no one shall decide, what the public safety does require in cases of rebellion or invasion.

"The Constitution contemplates the question as likely to occur for decision, but it does not expressly declare who is to decide it. By necessary implication, when rebellion or invasion comes, the decision is to be made from time to time; and I think the man whom, for the time, the people have, under the Constitution, made the Commander-in-chief of their army and navy, is the man who holds the power and bears the responsibility of making it. If he uses the power justly, the same people will probably justify him; if he abuses it, he is in their hands to be dealt with by all the modes they have reserved to themselves in the Constitution."(17)

Browning's argument over again-the President can be brought to book by a plebiscite, while Congress can not. But Lincoln did not rest, as Browning did, on mere argument. The old-time jury lawyer revived. He was doing more than arguing a theorem of political science. He was on trial before the people, the great mass, which he understood so well. He must reach their imaginations and touch their hearts.

"Mr. Vallandigham avows his hostility to the war on the part of the Union, and his arrest was made because he was laboring with some effect, to prevent the raising of troops, to encourage desertions from the army, and to leave the rebellion without an adequate military force to sup-press it. He was not arrested because he was damaging the political prospects of the Administration or the personal interests of the Commanding General, but because he was damaging the army, upon the existence and vigor of which the life of the nation depends. He was warring upon the military, and this gave the military constitutional jurisdiction to lay hands upon him.

"I understand the meeting whose resolutions I am considering, to be in favor of suppressing the rebellion by military force-by armies. Long experience has shown that armies can not be maintained unless desertion shall be punished by the severe penalty of death. The case requires, and the Law and the Constitution sanction this punishment. Must I shoot a simple-minded soldier boy who deserts while I must not touch a hair of a wily agitator who induces him to desert?" (18)

Again, the ironical situation of the previous December; the wrathful Jacobins, the most dangerous because the most sincere enemies of the presidential dictatorship, silent, trapped, biding their time. But the situation had for them a distinct consolation. A hundred to one it had killed the hope of a Lincoln-Democratic alliance.

However, the President would not give up the Democrats without one last attempt to get round the Little Men. Again, he could think of no mode of negotiation except the one he had vainly attempted with Seymour. As earnest of his own good faith, he would once more renounce his own prospect of a second term. But since Seymour had failed him, who was there that could serve his purpose? The popularity of McClellan among those Democrats who were not Copperheads had grown with his misfortunes. There had been a wide demand for his restoration after Fredericksburg, and again after Chancellorsville. Lincoln justified his reputation for political insight by concluding that McClellan, among the Democrats, was the coming man. Again Weed was called in. Again he became an ambassador of renunciation. Apparently he carried a message to the effect that if McClellan would join forces with the Administration, Lincoln would support him for president a year later. But McClellan was too inveterate a partisan. Perhaps he thought that the future was his anyway.(19)

And so Lincoln's persistent attempt to win over the Democrats came to an end. The final sealing of their antagonism was effected at a great Democratic rally in New York on the Fourth of July. The day previous, a manifesto had been circulated through the city beginning, "Freemen, awake! In everything, and in most stupendous proportion, is this Administration abominable!"(20) Seymour reaffirmed his position of out-and-out partisan hostility to the Administration. Vallandigham's colleague, Pendleton of Ohio, formulated the Democratic doctrine: that the Constitution was being violated by the President's assumption of war powers. His cry was, "The Constitution as it is and the Union as it was." He thundered that "Congress can not, and no one else shall, interfere with free speech." The question was not whether we were to have peace or war, but whether or not we were to have free government; "if it be necessary to violate the Constitution in order to carry on the war, the war ought instantly to be stopped."(21)

Lincoln's political program had ended apparently in a wreck. But Fortune had not entirely deserted him. Hooker in a fit of irritation had offered his resignation. Lincoln had accepted it. Under a new commander, the army of the Potomac had moved against Lee. The orators at the Fourth of July meeting had read in the papers that same day Lincoln's announcement of the victory at Gettysburg.(22) Almost coincident with that announcement was the surrender of Vicksburg. Difficult as was the political problem ahead of him, the problem of finding some other plan for unifying his support without participating in a Vindictive Coalition, Lincoln's mood was cheerful. On the seventh of July he was serenaded. Serenades for the President were a feature of war-time in Washington, and Lincoln utilized the occasions to talk informally to the country. His remarks on the seventh were not distinctive, except for their tone, quietly, joyfully confident. His serene mood displayed itself a week later in a note to Grant which is oddly characteristic. Who else would have had the impulse to make this quaint little confession? But what, for a general who could read between the lines, could have been more delightful?(23)

"My dear General: I do not remember that you and I ever met personally. I write this now as a grateful acknowledgment for the almost inestimable service you have done the country. I wish to say a word further. When you first reached the vicinity of Vicksburg, I thought you should do what you finally did-march the troops across the neck, run the batteries with the transports, and thus go below; and I never had any faith except a general hope that you knew better than I, that the Yazoo Pass expedition and the like could succeed. When you got below and took Port Gibson, Grand Gulf and the vicinity, I thought you should go down the river and join General Banks, and when you turned Northward, east of the Big Black, I feared it was a mistake. I now wish to make the personal acknowledgment that you were right and I was wrong.

"Very truly,

"A. LINCOLN."

XXVII
THE TRIBUNE OF THE PEOPLE

Between March and December, 1863, Congress was not in session. Its members were busy "taking the sense of the country" as they would have said: "putting their ears to the ground," as other people would say. A startling tale the ground told them. It was nothing less than that Lincoln was the popular hero; that the people believed in him; that the politicians would do well to shape their ways accordingly. When they reassembled, they were in a sullen, disappointed frame of mind. They would have liked to ignore the ground's mandate; but being politicians, they dared not.

What an ironical turn of events! Lincoln's well-laid plan for a coalition of Moderates and Democrats had come to nothing. Logically, he ought now to be at the mercy of the Republican leaders. But instead, those leaders were beginning to be afraid of him, were perceiving that he had power whereof they had not dreamed. Like Saul the son of Kish, who had set out to find his father's asses, he had found instead a kingdom. How had he done it?

On a grand scale, it was the same sort of victory that had made him a power, so long before, on the little stage at Springfield. It was personal politics. His character had saved him. A multitude who saw nothing in the fine drawn constitutional issue of the war powers, who sensed the war in the most simple and elementary way, had formed, somehow, a compelling and stimulating idea of the President. They were satisfied that "Old Abe," or "Father Abraham," was the man for them. When, after one of his numerous calls for fresh troops, their hearts went out to him, a new song sprang to life, a ringing, vigorous, and yet a touching song with the refrain, "We're coming, Father Abraham, three hundred thousand more."

But how has he done it, asked the bewildered politicians, one of another. How had he created this personal confidence? They, Wade, Chandler, Stevens, Davis, could not do it; why could he?

Well, for one thing, he was a grand reality. They, relatively, were shadows. The wind of destiny for him was the convictions arising out of his own soul; for them it was vox populi. The genuineness of Lincoln, his spiritual reality, had been perceived early by a class of men whom your true politician seldom understands. The Intellectuals—"them literary fellers," in the famous words of an American Senator—were quick to see that the President was an extraordinary man; they were not long in concluding that he was a genius. The subtlest intellect of the time, Hawthorne, all of whose prejudices were enlisted against him, said in the Atlantic of July, 1863: "He is evidently a man of keen faculties, and what is still more to the purpose, of powerful character. As to his integrity, the people have that intuition of it which is never deceived he has a flexible mind capable of much expansion." And this when Trumbull chafed in spirit because the President was too "weak" for his part and Wade railed at him as a despot. As far back as 1860, Lowell, destined to become one of his ablest defenders, had said that Lincoln had "proved both his ability and his integrity; he . . . had experience enough in public affairs to make him a statesman, and not enough to make him a politician." To be sure, there were some Intellectuals who could not see straight nor think clear. The world would have more confidence in the caliber of Bryant had he been able to rank himself in the Lincoln following. But the greater part of the best intelligence of the North could have subscribed to Motley's words, "My respect for the character of the President increases every day."(1) The impression he made on men of original mind is shadowed in the words of Walt Whitman, who saw him often in the streets of Washington: "None of the artists or pictures have caught the subtle and indirect expression of this man's face. One of the great portrait painters of two or three centuries ago is needed."(2)

Lincoln's popular strength lay in a combination of the Intellectuals and the plain people against the politicians. He reached the masses in three ways: through his general receptions which any one might attend; through the open-door policy of his office, to which all the world was permitted access; through his visits to the army. Many thousand men and women, in one or another of these ways, met the President face to face, often in the high susceptibility of intense woe, and carried away an impression which was immediately circulated among all their acquaintances.

It would be impossible to exaggerate the grotesque miscellany of the stream of people flowing ever in and out of the President's open doors. Patriots eager to serve their country but who could find no place in the conventional requirements of the War Office; sharpers who wanted to inveigle him into the traps of profiteers; widows with all their sons in service, pleading for one to be exempted; other parents struggling with the red tape that kept them from sons in hospitals; luxurious frauds prating of their loyalty for the sake of property exemptions; inventors with every imaginable strange device; politicians seeking to cajole him; politicians bluntly threatening him; cashiered officers demanding justice; men with grievances of a myriad sorts; nameless statesmen who sought to teach him his duty; clergymen in large numbers, generally with the same purpose; deputations from churches, societies, political organizations, commissions, trades unions, with every sort of message from flattery to denunciation; and best of all, simple, confiding people who wanted only to say, "We trust you—God bless you!"

There was a method in this madness of accessibility. Its deepest inspiration, to be sure, was kindness. In reply to a protest that he would wear himself out listening to thousands of requests most of which could not be granted, he replied with one of those smiles in which there was so much sadness, "They don't want much; they get but little, and I must see them."(3)

But there was another inspiration. His open doors enabled him to study the American people, every phase of it, good and bad. "Men moving only in an official circle," said he, "are apt to become merely official—not to say arbitrary—in their ideas, and are apter and apter with each passing day to forget that they only hold power in a representative capacity. . . . Many of the matters brought to my notice are utterly frivolous, but others are of more or less importance, and all serve to renew in me a clearer and more vivid image of that great popular assemblage out of which I sprung, and to which at the end of two years I must return. . . . I call these receptions my public opinion baths; for I have but little time to read the papers, and gather public opinion that way; and though they may not be pleasant in all their particulars, the effect as a whole, is renovating and invigorating to my perceptions of responsibility and duty."(4)

He did not allow his patience to be abused with evil intent. He read his suppliants swiftly. The profiteer, the shirk, the fraud of any sort, was instantly unmasked. "I'll have nothing to do with this business," he burst out after listening to a gentlemanly profiteer; "nor with any man who comes to me with such degrading propositions. What! Do you take the President of the United States to be a commission broker? You have come to the wrong place, and for you and for every one who comes for the same purpose, there is the door."(5)

Lincoln enjoyed this indiscriminate mixing with people. It was his chief escape from care. He saw no reason why his friends should Commiserate him because of the endless handshaking. That was a small matter compared with the interest he took in the ever various stream of human types. Sometimes, indeed, he would lapse into a brown study in the midst of a reception. Then he "would shake hands with thousands of people, seemingly unconscious of what he was doing, murmuring monotonous salutations as they went by, his eye dim, his thoughts far withdrawn. . . . Suddenly, he would see some familiar face — his memory for faces was very good-and his eye would brighten and his whole form grow attentive; he would greet the visitor with a hearty grasp and a ringing word and dismiss him with a cheery laugh that filled the Blue Room with infectious good nature."(6) Carpenter, the portrait painter, who for a time saw him daily, says that "his laugh stood by itself. The neigh of a wild horse on his native prairie is not more undisguised and hearty." An intimate friend called it his "life preserver."(7)

Lincoln's sense of humor delighted in any detail of an event which suggested comedy. His genial awkwardness amused himself quite as much as it amused the world. At his third public reception he wore a pair of white kid gloves that were too small. An old friend approached. The President shook hands so heartily that his glove burst with a popping sound. Holding up his hand, Lincoln gazed at the ruined glove with a droll air while the arrested procession came to a standstill. "Well, my old friend," said he, "this is a general bustification; you and I were never intended to wear these things. If they were stronger they might do to keep out the cold, but they are a failure to shake hands with between old friends like us. Stand aside, Captain, and I'll see you shortly."(8)

His complete freedom from pose, and from the sense of place, was glimpsed by innumerable visitors. He would never allow a friend to address him by a title. "Call me Lincoln," he would say; "Mr. President is entirely too formal for us."(9)

In a mere politician, all this might have been questioned. But Hawthorne was right as to the people's intuition of Lincoln's honesty. He hated the parade of eminence. Jefferson was his patron saint, and "simplicity" was part of his creed. Nothing could induce him to surround himself with pomp, or even — as his friends thought — with mere security. Rumors of plots against his life were heard almost from the beginning. His friends begged long and hard before he consented to permit a cavalry guard at the gates of the White House. Very soon he countermanded his consent. "It would never do," said he, "for a president to have guards with drawn sabers at his door, as if he fancied he were, or were trying to be, or were assuming to be, an emperor."(10)

A military officer, alarmed for his safety, begged him to consider "the fact that any assassin or maniac seeking his life, could enter his presence without the interference of a single armed man to hold him back. The entrance doors, and all doors on the official side of the building, were open at all hours of the day and very late into the evening; and I have many times entered the mansion and walked up to the rooms of the two private secretaries as late as nine or ten o'clock at night, without Seeing, or being challenged by a single soul." But the officer pleaded in vain. Lincoln laughingly paraphrased Charles II, "Now as to political assassination, do you think the Richmond people would like to have Hannibal Hamlin here any more than myself? . . . As to the crazy folks, Major, why I must only take my chances-the most crazy people at present, I fear, being some of my own too zealous adherents."(11) With Carpenter, to whom he seems to have taken a liking, he would ramble the streets of Washington, late at night, "without escort or even the company of a servant."(12) Though Halleck talked him into accepting an escort when driving to and fro between Washington and his summer residence at the Soldiers' Home, he would frequently give it the slip and make the journey on horseback alone. In August of 1862 on one of these solitary rides, his life was attempted. It was about eleven at night; he was "jogging along at a slow gait immersed in deep thought" when some one fired at him with a rifle from near at hand. The ball missed its aim and the President's horse, as Lincoln confided to his familiars, "gave proof of decided dissatisfaction at the racket, and with one reckless bound, he unceremoniously separated me from my eight-dollar plug hat . . . At break-neck speed we reached a haven of safety. Meanwhile, I was left in doubt whether death was more desirable from being thrown from a runaway Federal horse, or as the tragic result of a rifle ball fired by a disloyal bushwhacker in the middle of the night"(13)

While carrying his life in his hands in this oddly reckless way, he belied himself, as events were to show, by telling his friends that he fancied himself "a great coward physically," that he felt sure he would make a poor soldier. But he was sufficiently just to himself to add, "Moral cowardice is something which I think I never had."(14)

Lincoln's humor found expression in other ways besides telling stories and laughing at himself. He seized every opportunity to convert a petition into a joke, when this could be done without causing pain. One day, there entered a great man with a long list of favors which he hoped to have granted. Among these was "the case of Betsy Ann Dougherty, a good woman," said the great man. "She lived in my county and did my washing for a long time. Her husband went off and joined the Rebel army and I wish you would give her a protection paper." The pompous gravity of the way the case was presented struck Lincoln as very funny. His visitor had no humor. He failed to see jokes while Lincoln quizzed him as to who and what was Betsy Ann. At length the President wrote a line on a card and handed it to the great man. "Tell Betsy Ann to put a string in this card and hang it round her neck," said he. "When the officers (who may have doubted her affiliations) see this they will keep their hands off your Betsy Ann." On the card was written, "Let Betsy Ann Dougherty alone as long as she behaves herself. A. Lincoln."(15)

This eagerness for a joke now and then gave offense. On one occasion, a noted Congressman called on the President shortly after a disaster. Lincoln began to tell a story. The Congressman jumped up. "Mr. President, I did not come here this morning to hear stories. It is too serious a time." Lincoln's face changed. "Ashley," said he, "sit down! I respect you as an earnest, sincere man. You can not be more anxious than I have been constantly since the beginning of the war; and I say to you now, that were it not for this occasional vent, I should die."(16) Again he said, "When the Peninsula Campaign terminated suddenly at Harrison's Landing, I was as near inconsolable as I could be and live."(17)

Lincoln's imaginative power, the ineradicable artist in him, made of things unseen true realities to his sensibility. Reports of army suffering bowed his spirit. "This was especially' the case when the noble victims were of his own acquaintance, or of the narrower circle of his familiar friends; and then he seemed for the moment possessed of a sense of personal responsibility for their individual fate which was at once most unreasonable and most pitiful." On hearing that two sons of an old friend were desperately wounded and would probably die, he broke out with: "Here, now, are these dear brave boys killed in this cursed war. My God! My God! It is too bad! They worked hard to earn money to educate themselves and this is the end! I loved them as if they were my own."(18) He was one of the few who have ever written a beautiful letter of condolence. Several of his letters attempting this all but impossible task, come as near their mark as such things can. One has become a classic:

"I have been shown," he wrote to Mrs. Bixby, "in the files of the War Department a statement of the Adjutant-General of Massachusetts that you are the mother of five sons who have died gloriously on the field of battle. I feel how weak and fruitless must be any words of mine which should attempt to beguile you from the grief of a loss so overwhelming. But I can not refrain from tendering to you the consolation that may be found in the thanks of the Republic they died to save. I pray that our heavenly Father may assuage the anguish of your bereavement, and leave you only the cherished memory of the loved and lost, and the solemn pride that must be yours to have laid so costly a sacrifice upon the altar of freedom."(19)

All these innumerable instances of his sympathy passed from mouth to mouth; became part of a floating propaganda that was organizing the people in his support. To these were added many anecdotes of his mercy. The American people had not learned that war is a rigorous thing. Discipline in the army was often hard to maintain. Impulsive young men who tired of army life, or who quarreled with their officers, sometimes walked away. There were many condemnations either for mutiny or desertion. In the stream of suppliants pouring daily through the President's office, many were parents imploring mercy for rash sons. As every death-warrant had to be signed by the President, his generals were frequently enraged by his refusal to carry out their decisions. "General," said he to an angry commander who charged him with destroying discipline, "there are too many weeping widows in the United States now.-For God's sake don't ask me to add to the number; for I tell you plainly I won't do it."(20)

Here again, kindness was blended with statecraft, mercy with shrewdness. The generals could not grasp the political side of war. Lincoln tried to make them see it. When they could not, he quietly in the last resort counteracted their influence. When some of them talked of European experience, he shook his head; it would not do; they must work with the tools they had; first of all with an untrained people, intensely sensitive to the value of human life, impulsive, quick to forget offenses, ultra-considerate of youth and its rashness. Whatever else the President did, he must not allow the country to think of the army as an ogre devouring its sons because of technicalities. The General saw only the discipline, the morale, of the soldiers; the President saw the far more difficult, the more roundabout matter, the discipline and the morale of the citizens. The one believed that he could compel; the other with his finger on the nation's pulse, knew that he had to persuade.

However, this flowing army of the propaganda did not always engage him on the tragic note. One day a large fleshy man, of a stern but homely countenance and a solemn and dignified carriage, immaculate dress— "swallow-tailed coat, ruffled shirt of faultless fabric, white cravat and orange-colored gloves" — entered with the throng. Looking at him Lincoln was somewhat appalled. He expected some formidable demand. To his relief, the imposing stranger delivered a brief harangue on the President's policy, closing with, "I have watched you narrowly ever since your inauguration. . . . As one of your constituents, I now say to you, do in future as you damn please, and I will support you." "Sit down, my friend," said Lincoln, "sit down. I am delighted to see you. Lunch with us today. Yes, you must stay and lunch with us, my friend, for I have not seen enough of you yet."(21) There were many of these informal ambassadors of the people assuring the President of popular support. And this florid gentleman was not the only one who lunched with the President on first acquaintance.

This casual way of inviting strangers to lunch with him was typical of his mode of life, which was exceedingly simple. He slept lightly and rose early. In summer when he used the Soldiers' Home as a residence, he was at his desk in the White House at eight o'clock in the morning. His breakfast was an egg and a cup of coffee; luncheon was rarely more than a glass of milk and a biscuit with a plate of fruit in season; his dinner at six o'clock, was always a light meal. Though he had not continued a total abstainer, as in the early days at Springfield, he very seldom drank wine. He never used tobacco. So careless was he with regard to food that when Mrs. Lincoln was away from home, there was little regularity in his meals. He described his habits on such occasions as "browsing around."(22)

Even when Mrs. Lincoln was in command at the White House, he was not invariably dutiful. An amusing instance was observed by some high officials. The luncheon hour arrived in the midst of an important conference. Presently, a servant appeared reminding Mr. Lincoln of the hour, but he took no notice. Another summons, and again no notice. After a short interval, the door of the office flew open and the titular "First Lady" flounced into the room, a ruffled, angry little figure, her eyes flashing. With deliberate quiet, as if in a dream, Lincoln rose slowly, took her calmly, firmly by the shoulders, lifted her, carried her through the doorway, set her down, closed the door, and went on with the conference as if unconscious of an interruption.(23) Mrs. Lincoln did not return. The remainder of the incident is unknown.

The burden of many anecdotes that were included in the propaganda was his kindness to children. It began with his own. His little rascal "Tad," after Willie's death, was the apple of his eye. The boy romped in and out of his office. Many a time he was perched on his father's knee while great affairs of state were under discussion.(24) Lincoln could persuade any child from the arms of its mother, nurse, or play fellow, there being a "peculiar fascination in his voice and manner which the little one could not resist."(25)

All impressionable, imaginative young people, brought into close association with him, appear to have felt his spell. His private secretaries were his sworn henchmen. Hay's diary rings with admiration—the keen, discriminating, significant admiration of your real observer. Hay refers to him by pet name-"The Ancient," "The Old Man," "The Tycoon." Lincoln's entire relation with these gifted youngsters may be typified by one of Hay's quaintest anecdotes. Lincoln had gone to bed, as so often he did, with a book. "A little after midnight as I was writing, the President came into the office laughing, with a volume of Hood's Works in his hand, to show Nicolay and me the little caricature, 'An Unfortunate Being'; seemingly utterly unconscious that he, with his short shirt hanging about his long legs, and setting out behind like the tail feathers of an enormous ostrich, was infinitely funnier than anything in the book he was laughing at. What a man it is! occupied all day with matters of vast moment, deeply anxious about the fate of the greatest army of the world, with his own plans and future hanging on the events of the passing hour, he yet has such a wealth of simple bonhomie and good fellowship that he gets out of bed and perambulates the house in his shirt to find us that we may share with him the fun of poor Hood's queer little conceits."(26)

In midsummer, 1863, "The Tycoon is in fine whack. I have rarely seen him more serene and busy. He is managing this war, the draft, foreign relations, and planning a reconstruction of the Union, all at once. I never knew with what a tyrannous authority he rules the Cabinet, until now. The most important things he decides and there is no cavil. I am growing more convinced that the good of the country demands that he should be kept where he is till this thing is over. There is no man in the country so wise, so gentle, and so firm."(27)

And again, "You may talk as you please of the Abolition Cabal directing affairs from Washington; some well-meaning newspapers advise the President to keep his fingers out of the military pie, and all that sort of thing. The truth is, if he did, the pie would be a sorry mess. The old man sits here and wields, like a backwoods Jupiter, the bolts of war and the machinery of government with a hand especially steady and equally firm. . . I do not know whether the nation is worthy of him for another term. I know the people want him. There is no mistaking that fact. But the politicians are strong yet, and he is not their 'kind of a cat.' I hope God won't see fit to scourge us for our sins by any of the two or three most prominent candidates on the ground."(28) This was the conclusion growing everywhere among the bulk of the people. There is one more cause of it to be reckoned with. Lincoln had not ceased to be the literary statesman. In fact, he was that more effectively than ever. His genius for fable-making took a new turn. Many a visitor who came to find fault, went home to disseminate the apt fable with which the President had silenced his objections and captured his agreement. His skill in narration also served him well. Carpenter repeats a story about Andrew Johnson and his crude but stern religion which in mere print is not remarkable. "I have elsewhere insinuated," comments Carpenter, "that Mr. Lincoln was capable of much dramatic power. . . . It was shown in his keen appreciation of Shakespeare, and unrivaled faculty of Storytelling. The incident just related, for example, was given with a thrilling effect which mentally placed Johnson, for the time being, alongside Luther and Cromwell. Profanity or irreverence was lost sight of in a fervid utterance of a highly wrought and great-souled determination, united with a rare exhibition of pathos and self-abnegation."(29)

In formal literature, he had done great things upon a far higher level than any of his writings previous to that sudden change in his style in 1860. For one, there was the Fast Day Proclamation. There was also a description of his country, of the heritage of the nation, in the third message. Its aim was to give imaginative reality to the national idea; just as the second message had aimed to give argumentative reality.

"There is no line, straight or crooked, suitable for a national boundary upon which to divide. Trace through from east to west, upon the line between the free and the slave Country and we shall find a little more than one-third of its length are rivers, easy to be crossed, and populated, or soon to be populated, thickly upon both sides; while nearly all its remaining length are merely surveyors' lines, over which people may walk back and forth without any consciousness of their presence. No part of this line can be made any more difficult to pass by writing it down on paper or parchment as a national boundary.

"But there is another difficulty. The great interior region, bounded east by the Alleghanies, north by the British dominions, west by the Rocky Mountains, and south by the line along which the culture of corn and cotton meets, and which includes part of Virginia, part of Tennessee, all of Kentucky, Ohio, Indiana, Michigan, Wisconsin, Illinois, Missouri, Kansas, Iowa, Minnesota, and the Territories of Dakota, Nebraska, and part of Colorado, already has above ten millions of people, and will have fifty millions within fifty years, if not prevented by any political folly or mistake. It contains more than one-third of the Country owned by the United States—certainly more than one million square miles. Once half as populous as Massachusetts already is, it would have more than seventy-five millions of people. A glance at the map shows that, territorially speaking, it is the great body of the republic. The other parts are but marginal borders to it, the magnificent region sloping west from the Rocky Mountains to the Pacific being the deepest and also the richest in undeveloped resources. In the production of provisions, grains, grasses, and all which proceed from them, this great interior region is naturally one of the most important in the world. Ascertain from the statistics the small proportion of the region which has, as yet, been brought into cultivation, and also the large and rapidly increasing amount of its products and we shall be overwhelmed with the magnitude of the prospect presented; and yet, this region has no seacoast, touches no ocean anywhere. As part of one nation, its people now find, and may forever find, their way to Europe by New York, to South America and Africa by New Orleans, and to Asia by San Francisco. But separate our common country into two nations as designed by the present rebellion, and every man of this great interior region is thereby cut off from some one or more of these outlets-not, perhaps, by a physical barrier, but by embarrassing and onerous trade regulations.

"And this is true wherever a dividing or boundary line may be fixed. Place it between the now free and slave country, or place it south of

Kentucky or north of Ohio, and still the truth remains that none south of it can trade to any port or place north of it, and none north of it can trade to any port or place south of it, except upon terms dictated by a government foreign to them. These outlets east, west, and south, are indispensable to the well-being of the people inhabiting and to inhabit, this vast interior region. Which of the three may be the best is no proper question. All are better than either; and all of right belong to that people and to their Successors forever. True to themselves, they will not ask where a line of separation shall be, but will vow rather that there shall be no such line. Nor are the marginal regions less interested in these communications to and through them to the great outside world. They, too, and each of them, must have access to this Egypt of the West without paying toll at the crossing of any national boundary.

"Our national strife springs not from our permanent part, not from the land we inhabit, not from our national homestead. There is no possible severing of this but would multiply, and not mitigate, evils among us. In all its adaptations and aptitudes it demands union and abhors separation. In fact, it would ere long, force reunion, however much of blood and treasure the separation might have cost." (30)

A third time he made a great literary stroke, gave utterance, in yet another form, to his faith that the national idea was the one constant issue for which he had asked his countrymen, and would continue to ask them, to die. It was at Gettysburg, November 19, 1863, in consecration of a military burying-ground, that he delivered, perhaps, his greatest utterance:

"But, in a larger sense, we can not dedicate—we can not consecrate—we can not hallow—this ground. The brave men, living and dead, who struggled here, have consecrated it far above our poor power to add or detract. The world will little note nor long remember what we say here, but it can never forget what they did here. It is for us, the living, rather, to be dedicated here to the unfinished work which they who fought here have thus far so nobly advanced. It is rather for us to be here dedicated to the great task remaining before us—that from these honored dead we take increased devotion to that cause for which they gave the last full measure of devotion; that we here highly resolve that these dead shall not have died in vain; that this nation under God, shall have a new birth of freedom; and that government of the people, for the people, by the people, shall not perish from the earth." (31)

XXVIII
APPARENT ASCENDENCY

Toward the end of 1863, Lowell prepared an essay on "The President's Policy." It might almost be regarded as a manifesto of the Intellectuals. That there was now a prospect of winning the war "was mainly due to the good sense, the good humor, the sagacity, the large-mindedness, and the unselfish honesty of the unknown man whom a blind fortune, as it seemed, had lifted from the crowd to the most dangerous and difficult eminence of modern times." When the essay appeared in print, Lincoln was greatly pleased. He wrote to the editors of the North American Review, "I am not the most impartial judge; yet with due allowance for this, I venture to hope that the article entitled 'The President's Policy' will be of value to the country. I fear I am not quite worthy of all which is therein so kindly said of me personally."(1)

This very able defense of his previous course appeared as he was announcing to the country his final course. He was now satisfied that winning the war was but a question of time. What would come after war was now in his mind the overshadowing matter. He knew that the vindictive temper had lost nothing of its violence. Chandler's savagery — his belief that the Southerners had forfeited the right to life, liberty and the pursuit of happiness — was still the Vindictive creed. 'Vae victi'! When war ended, they meant to set their feet on the neck of the vanquished foe. Furthermore, Lincoln was not deceived as to why they were lying low at this particular minute. Ears had been flattened to the ground and they were heeding what the ground had said. The President was too popular for them to risk attacking him without an obvious issue. Their former issue had been securely appropriated by the Democrats. Where could they find another? With consummate boldness Lincoln presented them an issue. It was reconstruction. When Congress met, he communicated the text of a "Proclamation of Amnesty and Reconstruction."(2) This great document on which all his concluding policy was based, offered "a full pardon" with "restoration of all rights of property, except as to slaves, or in property cases, where rights of third persons shall have intervened" upon subscribing to an oath of allegiance which required only a full acceptance of the authority of the United States. This amnesty was to be extended to all persons except a few groups, such as officers above the rank of colonel and former officials of the United States. The Proclamation also provided that whenever, in any Seceded State, the new oath should be taken by ten per cent. of all those who were qualified to vote under the laws of 1860, these ten per cent. should be empowered to set up a new State government.

From the Vindictive point of view, here was a startling announcement. Lincoln had declared for a degree of magnanimity that was as a red rag to a bull. He had also carried to its ultimate his assumption of war powers. No request was made for congressional cooperation. The message which the Proclamation accompanied was informative only.

By this time, the Vindictive Coalition of 1861 was gradually coming together again. Or, more truly, perhaps, various of its elements were fusing into a sort of descendant of the old coalition. The leaders of the new Vindictive group were much the same as the leaders of the earlier group. There was one conspicuous addition. During the next six months, Henry Winter Davis held for a time the questionable distinction of being Lincoln's most inveterate enemy. He was a member of the House. In the House many young and headstrong politicians rallied about him. The Democrats at times craftily followed his lead. Despite the older and more astute Vindictives of the Senate, Chandler, Wade and the rest who knew that their time had not come, Davis, with his ardent followers, took up the President's challenge. Davis brought in a bill designed to complete the reorganization of the old Vindictive Coalition. It appealed to the enemies of presidential prerogative, to all those who wanted the road to reconstruction made as hard as possible, and to the Abolitionists. This bill, in so many words, transferred the whole matter of reconstruction from the President to Congress; it required a majority (instead of one-tenth) of all the male citizens of a Seceded State as the basis of a new government; it exacted of this majority a pledge never to pay any State debt contracted during the Confederacy, and also the perpetual prohibition of slavery in their State constitution.

Davis got his bill through the House, but his allies in the Senate laid it aside. They understood the country too well not to see that they must wait for something to happen. If the President made any mistake, if anything went wrong with the army—they remembered the spring of 1862, McClellan's failure, and how Chandler followed it up. And at this moment no man was chafing more angrily because of what the ground was saying, no man was watching the President more keenly, than Chandler. History is said to repeat itself, and all things are supposed to come to him who waits. While Davis's bill was before the House, Lincoln accepted battle with the Vindictives in a way that was entirely unostentatious, but that burned his bridges. He pressed forward the organization of a new State government in Louisiana under Federal auspices. He wrote to Michael Hahn, the newly chosen governor of this somewhat fictitious State: "I congratulate you on having fixed your name in history as the first Free State governor of Louisiana."(3)

Meanwhile, the hotheads of the House again followed Davis's lead and flung defiance in Lincoln's face. Napoleon, who had all along coquetted alarmingly with the Confederates, had also pushed ahead with his insolent conquest of Mexico. Lincoln and Seward, determined to have but one war on their hands at a time, had skilfully evaded committing themselves. The United States had neither protested against the action of Napoleon, nor in any way admitted its propriety. Other men besides the Vindictives were biding their time. But here the hotheads thought they saw an opportunity. Davis brought in a resolution which amounted to a censure of the Administration for not demanding the retirement of the French from Mexico. This was one of those times when the Democrats played politics and followed Davis. The motion was carried unanimously.(4) It was so much of a sensation that the 'American Minister at Paris, calling on the Imperial Minister of Foreign Affairs, was met by the curt question, "Do you bring peace or war?"

But it was not in the power of the House to draw Lincoln's fire until he chose to be drawn. He ignored its action. The Imperial Government was informed that the acts of the House of Representatives were not the acts of the President, and that in relation to France, if the President should change his policy, the imperial Government would be duly in formed.(5)

It was Lincoln's fate to see his policy once again at the mercy of his Commanding General. That was his situation in the spring of 1862 when everything hung on McClellan who failed him; again in the autumn of the year when McClellan so narrowly saved him. The spring of 1864 paralleled, in this respect, that other spring two years earlier. To be sure, Lincoln's position was now much stronger; he had a great personal following on which he relied. But just how strong it was he did not know. He was taking a great risk forcing a policy high-handed in defiance of Congress, where all his bitterest enemies were entrenched, glowering. If his General failed him now —

The man on whom this huge responsibility rested was Grant. Lincoln had summoned him from the West and placed him at the head of all the armies of the Republic. As to Halleck who had long since proved himself perfectly useless, he was allowed to lapse into obscurity.

Grant has preserved in his Memoirs his first confidential talk with Lincoln: "He told me he did not want to know what I proposed to do. But he submitted a plan of campaign of his own that he wanted me to hear and then do as I pleased about. He brought out a map of Virginia on which he had evidently marked every position occupied by the Federal and Confederate armies up to that time. He pointed out on the map two streams which empty into the Potomac, and suggested that an army might be moved on boats and landed between the mouths of those streams. We would then have the Potomac to bring our supplies, and the tributaries would protect our flanks while we moved out. I listened respectfully, but did not suggest that the same streams would protect Lee's flanks while he was shutting us up."(6)

Grant set out for the front in Virginia. Lincoln's parting words were this note: "Not expecting to see you again before the spring campaign opens, I wish to express in this way my entire satisfaction with what you have done up to this time, so far as I understand it. The particulars of your plans I neither know nor seek to know. You are vigilant and self-reliant; and, pleased with this, I wish not to obtrude any constraints or restraints upon you. While I am very anxious that any great disaster or capture of our men in great numbers shall be avoided, I know these points are less likely to escape your attention than they would be mine. If there is anything wanting which is within my power to give, do not fail to let me know it. And now, with a brave army and a just cause, may God sustain you."(7)

XXIX
CATASTROPHE

If the politicians needed a definite warning, in addition to what the ground was saying, it was given by an incident that centered upon Chase. A few bold men whose sense of the crowd was not so acute as it might have been, attempted to work up a Chase boom. At the instance of Senator Pomeroy, a secret paper known to-day as the Pomeroy Circular, was started on its travels. The Circular aimed to make Chase the Vindictive candidate. Like all the other anti-Lincoln moves of the early part of 1864, it was premature. The shrewd old Senators who were silently marshaling the Vindictive forces, let it alone.

Chase's ambition was fully understood at the White House. During the previous year, his irritable self-consciousness had led to quarrels with the President, generally over patronage, and more than once he had offered his resignation. On one occasion, Lincoln went to his house and begged him to reconsider. Alone among the Cabinet, Chase had failed to take the measure of Lincoln and still considered him a second-rate person, much his inferior. He rated very high the services to his country of the Secretary of the Treasury whom he considered the logical successor to the Presidency.

Lincoln refused to see what Chase was after. "I have determined," he told Hay, "to shut my eyes as far as possible to everything of the sort. Mr. Chase makes a good secretary and I shall keep him where he is."(1) In lighter vein, he said that Chase's presidential ambition was like a "chin fly" pestering a horse; it led to his putting all the energy he had into his work.(2)

When a copy of the Circular found its way to the White House, Lincoln refused to read it.(3) Soon afterward it fell into the hands of an unsympathetic or indiscreet editor and was printed. There was a hubbub. Chase offered to resign. Lincoln wrote to him in reply:

"My knowledge of Mr. Pomeroy's letter having been made public came to me only the day you wrote but I had, in Spite of myself, known of its existence several days before. I have not yet read it, and I think I shall not. I was not shocked or surprised by the appearance of the letter because I had had knowledge of Mr. Pomeroy's committee, and of secret issues which I supposed came from it, and of secret agents who I supposed were sent out by it, for several weeks. I have known just as little of these things as my friends have allowed me to know. They bring the documents to me, but I do not read them; they tell me what they think fit to tell me, but I do not inquire for more. I fully concur with you that neither of us can be justly held responsible for what our respective friends may do without our instigation or countenance; and I assure you, as you have assured me, that no assault has been made upon you by my instigation or with my countenance. Whether you shall remain at the head of the Treasury Department is a question which I will not allow myself to consider from any standpoint other than my judgment of the public service, and in that view, I do not perceive occasion for a change."(4) But this was not the end of the incident. The country promptly repudiated Chase. His own state led the way. A caucus of Union members of the Ohio Legislature resolved that the people and the soldiers of Ohio demanded the reelection of Lincoln. In a host of similar resolutions, Legislative caucuses, political conventions, dubs, societies, prominent individuals not in the political machine, all ringingly declared for Lincoln, the one proper candidate of the "Union party"-as the movement was labeled in a last and relatively successful attempt to break party lines.

As the date of the "Union Convention" approached, Lincoln put aside an opportunity to gratify the Vindictives. Following the Emancipation Proclamation, the recruiting offices had been opened to negroes. Thereupon the Confederate government threatened to treat black soldiers as brigands, and to refuse to their white officers the protection of the laws of war. A cry went up in the North for reprisal. It was not the first time the cry had been raised. In 1862 Lincoln's spokesman in Congress, Browning, had withstood a proposal for the trial of General Buckner by the civil authorities of Kentucky. Browning opposed such a course on the ground that it would lead to a policy of retaliation, and make of the war a gratification of revenge. (5) The Confederate threat gave a new turn to the discussion. Frederick Douglas, the most influential negro of the time, obtained an audience with Lincoln and begged for reprisals. Lincoln would not consent. So effective was his argument that even the ardent negro, convinced that his race was about to suffer persecution, was satisfied.

"I shall never forget," Douglas wrote, "the benignant expression of his face, the tearful look of his eye, the quiver in his voice, when he deprecated a resort to retaliatory measures. 'Once begun,' said he, 'I do not know where such a measure would stop.' He said he could not take men out and kill them in cold blood for what was done by others. If he could get hold of the persons who were guilty of killing the colored prisoners in cold blood, the case would be different, but he could not kill the innocent for the guilty."(6)

In April, 1864, the North was swept by a wild rumor of deliberate massacre of prisoners at Fort Pillow. Here was an opportunity for Lincoln to ingratiate himself with the Vindictives. The President was to make a speech at a fair held in Baltimore, for the benefit of the Sanitary Commission. The audience was keen to hear him denounce the reputed massacre, and eager to applaud a promise of reprisal. Instead, he deprecated hasty judgment; insisting that the rumor had not been verified; that nothing should be done on the strength of mere report.

"It is a mistake to suppose the government is indifferent in this matter, or is not doing the best it can in regard to it. We do not to-day know that a colored soldier or white officer commanding colored soldiers has been massacred by the Rebels when made a prisoner. We fear it — believe it, I may say-but we do not know it To take the life of one of their prisoners on the assumption that they murder ours, when it is short of certainty that they do murder ours, might be too serious, too cruel a mistake."(7)

What a tame, spiritless position in the eyes of the Vindictives! A different opportunity to lay hold of public opinion he made the most of. And yet, here also, he spoke in that carefully guarded way, making sure he was not understood to say more than he meant, which most politicians would have pronounced over-scrupulous. A deputation of working men from New York were received at the White House. "The honorary membership in your association," said he, "as generously tendered, is gratefully accepted. . . . You comprehend, as your address shows, that the existing rebellion means more, and tends to more, than the perpetuation of African slavery-that it is, in fact, a war upon the rights of all working people."

After reviewing his own argument on this subject in the second message, he concluded:

"The views then expressed now remain unchanged, nor have I much to add. None are so deeply interested to resist the present rebellion as the working people. Let them beware of prejudices, working division and hostility among themselves. The most notable feature of a disturbance in your city last summer was the hanging of some working people by other working people. It should never be so. The strongest bond of human sympathy outside of the family relation, should be one uniting all working people, of all nations, and tongues, and kindreds. Nor should this lead to a war upon property, or the owners of property. Property is the fruit of labor; property is desirable; is a positive good in the world. That some should be rich shows that others may become rich, and hence is just encouragement to industry and enterprise. Let not him who is houseless pull down the house of another, but let him work diligently and build one for himself, thus by example assuming that his own shall be safe from violence when built."(8)

Lincoln was never more anxious than in this fateful spring when so many issues were hanging in the balance. Nevertheless, in all his relations with the world, his firm serenity was not broken. Though subject to depression so deep that his associates could not penetrate it, he kept it sternly to himself.(9) He showed the world a lighter, more graceful aspect than ever before. 'A precious record of his later mood is the account of him set down by Frank B. Carpenter, the portrait painter, a man of note in his day, who was an inmate of the White House during the first half of 1864. Carpenter was painting a picture of the "Signing of the Emancipation Proclamation." He saw Lincoln informally at all sorts of odd times, under all sorts of conditions. "All familiar with him," says Carpenter, "will remember the weary air which became habitual during his last years. This was more of the mind than of the body, and no rest and recreation which he allowed himself could relieve it. As he sometimes expressed it, 'no remedy seemed ever to reach the tired spot."(10)

A great shadow was darkening over him. He was more than ever convinced that he had not long to live. None the less, his poise became more conspicuous, his command over himself and others more distinguished, as the months raced past. In truth he had worked through a slow but profound transformation. The Lincoln of 1864 was so far removed from the Lincoln of Pigeon Creek-but logically, naturally removed, through the absorption of the outer man by the inner—that inevitably one thinks of Shakespeare's change "into something rich and strange."

Along with the weakness, the contradictions of his earlier self, there had also fallen away from him the mere grossness that had belonged to him as a peasant. Carpenter is unconditional that in six months of close intimacy, seeing him in company with all sorts of people, he never heard from Lincoln an offensive story. He quotes Seward and Lincoln's family physician to the same effect.(11)

The painter, like many others, was impressed by the tragic cast of his expression, despite the surface mirth.

"His complexion, at this time, was inclined to sallowness his eyes were bluish gray in color—always in deep shadow, however, from the upper lids which were unusually heavy (reminding me in this respect of Stuart's portrait of Washington) and the expression was remarkably pensive and tender, often inexpressibly sad, as if the reservoir of tears lay very near the surface—a fact proved not only by the response which accounts of suffering and sorrow invariably drew forth, but by circumstances which would ordinarily affect few men in his position." (12) As a result of the great strain to which he was subjected "his demeanor and disposition changed-so gradually that it would be impossible to say when the change began. . . . He continued always the same kindly, genial, and cordial spirit he had been at first; but the boisterous laughter became less frequent, year by year; the eye grew veiled by constant meditation on momentous subjects; the air of reserve and detachment from his surroundings increased. He aged with great rapidity." (13)

Every Saturday afternoon the Marine Band gave an open-air concert in the grounds of the White House. One afternoon Lincoln appeared upon the portico. There was instant applause and cries for a speech. "Bowing his thanks and excusing himself, he stepped back into the retirement of the circular parlor, remarking (to Carpenter) with a disappointed air, as he reclined on a sofa, 'I wish they would let me sit there quietly and enjoy the music.' His kindness to others was unfailing. It was this harassed statesman who came into the studio one day and found (Carpenter's) little boy of two summers playing on the floor. A member of the Cabinet was with him; but laying aside all restraint, he took the little fellow in his arms and they were soon on the best of terms." While his younger son "Tad" was with his mother on a journey, Lincoln telegraphed: "Tell Tad, father and the goats are well, especially the goats." (14) He found time one bright morning in May to review the Sunday-school children of Washington who filed past "cheering as if their very lives depended upon it," while Lincoln stood at a window "enjoying the scene... making pleasant remarks about a face that now and then struck him." (15) Carpenter told him that no other president except Washington had placed himself so securely in the hearts of the people. "Homely, honest, ungainly Lincoln," said Asa Gray, in a letter to Darwin, "is the representative man of the country."

However, two groups of men in his own party were sullenly opposed to him—the relentless Vindictives and certain irresponsible free lances who named themselves the "Radical Democracy." In the latter group, Fremont was the hero; Wendell Phillips, the greatest advocate. They were extremists in all things; many of them Agnostics. Furious against Lincoln, but unwilling to go along with the waiting policy of the Vindictives, these visionaries held a convention at Cleveland; voted down a resolution that recognized God as an ally; and nominated Fremont for the Presidency. A witty comment on the movement—one that greatly amused Lincoln—was the citation of a verse in first Samuel: "And every one that was in distress, and every one that was in debt, and every one that was discontented, gathered themselves unto him; and he became a captain over them; and there were with him about four hundred men."

If anything was needed to keep the dissatisfied Senators in the party ranks, it was this rash "bolt." Though Fremont had been their man in the past, he had thrown the fat in the fire by setting up an independent ticket. Silently, the wise opportunists of the Senate and all their henchmen, stood aside at the "Union convention"—which they called the Republican Convention—June seventh, and took their medicine.

There was no doubt of the tempest of enthusiasm among the majority of the delegates. It was a Lincoln ovation.

In responding the next day to a committee of congratulation, Lincoln said: "I am not insensible at all to the personal compliment there is in this, and yet I do not allow myself to believe that any but a small portion of it is to be appropriated as a personal compliment. . . . I do not allow myself to suppose that either the Convention or the (National Union) League have concluded to decide that I am the greatest or best man in America, but rather they have concluded that it is best not to swap horses while crossing the river, and have further concluded that I am not so poor a horse that they might not make a botch of it trying to swap."(16)

Carpenter records another sort of congratulation a few days later that brought out the graceful side of this man whom most people still supposed to be hopelessly awkward. It happened on a Saturday. Carpenter had invited friends to sit in his painting room and oversee the crowd while listening to the music. "Towards the close of the concert, the door suddenly opened, and the President came in, as he was in the habit of doing, alone. Mr. and Mrs. Cropsey had been presented to him in the course of the morning; and as he came forward, half hesitatingly, Mrs. C., who held a bunch of beautiful flowers in her hand, tripped forward playfully, and said: 'Allow me, Mr. President, to present you with a bouquet!' The situation was momentarily embarrassing; and I was puzzled to know how 'His Excellency' would get out of it. With no appearance of discomposure, he stooped down, took the flowers, and, looking from them into the sparkling eyes and radiant face of the lady, said, with a gallantry I was unprepared for 'Really, madam, if you give them to me, and they are mine, I think I can not possibly make so good use of them as to present them to you, in return!'"(17)

In gaining the nomination, Lincoln had not, as yet, attained security for his plans. Grant was still to be reckoned with. By a curious irony, the significance of his struggle with Lee during May, his steady advance by the left flank, had been misapprehended in the North. Looking at the map, the country saw that he was pushing southward, and again southward, on Virginia soil. McClellan, Pope, Burnside, Hooker, with them it had been:

"He who fights and runs away
May live to fight another day."

But Grant kept on. He struck Lee in the furious battle of the Wilderness, and moved to the left, farther south. "Victory!" cried the Northern newspapers, "Lee isn't able to stop him." The same delusion was repeated after Spottsylvania where the soldiers, knowing more of war than did the newspapers, pinned to their coats slips of paper bearing their names; identification of the bodies might be difficult. The popular mistake continued throughout that dreadful campaign. The Convention was still under the delusion of victory.

Lincoln also appears to have stood firm until the last minute in the common error. But the report of Grant's losses, more than the whole of Lee's army, filled him with horror. During these days, Carpenter had complete freedom of the President's office and "intently studied every line and shade of expression in that furrowed face. In repose, it was the saddest face I ever knew. There were days when I could scarcely look into it without crying. During the first week of the battles of the Wilderness he scarcely slept at all. Passing through the main hall of the domestic apartment on one of these days, I met him, clad in a long, morning wrapper, pacing back and forth a narrow passage leading to one of the windows, his hands behind him, great black rings under his eyes, his head bent forward upon his breast-altogether such a picture of the effects of sorrow, care, and anxiety as would have melted the hearts of the worst of his adversaries, who so mistakenly applied to him the epithets of tyrant and usurper."(18)

Despite these sufferings, Lincoln had not the slightest thought of giving way. Not in him any likeness to the sentimentalists, Greeley and all his crew, who were exultant martyrs when things were going right, and shrieking pacifists the moment anything went wrong. In one of the darkest moments of the year, he made a brief address at a Sanitary Fair in Philadelphia.

"Speaking of the present campaign," said he, "General Grant is reported to have said, 'I am going to fight it out on this line if it takes all summer.' This war has taken three years; it was begun or accepted upon the line of restoring the national authority over the whole national domain, and for the American people, as far as my knowledge enables me to speak, I say we are going through on this line if it takes three years more."(19) He made no attempt to affect Grant's course. He had put him in supreme command and would leave everything to his judgment. And then came the colossal blunder at Cold Harbor. Grant stood again where McClellan had stood two years before. He stood there defeated. He could think of nothing to do but just what McClellan had wanted to do—abandon the immediate enterprise, make a great detour to the Southwest, and start a new campaign on a different plan. Two years with all their terrible disasters, and this was all that had come of it! Practically no gain, and a death-roll that staggered the nation. A wail went over the North. After all, was the war hopeless? Was Lee invincible? Was the best of the Northern manhood perishing to no result?

Greeley, perhaps the most hysterical man of genius America has produced, made his paper the organ of the wail. He wrote frantic appeals to the government to cease fighting, do what could be done by negotiation, and if nothing could be done—at least, stop "these rivers of human blood."

The Vindictives saw their opportunity. They would capitalize the wail. The President should be dealt with yet.

XXX
THE PRESIDENT VERSUS
THE VINDICTIVES

Now that the Vindictives had made up their minds to fight, an occasion was at their hands. Virtually, they declared war on the President by refusing to recognize a State government which he had set up in Arkansas. Congress would not admit Senators or Representatives from the Reconstructed State. But on this issue, Lincoln was as resolute to fight to a finish as were any of his detractors. He wrote to General Steele, commanding in Arkansas:

"I understand that Congress declines to admit to seats the persons sent as Senators and Representatives from Arkansas. These persons apprehend that, in consequence, you may not support the new State government there as you otherwise would. My wish is that you give that government and the people there the same support and protection that you would if the members had been admitted, because in no event, nor in any view of the case, can this do harm, while it will be the best you can do toward suppressing the rebellion."(1)

The same day Chase resigned. The reason he assigned was, again, the squabble over patronage. He had insisted on an appointment of which the President disapproved. Exactly what moved him may be questioned. Chase never gave his complete confidence, not even to his diary. Whether he thought that the Vindictives would now take him up as a rival of Lincoln, continues doubtful. Many men were staggered by his action. Crittenden, the Registrar of the Treasury, was thrown into a panic. "Mr. President," said he, "this is worse than another Bull Run. Pray let me go to Secretary Chase and see if I can not induce him to withdraw his resignation. Its acceptance now might cause a financial panic." But Lincoln was in a fighting mood. "Chase thinks he has become indispensable to the country," he told Chittenden.

"He also thinks he ought to be President; he has no doubt whatever about that. He is an able financier, a great statesman, and at the bottom a patriot . . he is never perfectly happy unless he is thoroughly miserable and able to make everybody else just as uncomfortable as he is himself. . He is either determined to annoy me or that I shall pat him on the shoulder and coax him to stay. I don't think I ought to do it. I will take him at his word."(2)

He accepted the resignation in a note that was almost curt: "Of all I have said in commendation of your ability and fidelity, I have nothing to unsay; and yet you and I have reached a point of mutual embarrassment in our official relations which it seems can not be overcome or longer sustained consistently with the public service."(3)

The selection of a successor to Chase was no easy matter. The Vindictives were the leaders of the moment. What if they persuaded the Senate not to confirm Lincoln's choice of Secretary. "I never saw the President," says Carpenter, "under so much excitement as on the day following this event" On the night of July first, Lincoln lay awake debating with himself the merits of various candidates. At length, he selected his man and immediately went to sleep.

"The next morning he went to his office and wrote the nomination. John Hay, the assistant private secretary, had taken it from the President on his way to the Capitol, when he encountered Senator Fessenden upon the threshold of the room. As chairman of the Finance Committee, he also had passed an anxious night, and called this early to consult with the President, and offer some suggestions. After a few moments' conversation, Mr. Lincoln turned to him with a smile and said: 'I am obliged to you, Fessenden, but the fact is, I have just sent your own name to the Senate for Secretary of the Treasury. Hay had just received the nomination from my hand as you entered.' Mr. Fessenden was taken completely by surprise, and, very much agitated, protested his inability to accept the position. The state of his health, he said, if no other consideration, made it impossible. Mr. Lincoln would not accept the refusal as final. He very justly felt that with Mr. Fessenden's experience and known ability at the head of the Finance Committee, his acceptance would go far toward reestablishing a feeling of security. He said to him, very earnestly, 'Fessenden, the Lord has not deserted me thus far, and He is not going to now — you must accept!'

"They separated, the Senator in great anxiety of mind. Throughout the day, Mr. Lincoln urged almost all who called to go and see Mr. Fessenden, and press upon him the duty of accepting. Among these, was a delegation of New York bankers, who, in the name of the banking community, expressed their satisfaction at the nomination. This was especially gratifying to the President; and in the strongest manner, he entreated them to 'see Mr. Fessenden and assure him of their support.'"(4)

In justification of his choice, Lincoln said to Hay: — "Thinking over the matter, two or three points occurred to me: first his thorough acquaintance with the business; as chairman of the Senate Committee of Finance, he knows as much of this special subject as Mr. Chase; he possesses a national reputation and the confidence of the country; he is a Radical without the petulance and fretfulness of many radicals."(5) In other words, though he was not at heart one of them, he stood for the moment so close to the Vindictives that they would not make an issue on his confirmation.

Lincoln had scored a point in his game with the Vindictives. But the point was of little value. The game's real concern was that Reconstruction Bill which was now before the Senate with Wade as its particular sponsor. The great twin brethren of the Vindictives were Wade and Chandler. Both were furious for the passage of the bill. "The Executive," said Wade angrily, "ought not to be allowed to handle this great question of his own liking."

On the last day of the session, Lincoln was in the President's room at the Capitol Signing bills. The Reconstruction Bill, duly passed by both Houses, was brought to him. Several Senators, friends of the bill and deeply anxious, had come into the President's room hoping to see him affix his signature. To their horror, he merely glanced at the bill and laid it aside. Chandler, who was watching him, bluntly demanded what he meant to do. "This bill," said Lincoln, "has been placed before me a few minutes before Congress adjourns. It is a matter of too much importance to be swallowed in that way."

"If it is vetoed," said Chandler, whose anger was mounting, "it will damage us fearfully in the Northwest. The important point is that one prohibiting slavery in the Reconstructed States."

"That is the point," replied the President, "on which I doubt the authority of Congress to act."

"It is no more than you have done yourself," retorted Chandler.

Lincoln turned to him and said quietly but with finality: "I conceive that I may in an emergency do things on military grounds which can not constitutionally be done by Congress."

Chandler angrily left the room. To those who remained, Lincoln added: "I do not see how any of us now can deny and contradict what we have always said, that Congress has no constitutional power over slavery in the States."(6)

In a way, he was begging the question. The real issue was not how a State should be constitutionally reconstructed, but which, President or Congress, had a right to assume dictatorial power. At last the true Vindictive issue, lured out of their arms by the Democrats, had escaped like a bird from a snare and was fluttering home. Here was the old issue of the war powers in a new form that it was safe for them to press. And the President had squarely defied them. It was civil war inside the Union party. And for both sides, President and Vindictives, there could now be nothing but rule or ruin.

In this crisis of factional politics, Lincoln was unmoved, self-contained, lofty, deliberate. "If they (the Vindictives) choose to make a point on this, I do not doubt that they can do harm. They have never been friendly to me. At all events, I must keep some consciousness of being somewhere near right. I must keep some standard of principle fixed within myself."

XXXI
A MENACING PAUSE

Lincoln had now reached his final stature. In contact with the world his note was an inscrutable serenity. The jokes which he continued to tell were but transitory glimmerings. They crossed the surface of his mood like quick flickers of golden light on a stormy March day, — witnesses that the sun would yet prevail, — in a forest-among mountain shadows. Or, they were lightning glimmers in a night sky; they revealed, they did not dispel, the dark beyond. Over all his close associates his personal ascendency was complete. Now that Chase was gone, the last callous spot in the Cabinet had been amputated. Even Stanton, once so domineering, so difficult to manage, had become as clay in his hands.

But Lincoln never used power for its own sake, never abused his ascendency. Always he got his end if he could without evoking the note of command. He would go to surprising lengths to avoid appearing peremptory. A typical remark was his smiling reply to a Congressman whom he had armed with a note to the Secretary, who had returned aghast, the Secretary having refused to comply with the President's request and having decorated his refusal with extraordinary language.

"Did Stanton say I was a damned fool?" asked Lincoln. "Then I dare say I must be one, for Stanton is generally right and he always says what he means."

Nevertheless, the time had come when Lincoln had only to say the word and Stanton, no matter how fierce his temper might' be, would acknowledge his master. General Fry, the Provost Marshal, witnessed a scene between them which is a curious commentary on the transformation of the Stanton of 1862. Lincoln had issued an order relative to the disposition of certain recruits. Stanton protested that it was unwarranted, that he would not put it into effect. The Provost Marshal was called in and asked to state at length all the facts involved. When he had finished Stanton broke out excitedly —

"'Now, Mr. President, those are the facts and you must see that your order can not be executed.'

"Lincoln sat upon a sofa with his legs crossed and did not say a word until the Secretary's last remark. Then he said in a somewhat positive tone, 'Mr. Secretary, I reckon you'll have to execute the order.'

"Stanton replied with asperity, 'Mr. President, I can not do it. The order is an improper one, and I can not execute it'."

Lincoln fixed his eye upon Stanton, and in a firm voice with an accent that clearly showed his determination, he said, "Mr. Secretary, it will have to be done."(1)

At this point, General Fry discreetly left the room. A few moments later, he received instructions from Stanton to execute the President's order.

In a public matter in the June of 1864 Lincoln gave a demonstration of his original way of doing things. It displayed his final serenity in such unexpected fashion that no routine politician, no dealer in the catchwords of statecraft, could understand it. Since that grim joke, the deportation of Vallandigham, the Copperhead leader had not had happy time. The Confederacy did not want him. He had made his way to Canada. Thence, in the spring of 1864 he served notice on his country that he would perform a dramatic Part, play the role of a willing martyr—in a word, come home and defy the government to do its worst. He came. But Lincoln did nothing. The American sense of humor did the rest. If Vallandigham had not advertised a theatrical exploit, ignoring him might have been dangerous. But Lincoln knew his people. When the show did not come off, Vallandigham was transformed in an instant from a martyr to an anticlimax. Though he went busily to work, though he lived to attend the Democratic National Convention and to write the resolution that was the heart of its platform, his tale was told.

Turning from Vallandigham, partly in amusement, partly in contempt, Lincoln grappled with the problem of reinforcing the army. Since the Spring of 1863 the wastage of the army had been replaced by conscription. But the system had not worked well. It contained a fatal provision. A drafted man might escape service by paying three hundred dollars. Both the Secretary of War and the Provost Marshal had urged the abolition of this detail. Lincoln had communicated their arguments to Congress with his approval and a new law had been drawn up accordingly. Nevertheless, late in June, the House amended it by restoring the privilege of commuting service for money.(2) Lincoln bestirred himself. The next day he called together the Republican members of the House. "With a sad, mysterious light in his melancholy eyes, as if they were familiar with things hidden from mortals" he urged the Congressmen to reconsider their action. The time of three hundred eighty thousand soldiers would expire in October. He must have half a million to take their places. A Congressman objected that elections were approaching; that the rigorous law he proposed would be intensely unpopular; that it might mean the defeat, at the polls, of many Republican Representatives; it might even mean the President's defeat. He replied that he had thought of all that.

"My election is not necessary; I must put down the rebellion; I must have five hundred thousand more men."(3)

He raised the timid politicians to his own level, inspired them with new courage. Two days later a struggle began in the House for carrying out Lincoln's purpose. On the last day of the session along with the offensive Reconstruction Bill, he received the new Enrollment Act which provided that "no payment of money shall be accepted or received by the Government as commutation to release any enrolled or drafted man from personal obligation to per-form military service."

Against this inflexible determination to fight to a finish, this indifference to the political consequences of his determination, Lincoln beheld arising like a portentous specter, a fury of pacifism. It found expression in Greeley. Always the swift victim of his own affrighted hope, Greeley had persuaded himself that both North and South had lost heart for the war; that there was needed only a moving appeal, and they would throw down their arms and the millennium would come. Furthermore, on the flimsiest sort of evidence, he had fallen into a trap designed to place the Northern government in the attitude of suing for peace. He wrote to Lincoln demanding that he send an agent to confer with certain Confederate officials who were reported to be then in Canada; he also suggested terms of peace.(4) Greeley's terms were entirely acceptable to Lincoln; but he had no faith in the Canadian mare's nest. However, he decided to give Greeley the utmost benefit of the doubt, and also to teach him a lesson. He commissioned Greeley himself to proceed to Canada, there to discover "if there is or is not anything in the affair." He wrote to him, "I not only intend a sincere effort for peace, but I intend that you shall be a personal witness that it is made."(5)

Greeley, who did not want to have any responsibility for anything that might ensue, whose joy was to storm and to find fault, accepted the duty he could not well refuse, and set out in a bad humor.

Meanwhile two other men had conceived an undertaking somewhat analogous but in a temper widely different. These were Colonel Jaquess, a clergyman turned soldier, a man of high simplicity of character, and J. R. Gilmore, a writer, known by the pen name of Edmund Kirke. Jaquess had told Gilmore of information he had received from friends in the Confederacy; he was convinced that nothing would induce the Confederate government to consider any terms of peace that embraced reunion, whether with or without emancipation. "It at once occurred to me," says Gilmore, "that if this declaration could be got in such a manner that it could be given to the public, it would, if scattered broadcast over the North, destroy the peace-party and reelect Mr. Lincoln." Gilmore went to Washington and obtained an interview with the President. He assured him—and he was a newspaper correspondent whose experience was worth considering—that the new pacifism, the incipient "peace party," was schooling the country in the belief that an offer of liberal terms would be followed by a Southern surrender. The masses wanted peace on any terms that would preserve the Union; and the Democrats were going to tell them in the next election that Lincoln could save the Union by negotiation, if he would. Unless the popular mind were disabused of this fictitious hope, the Democrats would prevail and the Union would collapse. But if an offer to negotiate should be made, and if "Davis should refuse to negotiate—as he probably would, except on the basis of Southern independence—that fact alone would reunite the North, reelect Lincoln, and thus save the Union."(6)

"Then," said Lincoln, "you would fight the devil with fire. You would get that declaration from Davis and use it against him."

Gilmore defended himself by proposing to offer extremely liberal terms. There was a pause in the conversation. Lincoln who was seated at his desk "leaned slightly forward looking directly into (Gilmore's) eyes, but with an absent, far-away gaze as if unconscious of (his) presence." Suddenly, relapsing into his usual badinage, he said, "God selects His own instruments and some times they are queer ones: for instance, He chose me to see the ship of state through a great crisis."(7) He went on to say that Gilmore and Jaquess might be the very men to serve a great purpose at this moment. Gilmore knew the world; and anybody could see at a glance that Jaquess never told anything that wasn't true. If they would go to Richmond on their own responsibility, make it plain to President Davis that they were not official agents, even taking the chance of arrest and imprisonment, they might go. This condition was accepted. Lincoln went on to say that no advantage should be taken of Mr. Davis; that nothing should be proposed which if accepted would not be made good. After considerable further discussion he drew up a memorandum of the terms upon which he would consent to peace. There were seven items:

1. The immediate dissolution of the armies.

2. The abolition of slavery.

3. A general amnesty.

4. The Seceded States to resume their functions as states in the Union as if no secession had taken place.

5. Four hundred million dollars to be appropriated by Congress as compensation for loss of slave property; no slaveholder, however, to receive more than one-half the former value of his slaves.

6. A national convention to be called for readjustment of all other difficulties.

7. It to be understood that the purpose of negotiation was a full restoration of the Union as of old.(8)

Gilmore and Jaquess might say to Davis that they had private but sure knowledge that the President of the United States would agree to peace on these terms. Thus provided, they set forth.

Lincoln's thoughts were speedily claimed by an event which had no Suggestion of peace. At no time since Jackson threw the government into a panic in the spring of 1862, had Washington been in danger of capture. Now, briefly, it appeared to be at the mercy of General Early. In the last act of a daring raid above the Potomac, he came sweeping down on Washington from the North. As Grant was now the active commander-in-chief, responsible for all the Northern armies, Lincoln with a fatalistic calm made no move to take the capital out of his hands. When Early was known to be headed toward Washington, Lincoln drove out as usual to spend the night at the Soldiers' Home beyond the fortifications. Stanton, in whom there was a reminiscence at least of the hysterical Secretary of 1862, sent after him post haste and insisted on his returning. The next day, the eleventh of July, 1864, Washington was invested by the Confederate forces. There was sharp firing in front of several forts. Lincoln—and for that matter, Mrs. Lincoln also—made a tour of the defenses. While Fort Stevens was under fire, he stood on the parapet, "apparently unconscious of danger, watching with that grave and passive countenance the progress of the fight, amid the whizzing bullets of the sharp shooters, until an officer fell mortally wounded within three feet of him, and General Wright peremptorily represented to him the needless risk he was running." Hay recorded in his diary "the President in good feather this evening . . . not concerned about Washington's safety . . . only thought, can we bag or destroy the force in our front." He was much disappointed when Early eluded the forces which Grant hurried to the Capitol. Mrs. Lincoln was outspoken to the same effect. The doughty little lady had also been under fire, her temper being every whit as bold as her husband's. When Stanton with a monumental playfulness proposed to have her portrait painted in a commanding attitude on the parapet of Fort

Stevens, she gave him the freedom of her tongue, because of the inadequacy of his department.(9)

This incident had its aftermath. A country-place belonging to the Postmaster General had been laid waste. Its owner thought that the responsibility for permitting Early to come so near to Washington fell chiefly on General Halleck. He made some sharp criticisms which became public the General flew into a rage and wrote to the Secretary of War: "The Postmaster General ought to be dismissed by the President from the Cabinet." Stanton handed his letter to the President, from whom the next day the General received this note: "Whether the remarks were made I do not know, nor do I suppose such knowledge is necessary to a correct response. If they were made, I do not approve them; and yet, under the circumstances, I would not dismiss a member of the Cabinet therefor. I do not consider what may have been hastily said in a moment of vexation at so severe a loss is sufficient ground for so grave a step. Besides this, truth is generally the best vindication against slander. I propose continuing to be myself the judge as to when a member of the Cabinet shall be dismissed." Lincoln spoke of the affair at his next conference with his Ministers. "I must, myself, be the judge," said he, "how long to retain in and when to remove any of you from his position. It would greatly pain me to discover any of you endeavoring to procure another's removal, or in any way to prejudice him before the public. Such an endeavor would be a wrong to me, and much worse, a wrong to the country. My wish is that on this subject no remark be made nor question asked by any of you, here or elsewhere, now or hereafter."(10)

Not yet had anything resulted either from the Canadian mission of Greeley, or from the Richmond adventure of Gilmore and Jaquess. There was a singular ominous pause in events. Lincoln could not be blind to the storm signals that had attended the close of Congress. What were the Vindictives about? As yet they had made no Sign. But it was incredible that they could pass over his defiance without a return blow. When would it come? What would it be?

He spent his nights at the Soldiers' Home. As a rule, his family were with him. Sometimes, however, Mrs. Lincoln and his sons would be absent and his only companion was one of the ardent young secretaries. Then he would indulge in reading Shakespeare aloud, it might be with such forgetfulness of time that only the nodding of the tired young head recalled him to himself and brought the reading to an end. A visitor has left this charming picture of Lincoln at the Soldiers' Home in the sad sweetness of a summer night:

"The Soldiers' Home is a few miles out of Washington on the Maryland side. It is situated on a beautiful wooded hill, which you ascend by a winding path, shaded on both sides by wide-spread branches, forming a green arcade above you. When you reach the top you stand between two mansions, large, handsome and substantial, but with nothing about them to indicate the character of either. That on the left is the Presidential country house; that directly before you, is the 'Rest,' for soldiers who are too old for further service . . . In the graveyard near at hand there are numberless graves — some without a spear of grass to hide their newness — that hold the bodies of volunteers.

"While we stood in the soft evening air, watching the faint trembling of the long tendrils of waving willow, and feeling the dewy coolness that was flung out by the old oaks above us, Mr. Lincoln joined us, and stood silent, too, taking in the scene.

"'How sleep the brave who sink to rest, By all their country's wishes blest,'' he said, softly. . .

"Around the 'Home' grows every variety of tree, particularly of the evergreen class. Their branches brushed into the carriage as we passed along, and left us with that pleasant woody smell belonging to leaves. One of the ladies, catching a bit of green from one of these intruding branches, said it was cedar, and another thought it spruce.

"'Let me discourse on a theme I understand,' said the President. 'I know all about trees in right of being a backwoodsman. I'll show you the difference between spruce, pine and cedar, and this shred of green, which is neither one nor the other, but a kind of illegitimate cypress. He then proceeded to gather specimens of each, and explain the distinctive formation of foliage belonging to each."(11)

Those summer nights of July, 1864, had many secrets which the tired President musing in the shadows of the giant trees or finding solace with the greatest of earthly minds would have given much to know. How were Gilmore and Jaquess faring? What was really afoot in Canada? And that unnatural silence of the Vindictives, what did that mean? And the two great armies, Grant's in Virginia, Sherman's in Georgia, was there never to be stirring news of either of these? The hush of the moment, the atmosphere of suspense that seemed to envelop him, it was just what had always for his imagination had such strange charm in the stories of fated men. He turned again to Macbeth, or to Richard II, or to Hamlet. Shakespeare, too, understood these mysterious pauses — who better!

The sense of the impending was strengthened by the alarms of some of his best friends. They besought him to abandon his avowed purpose to call for a draft of half a million under the new Enrollment Act. Many voices joined the one chorus: the country is on the verge of despair; you will wreck the cause by demanding another colossal sacrifice. But he would not listen. When, in desperation, they struck precisely the wrong note, and hinted at the ruin of his political prospects, he had his calm reply: "it matters not what becomes of me. We must have men. If I go down, I intend to go like the Cumberland, with my colors flying."(12)

Thus the days passed until the eighteenth of July. Meanwhile the irresponsible Greeley had made a sad mess of his Canadian adventure. Though Lincoln had given him definite instructions, requiring him to negotiate only with agents who could produce written authority from Davis, and who would treat on the basis of restoration of the Union and abandonment of slavery, Greeley ignored both these unconditional requirements.(13) He had found the Confederate agents at Niagara. They had no credentials. Nevertheless, he invited them to come to Washington and open negotiations. Of the President's two conditions, he said not a word. This was just what the agents wanted. It could easily be twisted into the semblance of an attempt by Lincoln to sue for peace. They accepted the invitation. Greeley telegraphed to Lincoln reporting what he had done. Of course, it was plain that he had misrepresented Lincoln; that he had far exceeded his authority; and that his perverse unfaithfulness must be repudiated. On July eighteenth, Hay set out for Niagara with this paper in Lincoln's handwriting.(14)

"To whom it may concern: Any proposition which embraces the restoration of peace, the integrity of the whole Union, and the abandonment of slavery, and which comes by and with an authority that can control the armies now at war against the United States, will be received and considered by the executive government of the United States, and will be met by liberal terms on other substantial and collateral points and the bearer or bearers thereof shall have, safe conduct both ways. ABRAHAM LINCOLN."

This was the end of the negotiation. The agents could not accept these terms. Immediately, they published a version of what had happened: they had been invited to come to Washington; subsequently, conditions had been imposed which made it impossible for them to accept Was not the conclusion plain? The Washington government was trying to open negotiations but it was also in the fear of its own supporters playing craftily a double game. These astute diplomats saw that there was a psychological crisis in the North. By adding to the confusion of the hour they had well served their cause. Greeley's fiasco was susceptible of a double interpretation. To the pacifists it meant that the government, whatever may have been intended at the start, had ended by setting impossible conditions of peace. To the supporters of the war, it meant that whatever were the last thoughts of the government, it had for a time contemplated peace without any conditions at all. Lincoln was severely condemned, Greeley was ridiculed, by both groups of interpreters. Why did not Greeley come out bravely and tell the truth? Why did he not confess that he had suppressed Lincoln's first set of instructions; that it was he, on his own responsibility, who had led the Confederate agents astray; that he, not Lincoln was solely to blame for the false impression that was now being used so adroitly to injure the President? Lincoln proposed to publish their correspondence, but made a condition that was characteristic. Greeley's letters rang with cries of despair. He was by far the most influential Northern editor. Lincoln asked him to strike out these hopeless passages. Greeley refused. The correspondence must be published entire or not at all. Lincoln suppressed it. He let the blame of himself go on; and he said nothing in extenuation.(15)

He took some consolation in a "card" that appeared in the Boston Transcript, July 22. It gave a brief account of the adventure of Gilmore and Jaquess, and stated the answer given to them by the President of the Confederacy. That answer, as restated by the Confederate Secretary of State, was: "he had no authority to receive proposals for negotiations except by virtue of his office as President of an independent Confederacy and on this basis alone must proposals be made to him."(16)

There was another circumstance that may well have been Lincoln's consolation in this tangle of cross-purposes. Only boldness could extricate him from the mesh of his difficulties. The mesh was destined to grow more and more of a snare; his boldness was to grow with his danger. He struck the note that was to rule his conduct thereafter, when, on the day he sent the final instructions to Greeley, in defiance of his timid advisers, he issued a proclamation calling for a new draft of half a million men.(17)

XXXII
THE AUGUST CONSPIRACY

Though the Vindictives kept a stealthy silence during July, they were sharpening their claws and preparing for a tiger spring whenever the psychological moment should arrive. Those two who had had charge of the Reconstruction Bill prepared a paper, in some ways the most singular paper of the war period, which has established itself in our history as the Wade-Davis Manifesto. This was to be the deadly shot that should unmask the Vindictive batteries, bring their war upon the President out of the shadows into the open.

Greeley's fiasco and Greeley's mortification both played into their hands. The fiasco contributed to depress still more the despairing North. By this time, there was general appreciation of the immensity of Grant's failure, not only at Cold Harbor, but in the subsequent slaughter of the futile assault upon Petersburg. We have the word of a member of the Committee that the despair over Grant translated itself into blame of the Administration.(1) The Draft Proclamation; the swiftly traveling report that the government had wilfully brought the peace negotiations to a stand-still; the continued cry that the war was hopeless; all these produced, about the first of August, an emotional crisis—just the sort of occasion for which Lincoln's enemies were waiting.

Then, too, there was Greeley's mortification. The Administration papers made him a target for sarcasm. The Times set the pace with scornful demands for "No more back door diplomacy."(2) Greeley answered in a rage. He permitted himself to imply that the President originated the Niagara negotiation and that Greeley "reluctantly" became a party to it. That "reluctantly" was the truth, in a sense, but how falsely true! Wade and Davis had him where they wanted him. On the fifth of August, The Tribune printed their manifesto. It was an appeal to "the supporters of the Administration . . . to check the encroachment of the Executive on the authority of Congress, and to require it to confine itself to its proper sphere." It insinuated the basest motives for the President's interest in reconstruction, and for rejecting their own bill. "The President by preventing this bill from becoming a law, holds the electoral votes of the Rebel States at the dictation of his personal ambition. . . . If electors for President be allowed to be chosen in either of those States, a sinister light will be cast on the motives which induced the President to 'hold for naught' the will of Congress rather than his government in Louisiana and Arkansas."

After a long discussion of his whole course with regard to reconstruction, having heaped abuse upon him with shocking liberality, the Manifesto concluded:

"Such are the fruits of this rash and fatal act of the President—a blow at the friends of the Administration, at the rights of humanity, and at the principles of Republican government The President has greatly presumed on the forbearance which the supporters of his Administration have so long practised in view of the arduous conflict in which we are engaged, and the reckless ferocity of our political opponents. But he must understand that our support is of a 'cause' and not of a man; that the authority of Congress is paramount and must be respected; that the whole body of the Union men in Congress will not submit to be impeached by him of rash and unconstitutional legislation; and if he wishes our support he must confine him-self to his executive duties—to obey and execute, not make the laws— to suppress by arms, armed rebellion, and leave political reorganization to Congress. If the supporters of the government fail to insist on this they become responsible for the usurpations they fail to rebuke and are justly liable to the indignation of the people whose rights and security, committed to their keeping, they sacrifice. Let them consider the remedy of these usurpations, and, having found it, fearlessly execute it."

To these incredible charges, Lincoln made no reply. He knew, what some statesmen never appear to know, the times when one should risk all upon that French proverb, "who excuses, accuses." However, he made his futile attempt to bring Greeley to reason, to induce him to tell the truth about Niagara without confessing to the country the full measure of the despair that had inspired his course. When Greeley refused to do so, Lincoln turned to other matters, to preparation for the draft, and grimly left the politicians to do their worst. They went about it with zest. Their reliance was chiefly their power to infect the type of party man who is easily swept from his moorings by the cry that the party is in danger, that sacrifices must be made to preserve the party unity, that otherwise the party will go to pieces. By the middle of August, six weeks after Lincoln's defiance of them on the fourth of July, they were in high feather, convinced that most things were coming their way. American politicians have not always shown an ability to read clearly the American people. Whether the politicians were in error on August 14, 1864, and again on August twenty-third, two dates that were turning points, is a matter of debate to this day. As to August fourteenth, they have this, at least, in their defense. The country had no political observer more keen than the Scotch free lance who edited The New York Herald. It was Bennett's editorial view that Lincoln would do well to make a virtue of necessity and withdraw his candidacy because "the dissatisfaction which had long been felt by the great body of American citizens has spread even to his own supporters."(3) Confident that a great reaction against Lincoln was sweeping the country, that the Manifesto had been launched in the very nick of time, a meeting of conspirators was held in New York, at the house of David Dudley Field, August fourteenth. Though Wade was now at his home in Ohio, Davis was present. So was Greeley. It was decided to ask Lincoln to withdraw. Four days afterward, a "call" was drawn up and sent out confidentially near and far to be signed by prominent politicians. The "call" was craftily worded. It summoned a new Union Convention to meet in Cincinnati, September twenty-eighth, for the purpose either of rousing the party to whole-hearted support of Lincoln, or of uniting all factions on some new candidate. Greeley who could not attend the committee which drew up the "call" wrote that "Lincoln is already beaten."(4)

Meanwhile, the infection of dismay had spread fast among the Lincoln managers. Even before the meeting of the conspirators on the fourteenth, Weed told the President that he could not be reelected.(5)

One of his bravest supporters, Washburne, came to the dismal conclusion that "were an election to be held now in Illinois, we should be beaten." Cameron, who had returned from Russia and was working hard for Lincoln in Pennsylvania, was equally discouraging. So was Governor Morton in Indiana. From all his "stanchest friends," wrote his chief manager to Lincoln, "there was but one report. The tide is setting strongly against us."(6)

Lincoln's managers believed that the great host of free voters who are the balance of power in American politics, were going in a drove toward the camp of the Democrats. It was the business of the managers to determine which one, or which ones, among the voices of discontent, represented truly this controlling body of voters. They thought they knew. Two cries, at least, that rang loud out of the Babel of the hour, should be heeded. One of these harked back to Niagara. In the anxious ears of the managers it dinned this charge: "the Administration prevented negotiations for peace by tying together two demands, the Union must be restored and slavery must be abolished; if Lincoln had left out slavery, he could have had peace in a restored Union." It was ridiculous, as every one who had not gone off his head knew. But so many had gone off their heads. And some of Lincoln's friends were meeting this cry in a way that was raising up other enemies of a different sort. Even so faithful a friend as Raymond, editor of The Times and Chairman of the Republican National Executive Committee, labored hard in print to prove that because Lincoln said he "would consider terms that embraced the integrity of the Union and the abandonment of slavery, he did not say that he would not receive them unless they embraced both these conditions."(7) What would Sumner and all the Abolitionists say to that? As party strategy, in the moment when the old Vindictive Coalition seemed on the highroad to complete revival, was that exactly the tune to sing? Then too there was the other cry that also made a fearful ringing in the ears of the much alarmed Executive Committee. There was wild talk in the air of an armistice. The hysteric Greeley had put it into a personal letter to Lincoln. "I know that nine-tenths of the whole American people, North and South, are anxious for peace — peace on any terms — and are utterly sick of human slaughter and devastation. I know that, to the general eye, it now seems that the Rebels are anxious to negotiate and that we repulse their advances. . . . I beg you, I implore you to inaugurate or invite proposals for peace forthwith. And in case peace can not now be made, consent to an armistice for one year, each party to retain all it now holds, but the Rebel ports to be opened. Meantime, let a national convention be held and there will surely be no war at all events."(8)

This armistice movement was industriously advertised in the Democratic papers. It was helped along by the Washington correspondent of The Herald who sowed broadcast the most improbable stories with regard to it. Today, Secretary Fessenden was a convert to the idea; another day, Senator Wilson had taken it up; again, the President, himself, was for an armistice.(9)

A great many things came swiftly to a head within a few days before or after the twentieth of August. Every day or two, rumor took a new turn; or some startling new alignment was glimpsed; and every one reacted to the news after his kind. And always the feverish question, what is the strength of the faction that approves this? Or, how far will this go toward creating a new element in the political kaleidoscope? About the twentieth of August, Jaquess and Gilmore threw a splashing stone into these troubled waters. They published in The Atlantic a full account of their interview with Davis, who, in the clearest, most unfaltering way had told them that the Southerners were fighting for independence and for nothing else; that no compromise over slavery; nothing but the recognition of the Confederacy as a separate nation would induce them to put up their bright swords. As Lincoln subsequently, in his perfect clarity of speech, represented Davis: "He would accept nothing short of severance of the Union — precisely what we will not and can not give.... He does not attempt to deceive us. He affords us no excuse to deceive ourselves. He can not voluntarily reaccept the Union; we can not voluntarily yield it"(10)

Whether without the intrusion of Jaquess and Gilmore, the Executive Committee would have come to the conclusion they now reached, is a mere speculation. They thought they were at the point of desperation. They thought they saw a way out, a way that reminds one of Jaquess and Gilmore. On the twenty-second, Raymond sent that letter to Lincoln about "the tide setting strongly against us." He also proposed the Committee's way of escape: nothing but to offer peace to Davis "on the sole condition of acknowledging the supremacy of the Constitution—all other questions to be settled in a convention of the people of all the States."(11) He assumed the offer would be rejected. Thus the clamor for negotiation would be met and brought to naught. Having sent off his letter, Raymond got his committee together and started for Washington for a council of desperation.

And this brings us to the twenty-third of August. On that day, pondering Raymond's letter, Lincoln took thought with himself what he should say to the Executive Committee. A mere opportunist would have met the situation with some insincere proposal, by the formulation of terms that would have certainly been rejected. We have seen how Lincoln reasoned in such a connection when he drew up the memorandum for Jaquess and Gilmore. His present problem involved nothing of this sort. What he was thinking out was how best to induce the committee to accept his own attitude; to become for the moment believers in destiny; to nail their colors; turn their backs as he was doing on these devices of diplomacy; and as to the rest-permit to heaven.

Whatever his managers might think, the serious matter in Lincoln's mind, that twenty-third of August, was the draft. And back of the draft, a tremendous matter which probably none of them at the time appreciated. Assuming that they were right in their political forecast, assuming that he was not to be reelected, what did it signify? For him, there was but one answer: that he had only five months in which to end the war. And with the tide running strong against him, what could he do? But one thing: use the war powers while they remained in his hands in every conceivable way that might force a conclusion on the field of battle. He recorded his determination. A Cabinet meeting was held on the twenty-third. Lincoln handed his Ministers a folded paper and asked them to write their initials on the back. At the time he gave them no intimation what the paper contained. It was the following memorandum: "This morning, as for some days past, it seems exceedingly probable that this Administration will not be reelected.

Then it will be my duty to so cooperate with the President elect as to save the Union between the election and the inauguration, as he will have secured his election on such ground that he can not possibly save it afterward."(12)

He took into his confidence "the stronger half of the Cabinet, Seward, Stanton and Fessenden," and together they assaulted the Committee.(13) It was a reception amazingly different from what had been expected. Instead of terrified party diplomats shaking in their shoes, trying to face all points at once, morbid over possible political defeats in every quarter, they found what may have seemed to them a man in a dream; one who was intensely sad, but who gave no suggestion of panic, no solicitude about his own fate, no doubt of his ultimate victory. Their practical astuteness was disarmed by that higher astuteness attained only by peculiar minds which can discern through some sure interior test the rare moment when it is the part of wisdom not to be astute at all.

Backed by those strong Ministers, all entirely under his influence, Lincoln fully persuaded the Committee that at this moment, any overture for peace would be the worst of strategic blunders, "would be worse than losing the presidential contest—it would be ignominiously surrendering it in advance."(14)

Lincoln won a complete spiritual victory over the Committee. These dispirited men, who had come to Washington to beg for a policy of negotiation, went away in such a different temper that Bennett's Washington correspondent jeered in print at the "silly report" of their having assembled to discuss peace.(15) Obviously, they had merely held a meeting of the Executive Committee. The Tribune correspondent telegraphed that they were confident of Lincoln's reelection.(16)

On the day following the conference with Lincoln, The Times announced: "You may rest assured that all reports attributing to the government any movements looking toward negotiations for peace at present are utterly without foundation. . . . The government has not entertained or discussed the project of proposing an armistice with the Rebels nor has it any intention of sending commissioners to Richmond . . . its sole and undivided purpose is to prosecute the war until the rebellion is quelled. . . ." Of equal significance was the announcement by The Times, fairly to be considered the Administration organ: "The President stands firm against every solicitation to postpone the draft."(17)

XXXIII
THE RALLY TO THE PRESIDENT

The question insists upon rising again: were the anti-Lincoln politicians justified in their exultation, the Lincoln politicians justified in their panic? Nobody will ever know; but it is worth considering that the shrewd opportunist who expressed himself through The Herald changed his mind during a fortnight in August. By one of those odd coincidences of which history is full, it was on the twenty-third of the month that he warned the Democrats and jeered at the Republicans in this insolent fashion:

"Many of our leading Republicans are now furious against Lincoln. . . . Bryant of The Evening Post is very angry with Lincoln because Henderson, The Post's publisher, has been arrested for defrauding the government.

"Raymond is a little shaky and has to make frequent journeys to Washington for instructions. . . .

"Now, to what does all this amount? Our experience of politics convinces us that it amounts to nothing. The sorehead Republicans complain that Lincoln gives them either too little shoddy or too little nigger. What candidate can they find who will give them more of either?

"The Chicago (Democratic) delegates must very emphatically comprehend that they must beat the whole Re-publican party if they elect their candidate. It is a strong party even yet and has a heavy army vote to draw upon. The error of relying too greatly upon the weakness of the Republicans as developed in the quarrels of the Republican leaders, may prove fatal . . . the Republican leaders may have their personal quarrels, or their shoddy quarrels, or their nigger quarrels with Old Abe; but he has the whip hand of them and they will soon be bobbing back into the Republican fold, like sheep who have gone astray. The most of the fuss some of them kick up now, is simply to force Lincoln to give them their terms. .

"We have studied all classes of politicians in our day and we warn the Chicago Convention to put no trust in the Republican soreheads. Furiously as some of them denounce Lincoln now, and lukewarm as the rest of them are in his cause, they will all be shouting for him as the only true Union candidate as soon as the nominations have all been made and the chances for bargains have passed.

"Whatever they say now, we venture to predict that Wade and his tail; and Bryant and his tail; and Wendell Phillips and his tail; and Weed, Barney, Chase and their tails; and Winter Davis, Raymond, Opdyke and Forney who have no tails; will all make tracks for Old Abe's plantation, and will soon be found crowing and blowing, and vowing and writing, and swearing and stumping the state on his side, declaring that he and he alone, is the hope of the nation, the bugaboo of Jeff Davis, the first of Conservatives, the best of Abolitionists, the purest of patriots, the most gullible of mankind, the easiest President to manage, and the person especially predestined and foreordained by Providence to carry on the war, free the niggers, and give all the faithful a fair share of the spoils. The spectacle will be ridiculous; but it is inevitable."(1)

The cynic of The Herald had something to go upon besides his general knowledge of politicians and elections. The Manifesto had not met with universal acclaim. In the course of this month of surprises, there were several things that an apprehensive observer might interpret as the shadow of that hand of fate which was soon to appear upon the wall. In the Republican Convention of the Nineteenth Ohio District, which included Ashtabula County, Wade's county, there were fierce words and then with few dissenting votes, a resolution, "That the recent attack upon the President by Wade and Davis is, in our opinion, ill-timed, ill-tempered, and ill-advised . . . and inasmuch as one of the authors of said protest is a citizen of this Congressional District and indebted in no small degree to our friendship for the position, we deem it a duty no less imperative than disagreeable, to pronounce upon that disorganizing Manifesto our unqualified disapproval and condemnation."(2)

To be sure there were plenty of other voices from Ohio and elsewhere applauding "The War on the President." Nevertheless, there were signs of a reluctance to join the movement, and some of these in quarters where they had been least expected. Notably, the Abolitionist leaders were slow to come forward. Sumner was particularly slow. He was ready, indeed, to admit that a better candidate than Lincoln could be found, and there was a whisper that the better candidate was himself. However, he was unconditional that he would not participate in a fight against Lincoln. If the President could be persuaded to withdraw, that was one thing. But otherwise—no Sumner in the conspiracy.(3)

Was it possible that Chandler, Wade, Davis and the rest had jumped too soon? To rebuild the Vindictive Coalition, the group in which Sumner had a place was essential. This group was composed of Abolitionists, chiefly

New Englanders, and for present purpose their central figure was Andrew, the Governor of Massachusetts. During the latter half of August, the fate of the Conspiracy hung on the question, Can Andrew and his group be drawn in?

Andrew did not like the President. He was one of those who never got over their first impression of the strange new man of 1861. He insisted that Lincoln lacked the essential qualities of a leader. "To comprehend this objection," says his frank biographer, "which to us seems so astoundingly wide of the mark, we must realize that whenever the New Englander of that generation uttered the word 'leader' his mind's eye was filled with the image of Daniel Webster . . . his commanding presence, his lofty tone about affairs of state, his sonorous profession of an ideal, his whole ex cathedra attitude. All those characteristics supplied the aristocratic connotation of the word 'leader' as required by a community in which a considerable measure of aristocratic sympathy still lingered. Andrew and his friends were like the men of old who having known Saul before time, and beholding him prophesying, asked 'Is Saul also among the prophets?'"(4)

But Andrew stood well outside the party cabals that were hatched at Washington. He and his gave the conspirators a hearing from a reason widely different from any of theirs. They distrusted the Executive Committee. The argument that had swept the Committee for the moment off its feet filled the stern New Englanders with scorn. They were prompt to deny any sympathy with the armistice movement.(5) As Andrew put it, the chief danger of the hour was the influence of the Executive Committee on the President, whom he persisted in considering a weak man; the chief duty of the hour was to "rescue" Lincoln, or in some other way to "check the peace movement of the Republican managers."(6) if it were fairly certain that this could be effected only by putting the conspiracy through, Andrew would come in. But could he be clear in his own mind that this was the thing to do? While he hesitated, Jaquess and Gilmore did their last small part in American history and left the stage. They made a tour of the Northern States explaining to the various governors the purposes of their mission to Richmond, and reporting in full their audience with Davis and the impressions they had formed.(7) This was a point in favor of Lincoln—as Andrew thought. On the other hand, there were the editorials of The Times. As late as the twenty-fourth of August, the day before the Washington conference, The Times asserted that the President would waive all the objects for which the war had been fought, including Abolition, if any proposition of peace should come that embraced the integrity of the Union. To be sure, this was not consistent with the report of Jaquess and Gilmore and their statement of terms actually set down by Lincoln. And yet—it came from the Administration organ edited by the chairman of the Executive Committee. Was "rescue" of the President anything more than a dream?

It was just here that Lincoln intervened and revolutionized the whole situation. With what tense interest Andrew must have waited for reports of that conference held at Washington on the twenty-fifth. And with what delight he must have received them! The publication on the twenty-sixth of the sweeping repudiation of the negotiation policy; the reassertion that the Administration's "sole and undivided purpose was to prosecute the war." Simultaneous was another announcement, also in the minds of the New Englanders, of first importance: "So far as there being any probability of President Lincoln withdrawing from the canvass, as some have suggested, the gentlemen comprising the Committee express themselves as confident of his reelection."(8)

Meanwhile the letters asking for signatures to the pro-posed "call" had been circulated and the time had come to take stock of the result From Ohio, Wade had written in a sanguine mood. He was for issuing the call the moment the Democratic Convention had taken action.(9) On the twenty-ninth that convention met. On the thirtieth, the conspirators reassembled — again at the house of David Dudley Field — and Andrew attended. He had not committed himself either way.

And now Lincoln's firmness with the Executive Committee had its reward. The New Englanders had made up their minds. Personally, he was still obnoxious to them; but in light of his recent pronouncement, they would take their chances on "rescuing" him from the Committee; and since he would not withdraw, they would not cooperate in splitting the Union party. But they could not convince the conspirators. A long debate ended in an agreement to disagree. The New Englanders withdrew, confessed partisans of Lincoln.(10) It was the beginning of the end.

Andrew went back to Boston to organize New England for Lincoln. J. M. Forbes remained to organize New York.(11) All this, ignoring the Executive Committee. It was a new Lincoln propaganda, not in opposition to the Committee but in frank rivalry: "Since, or if, we must have Lincoln," said Andrew, "men of motive and ideas must get into the lead, must elect him, get hold of 'the machine' and 'run it' themselves."(12)

The bottom was out of the conspiracy; but the leaders at New York were slow to yield. Despite the New England secession, they thought the Democratic platform, on which McClellan had been invited to stand as candidate for the Presidency, gave them another chance, especially the famous resolution:

"That this Convention does explicitly declare, as the sense of the American people, after four years of failure to restore the Union by the experiment of war, during which, under the pretense of a military necessity, or war power higher than the Constitution, the Constitution itself has been disregarded in every part, and the public liberty and the private right alike trodden down and the material prosperity of the country essentially impaired, justice, humanity, liberty and the public welfare demand that immediate efforts be made for a cessation of hostilities, with a view to an ultimate convention of the States, or other peaceable means to the end that at the earliest practicable moment peace may be restored on the basis of the Federal Union of the States."

Some of the outlying conspirators also suffered a revival of hope. The Cincinnati Gazette came out flat foot for the withdrawal of Lincoln.(13) So did The Cincinnati Times, pressing hard for the new convention.(14) On the second of September, three New York editors, Greeley for The Tribune, Parke Godwin for The Post, and Tilton for The Independent, were busily concocting a circular letter to Governors of the States with a view to saving the conspiracy.(15)

But other men were at work in a different fashion, that same day. Lincoln's cause had been wrecked so frequently by his generals that whenever a general advanced, the event seems boldly dramatic. While the politicians at New York and Chicago thought they were loading the scales of fate, long lines of men in blue were moving through broken woodland and over neglected fields against the gray legions defending Atlanta. Said General Hood, it was "evident that General Sherman was moving with his main body to destroy the Macon road, and that the fate of Atlanta depended on our ability to defeat this movement." During the fateful pow-pow at the house of Dudley Field, Sherman's army like a colossal scythe was swinging round Atlanta, from the west and south, across Flint River, through the vital railway, on toward the city. On the second of September, the news that Atlanta was taken "electrified the people of the North."(16)

The first thought of every political faction, when, on the third, the newspapers were ringing with this great news, was either how to capitalize it for themselves, or how to forestall its capitalization by some one else. Forbes "dashed off" a letter to Andrew urging an immediate demonstration for Lincoln.(17) He was sure the Raymond group would somehow try to use the victory as a basis for recovering their leadership. Davis was eager to issue the "call" at once.(18) But his fellows hesitated. And while they hesitated, Andrew and the people acted. On the sixth, a huge Lincoln rally was held at Faneul Hall. Andrew presided. Sumner spoke.(19) That same day, Vermont held State elections and went Republican by a rousing majority. On the day following occurred the Convention of the Union party of New York. Enthusiastic applause was elicited by a telegram from Vermont. "The first shell that was thrown by Sherman into Atlanta has exploded in the Copperhead Camp in this State, and the Unionists have poured in a salute with shotted guns."(20) The mixed metaphors did not reduce the telegram's effect. The New York Convention formally endorsed Lincoln as the candidate of the Union party for President.

So much for the serious side of the swiftly changing political kaleidoscope. There was also a comic side. Only three days sufficed—from Davis's eagerness to proceed on the fourth to letters and articles written or printed on the seventh—only three days, and the leaders of the conspiracy began turning their coats. A typical letter of the seventh at Syracuse describes "an interview with Mr. Opdyke this morning, who told me the result of his efforts to obtain signatures to our call which was by no means encouraging. I have found the same sentiment prevailing here. A belief that it is too late to make any effectual demonstration, and therefore that it is not wise to attempt any. I presume that the new-born enthusiasm created by the Atlanta news will so encourage Lincoln that he can not be persuaded to withdraw."(21) Two days more and the anti-Lincoln newspapers began to draw in their horns. That Independent, whose editor had been one of the three in the last ditch but a week before, handsomely recanted, scuttling across to what now seemed the winning side. "The prospect of victory is brilliant. If a fortnight ago the prospect of Mr. Lincoln's reelection seemed doubtful, the case is now changed. The odious character of the Chicago platform, the sunshiny effect of the late victories, have rekindled the old enthusiasm in loyal hearts."(22) One day more, and Greeley sullenly took his medicine. The Tribune began printing "The Union Ticket—for President, Abraham Lincoln."

There remains the most diverting instance of the haste with which coats were turned. On the sixth of September, only three days after Atlanta!— the very day of the great Lincoln rally, the crown of Andrew's generalship, .at Fanuel Hall—a report was sent out from Washington that "Senator Wade is to take the stump for Mr. Lincoln."(23) Less than a week later The Washington Chronicle had learned "with satisfaction, though not with surprise, that Senator Wade, notwithstanding his signature to a celebrated Manifesto, had enrolled himself among the Lincoln forces."(24) Exactly two weeks after Atlanta, Wade made his first speech for Lincoln as President. It was a "terrific assault upon the Copperhead policy."(25)

The ship of the conspiracy was sinking fast, and on every hand was heard a scurrying patter of escaping politicians.

XXXIV
"FATHER ABRAHAM"

The key-notes of Lincoln's course with the Executive Committee, his refusal to do anything that appeared to him to be futile, his firmness not to cast about and experiment after a policy, his basing of all his plans on the vision in his own mind of their sure fruitage — these continued to be his key-notes throughout the campaign. They ruled his action in a difficult matter with which he was quickly forced to deal.

Montgomery Blair, the Postmaster General, was widely and bitterly disliked. Originally a radical Republican, he had quarreled with that wing of the party. In 1863 the Union League of Philadelphia, which elected all the rest of the Cabinet honorary members of its organization, omitted Blair. A reference to the Cabinet in the Union platform of 1864 was supposed to be a hint that the Postmaster General would serve his country, if he resigned. During the dark days of the summer of 1864, the President's mail was filled with supplications for the dismissal of Blair.(1) He was described as an incubus that might cause the defeat of the Administration.

If the President's secretaries were not prejudiced witnesses, Blair had worn out his welcome in the Cabinet. He had grown suspicious. He tried to make Lincoln believe that Seward was plotting with the Copperheads. Nevertheless, Lincoln turned a deaf ear to the clamor against him. Merely personal considerations were not compelling. If it was true, as for a while he believed it was, that his election was already lost, he did not propose to throw Blair over as a mere experiment. True to his principles he would not become a juggler with futility.

The turn of the tide in his favor put the matter in a new light. All the enemies of Blair renewed their attack on a slightly different line. One of those powerful New Englanders who had come to Lincoln's aid at such an opportune moment led off. On the second day following the news of Atlanta, Henry Wilson wrote to him, "Blair, every one hates. Tens of thousands of men will be lost to you, or will give you a reluctant vote because of the Blairs."(2)

If this was really true, the selfless man would not hesitate to' require of Blair the same sort of sacrifice he would, in other conditions, require of himself. Lincoln debated this in his own mind nearly three weeks.

Meanwhile, various other politicians joined the hue and cry. An old friend of Lincoln's, Ebenezer Peck, came east from Illinois to work upon him against Blair.(3) Chandler, who like Wade was eager to get out of the wrong ship, appeared at Washington as a friend of the Administration and an enemy of Blair.(4) But still Lincoln did not respond. After all, was it certain that one of these votes would change if Blair did not resign? Would anything be accomplished, should Lincoln require his resignation, except the humiliation of a friend, the gratification of a pack of malcontents? And then some one thought of a mode for giving definite political value to Blair's removal. Who did it? The anonymous author of the only biography of Chandler claims this doubtful honor for the great Jacobin. Lincoln's secretaries, including Colonel Stoddard who had charge of his correspondence, are ignorant on the subject.(5) It may well have been Chandler who negotiated a bargain with Fremont, if the story is to be trusted, which concerned Blair. A long-standing, relentless quarrel separated these two. That Fremont as a candidate was nobody had long been apparent; and yet it was worth while to get rid of him. Chandler, or another, extracted a promise from Fremont that if Blair were removed, he would resign. On the strength of this promise, a last appeal was made to Lincoln. Such is the legend. The known fact is that on September twenty-second Fremont withdrew his candidacy. The next day Lincoln sent this note to Blair:

"You have generously said to me more than once that whenever your resignation could be a relief to me, it was at my disposal. The time has come. You very well know that this proceeds from no dissatisfaction of mine, with you personally or officially. Your uniform kindness has been unsurpassed by that of any friend."(6)

No incident displays more clearly the hold which Lincoln had acquired on the confidence and the affection of his immediate associates. Blair at once tendered his resignation: "I can not take leave of you," said he, "without renewing the expression of my gratitude for the uniform kindness which has marked your course with regard to myself."(7) That he was not perfunctory, that his great chief had acquired over him an ascendency which was superior to any strain, was demonstrated a few days later in New York. On the twenty-seventh, Cooper Institute was filled with an enthusiastic Lincoln meeting. Blair was a speaker. He was received with loud cheers and took occasion to touch upon his relations with the President. "I retired," said he, "on the recommendation of my own father. My father has passed that period of life when its honors or its rewards, or its glories have any charm for him. He looks backward only, and forward only, to the grandeur of this nation and the happiness of this great people who have grown up under the prosperous condition of the Union; and he would not permit a son of his to stand in the way of the glorious and patriotic President who leads us on to success and to the final triumph that is in store for us."(8)

It was characteristic of this ultimate Lincoln that he offered no explanations, even in terminating the career of a minister; that he gave no confidences. Gently inexorable, he imposed his will in apparent unconsciousness that it might be questioned. Along with his overmastering kindness, he had something of the objectivity of a natural force. It was the mood attained by a few extraordinary men who have reached a point where, without becoming egoists, they no longer distinguish between themselves and circumstance; the mood of those creative artists who have lost themselves, in the strange way which the dreamers have, who have also found themselves.

Even in the new fascination of the probable turn of the tide, Lincoln did not waver in his fixed purpose to give all his best energies, and the country's best energies, to the war. In October, there was a new panic over the draft. Cameron implored him to suspend it in Pennsylvania until after the presidential election. An Ohio committee went to Washington with the same request. Why should not the arguments that had prevailed with him, or were supposed to have prevailed with him, for the removal of a minister, prevail also in the way of a brief flagging of military preparation? But Lincoln would not look upon the two cases in the same spirit. "What is the Presidency worth to me," he asked the Ohio committee, "if I have no country ?"(9)

From the active campaign he held himself aloof. He made no political speeches. He wrote no political letters. The army received his constant detailed attention. In his letters to Grant, he besought him to be unwavering in a relentless persistency.

As Hay records, he was aging rapidly. The immense strain of his labor was beginning to tell both in his features and his expression. He was moving in a shadow. But his old habit of merriment had not left him; though it was now, more often, a surface merriment. On the night of the October elections, Lincoln sat in the telegraph room of the War Office while the reports were coming in. "The President in a lull of despatches, took from his pocket the Naseby Papers and read several chapters of the Saint and Martyr, Petroleum V. They were immensely amusing. Stanton and Dana enjoyed them scarcely less than the President, who read on, con amore, until nine o'clock."(10)

The presidential election was held on the eighth of November. That night, Lincoln with his Secretary was again in the War Office. The early returns showed that the whole North was turning to him in enormous majorities. He showed no exultation. When the Assistant Secretary of the Navy spoke sharply of the complete effacement politically of Henry Winter Davis against whom he had a grudge, Lincoln said, "You have more of that feeling of personal resentment than I. Perhaps I have too little of it; but I never thought it paid. A man has no time to spend half his life in quarrels. If any man ceases to attack me I never remember the past against him." (11)

"Towards midnight," says Hay in his diary, "we had supper. The President went awkwardly and hospitably to work shovelling out the fried oysters. He was most agreeable and genial all the evening. . . . Captain Thomas came up with a band about half-past two and made some music. The President answered from a window with rather unusual dignity and effect, and we came home." (12)

"I am thankful to God," Lincoln said, in response to the serenade, "for this approval of the people; but while grateful for this mark of their confidence in me, if I know my heart, my gratitude is free from any taint of personal triumph. I do not impugn the motives of any one opposed to me. It is no pleasure to me to triumph over any one, but I give thanks to the Almighty for this evidence of the people's resolution to stand by free government and the rights of humanity." (13)

During the next few days a torrent of congratulations came pouring in. What most impressed the secretaries was his complete freedom from elation. "He seemed to deprecate his own triumph and sympathize rather with the beaten than the victorious party." His formal recognition of the event was a prepared reply to a serenade on the night of November tenth. A great crowd filled the space in front of the north portico of the White House. Lincoln appeared at a window. A secretary stood at his side holding a lighted candle while he read from a manuscript. The brief address is justly ranked among his ablest occasional utterances. As to the mode of the deliverance, he said to Hay, "Not very graceful, but I am growing old enough not to care much for the manner of doing things." (14)

XXXV
THE MASTER OF THE MOMENT

In Lincoln's life there are two great achievements.

One he brought to pass in time for him to behold his own victory. The other he saw only with the eyes of faith. The first was the drawing together of all the elements of nationalism in the American people and consolidating them into a driving force. The second was laying the foundation of a political temper that made impossible a permanent victory for the Vindictives. It was the sad fate of this nation, because Lincoln's hand was struck from the tiller at the very instant of the crisis, to suffer the temporary success of that faction he strove so hard to destroy. The transitoriness of their evil triumph, the eventual rally of the nation against them, was the final victory of the spirit of Lincoln.

The immediate victory he appreciated more fully and measured more exactly, than did any one else. He put it into words in the fifth message. While others were crowing with exaltation over a party triumph, he looked deeper to the psychological triumph. Scarcely another saw that the most significant detail of the hour was in the Democratic attitude. Even the bitterest enemies of nationalism, even those who were believed by all others to desire the breaking of the Union, had not thought it safe to say so. They had veiled their intent in specious words. McClellan in accepting the Democratic nomination had repudiated the idea of disunion. Whether the Democratic politicians had agreed with him or not, they had not dared to contradict him. This was what Lincoln put the emphasis on in his message: "The purpose of the people within the loyal States to maintain the Union was never more firm nor more nearly unanimous than now. . . . No candidate for any office, high or low, has ventured to seek votes on the avowal that he was for giving up the Union. There have been much impugning of motive and much heated controversy as to the proper means and best mode of advancing the Union cause; but on the distinct issue of Union or No Union the politicians have shown their instinctive knowledge that there is no diversity among the people. In affording the people the fair opportunity of showing one to another and to the world, this firmness and unanimity of purpose, the election has been of vast value to the national cause."(1)

This temper of the final Lincoln, his supreme detachment, the kind impersonality of his intellectual approach, has no better illustration in his state papers. He further revealed it in a more intimate way. The day he sent the message to Congress, he also submitted to the Senate a nomination to the great office of Chief Justice. When Taney died in the previous September, there was an eager stir among the friends of Chase. They had hopes but they felt embarrassed. Could they ask this great honor, the highest it is in the power of the American President to be-stow, for a man who had been so lacking in candor as Chase had been? Chase's course during the summer had made things worse. He had played the time-server. No one was more severe upon Lincoln in July; in August, he hesitated, would not quite commit himself to the conspiracy but would not discourage it; almost gave it his blessing; in September, but not until it was quite plain that the conspiracy was failing, he came out for Lincoln. However, his friends in the Senate overcame their embarrassment—how else could it be with Senators?—and pressed his case. And when Senator Wilson, alarmed at the President's silence, tried to apologize for Chase's harsh remarks about the President, Lincoln cut him short. "Oh, as to that, I care nothing," said he. The embarrassment of the Chase propaganda amused him. When Chase himself took a hand and wrote him a letter, Lincoln said to his secretary, "What is it about?" "Simply a kind and friendly letter," replied the secretary. Lincoln smiled. "File it with the other recommendations," said he.(2)

He regarded Chase as a great lawyer, Taney's logical successor. All the slights the Secretary had put upon the President, the intrigues to supplant him, the malicious sayings, were as if they had never occurred. When Congress assembled, it was Chase's name that he sent to the Senate. It was Chase who, as Chief Justice, administered the oath at Lincoln's second inauguration.

Long since, Lincoln had seen that there had ceased to any half-way house in the matter of emancipation. His thoughts were chiefly upon the future. And as mere strategy, he saw that slavery had to be got out of the way. It was no longer a question, who liked this, who did not. To him, the ultimate issue was the restoration of harmony among the States. Those States which had been defeated in the dread arbitrament of battle, would in any event encounter difficulties, even deadly perils, in the narrow way which must come after defeat and which might or might not lead to rehabilitation.

Remembering the Vindictive temper, remembering the force and courage of the Vindictive leaders, it was imperative to clear the field of the slavery issue before the reconstruction issue was fairly launched. It was highly desirable to commit to the support of the governments the whole range of influences that were in earnest about emancipation. Furthermore, the South itself was drifting in the same direction. In his interview with Gilmore and Jaquess, Davis had said: "You have already emancipated nearly two millions of our slaves; and if you will take care of them, you may emancipate the rest. I had a few when the war began. I was of some use to them; they never were of any to me."(3)

The Southern President had "felt" his constituency on the subject of enrolling slaves as soldiers with a promise of emancipation as the reward of military service.

The fifth message urged Congress to submit to the States an amendment to the Constitution abolishing slavery. Such action had been considered in the previous session, but nothing had been done. At Lincoln's suggestion, it had been recommended in the platform of the Union party. Now, with the President's powerful influence behind it, with his prestige at full circle, the amendment was rapidly pushed forward. Before January ended, it had been approved by both Houses. Lincoln had used all his personal influence to strengthen its chances in Congress where, until the last minute, the vote was still in doubt.(4)

While the amendment was taking its way through Congress, a shrewd old politician who thought he knew the world better than most men, that Montgomery Blair, Senior, who was father of the Postmaster General, had been trying on his own responsibility to open negotiations between Washington and Richmond. His visionary ideas, which were wholly without the results he intended, have no place here. And yet this fanciful episode had a significance of its own. Had it not occurred, the Confederate government probably would not have appointed commissioners charged with the hopeless task of approaching the Federal government for the purpose of negotiating peace between "the two countries."

Now that Lincoln was entirely in the ascendent at home, and since the Confederate arms had recently suffered terrible reverses, he was no longer afraid that negotiation might appear to be the symptom of weakness. He went so far as to consent to meet the Commissioners himself. On a steamer in Hampton Roads, Lincoln and Seward had a long conference with three members of the Confederate government, particularly the Vice-President, Alexander H. Stephens.

It has become a tradition that Lincoln wrote at the top of a sheet of paper the one word "Union"; that he pushed it across the table and said, "Stephens, write under that anything you want" There appears to be no foundation for the tale in this form. The amendment had committed the North too definitely to emancipation. Lincoln could not have proposed Union without requiring emancipation, also. And yet, with this limitation, the spirit of the tradition is historic. There can be no doubt that he presented to the commissioners about the terms which the year before he had drawn up as a memorandum for Gilmore and Jaquess: Union, the acceptance of emancipation, but also instantaneous restoration of political autonomy to the Southern States, and all the influence of the Administration in behalf of liberal compensation for the loss of slave property. But the commissioners had no authority to consider terms that did not recognize the existence of "two countries." However, this Hampton Roads Conference gave Lincoln a new hope. He divined, if he did not perceive, that the Confederates were on the verge of despair. If he had been a Vindictive, this would have borne fruit in ferocious telegrams to his generals to strike and spare not. What Lincoln did was to lay before the Cabinet this proposal: — that they advise Congress to offer the Confederate government the sum of four hundred million dollars, provided the war end and the States in secession acknowledge the authority of the Federal government previous to April 1, 1865. But the Cabinet, complete as was his domination in some respects, were not ripe for such a move as this. "'You are all against me,' said Lincoln sadly and in evident surprise at the want of statesmanlike liberality on the part of the executive council," to quote his Secretary, "folded and laid away the draft of his message."(5) Nicolay believes that the idea continued vividly in his mind and that it may be linked with his last public utterance — "it may be my duty to make some new announcement to the people of the South. I am considering and shall not fail to act when satisfied that action is proper."

It was now obvious to every one outside the Confederacy that the war would end speedily in a Northern victory. To Lincoln, therefore, the duty of the moment, overshadowing all else, was the preparation for what should come after. Reconstruction. More than ever it was of first importance to decide whether the President or Congress should deal with this great matter. And now occurred an event which bore witness at once to the beginning of Lincoln's final struggle with the Vindictives and to that personal ascendency which was steadily widening. One of those three original Jacobins agreed to become his spokesman in the Senate. As the third person of the Jacobin brotherhood, Lyman Trumbull had always been out of place. He had gone wrong not from perversity of the soul but from a mental failing, from the lack of inherent light, from intellectual conventionality. But he was a good man. One might apply to him Mrs. Browning's line: "Just a good man made a great man." And in his case, as in so many others, sheer goodness had not been sufficient in the midst of a revolution to save his soul. To quote one of the greatest of the observers of human life: "More brains, O Lord, more brains." Though Trumbull had the making of an Intellectual, politics had very nearly ruined him. For all his good intentions it took him a long time to see what Hawthorne saw at first sight-that Lincoln was both a powerful character and an original mind. Still, because Trumbull was really a good man, he found a way to recover his soul. What his insight was not equal to perceiving in 1861, experience slowly made plain to him in the course of the next three years. Before 1865 he had broken with the Vindictives; he had come over to Lincoln. Trumbull still held the powerful office of Chairman of the Senate Judiciary Committee. He now undertook to be the President's captain in a battle on the floor of the Senate for the recognition of Louisiana.

The new government in Louisiana had been in actual operation for nearly a year. Though Congress had denounced it; though the Manifesto had held it up to scorn as a monarchial outrage; Lincoln had quietly, steadily, protected and supported it. It was discharging the function of a regular State government. A governor had been elected and inaugurated-that Governor Hahn whom Lincoln had congratulated as Louisiana's first Free State Governor. He could say this because the new electorate which his mandate had created had assembled a constitutional convention and had abolished slavery. And it had also carried out the President's views with regard to the political status of freedmen. Lincoln was not a believer in general negro suffrage. He was as far as ever from the theorizing of the Abolitionists. The most he would approve was the bestowal of suffrage on a few Superior negroes, leaving the rest to be gradually educated into citizenship. The Louisiana Convention had authorized the State Legislature to make, when it felt prepared to do so, such a limited extension of suffrage. (6)

In setting up this new government, Lincoln had created a political vessel in which practically all the old electorate of Louisiana could find their places the moment they gave up the war and accepted the two requisites, union and emancipation. That electorate could proceed at once to rebuild the social-political order of the State without any interval of "expiation." All the power of the Administration would be with them in their labors. That this was the wise as well as the generous way to proceed, the best minds of the North had come to see. Witness the conversion of Trumbull. But there were four groups of fanatics who were dangerous: extreme Abolitionists who clamored for negro equality; men like Wade and Chandler, still mad with the lust of conquest, raging at the President who had stood so resolutely between them and their desire; the machine politicians who could never understand the President's methods, who regarded him as an officious amateur; and the Little Men who would have tried to make political capital of the blowing of the last trump. All these, each for a separate motive, attacked the President because of Louisiana.

The new government had chosen Senators. Here was a specific issue over which the Administration and its multiform opposition might engage in a trial of strength. The Senate had it in its power to refuse to seat the Louisiana Senators. Could the Vindictive leaders induce it to go to that length? The question took its natural course of reference to the Judiciary Committee. On the eighteenth of February, Trumbull opened what was destined to be a terrible chapter in American history, the struggle between light and darkness over reconstruction. Trumbull had ranged behind Lincoln the majority of his committee. With its authority he moved a joint resolution recognizing the new government of Louisiana.

And then began a battle royal. Trumbull's old associates were promptly joined by Sumner. These three rallied against the resolution all the malignancy, all the time-serving, all the stupidity, which the Senate possessed. Bitter language was exchanged by men who had formerly been as thick as thieves.

"You and I," thundered Wade, "did not differ formerly on this subject We considered it a mockery, a miserable mockery, to recognize this Louisiana organization as a State in the Union." He sneered fiercely, "Whence comes this new-born zeal of the Senator from Illinois? . . . Sir, it is the most miraculous conversion that has taken place since Saint Paul's time."(7)

Wade did not spare the President. Metaphorically speaking, he shook a fist in his face, the fist of a merciless old giant "When the foundation of this government is sought to be swept away by executive usurpation, it will not do to turn around to me and say this comes from a President I helped to elect. . . . If the President of the United States operating through his major generals can initiate a State government, and can bring it here and force us, compel us, to receive on this floor these mere mockeries, these men of straw who represent nobody, your Republic is at an end . . . talk not to me of your ten per cent. principle. A more absurd, monarchial and anti-American principle was never announced on God's earth."(8)

Amidst a rain of furious personalities, Lincoln's spokesman kept his poise. It was sorely tried by two things: by Sumner's frank use of every device of parliamentary obstruction with a view to wearing out the patience of the Senate, and by the cynical alliance, in order to balk Lincoln, of the Vindictives with the Democrats. What they would not risk in 1862 when their principles had to wait upon party needs, they now considered safe strategy. And if ever the Little Men deserved their label it was when they played into the hands of the terrible Vindictives, thus becoming responsible for the rejection of Lincoln's plan of reconstruction. Trumbull upbraided Sumner for "associating himself with those whom he so often denounced, for the purpose of calling the yeas and nays and making dilatory motions" to postpone action until the press of other business should compel the Senate to set the resolution aside. Sumner's answer was that he would employ against the measure every instrument he could find "in the arsenal of parliamentary warfare."

With the aid of the Democrats, the Vindictives carried the day. The resolution was "dispensed with."(9)

As events turned out it was a catastrophe. But this was not apparent at the time. Though Lincoln had been beaten for the moment, the opposition was made up of so many and such irreconcilable elements that as long as he could hold together his own following, there was no reason to suppose he would not in the long run prevail. He was never in a firmer, more self-contained mood than on the last night of the session.(10) Again, as on that memorable fourth of July, eight months before, he was in his room at the Capitol signing the last-minute bills. Stanton was with him. On receiving a telegram from Grant, the Secretary handed it to the President Grant reported that Lee had proposed a conference for the purpose of "a satisfactory adjustment of the present unhappy difficulties by means of a military convention." Without asking for the Secretary's opinion, Lincoln wrote out a reply which he directed him to sign and despatch immediately.

"The President directs me to say that he wishes you to have no conference with General Lee, unless it be for the capitulation of General Lee's army, or on some minor or purely military matter. He instructs me to say that you are not to decide, discuss, or confer upon any political questions, such questions the President holds in his own hands and will submit them to no military conferences or conventions. Meanwhile, you are to press to the utmost your military advantages."(11)

In the second inaugural (12) delivered the next day, there is not the faintest shadow of anxiety. It breathes a lofty confidence as if his soul was gazing meditatively downward upon life, and upon his own work, from a secure height. The world has shown a sound instinct in fixing upon one expression, "with malice toward none, with charity for all," as the key-note of the final Lincoln. These words form the opening line of that paragraph of unsurpassable prose in which the second inaugural culminates:

"With malice toward none; with charity for all; with firmness in the right as God gives us to see the right, let us strive on to finish the work we are in; to bind up the nation's wounds; to care for him who shall have borne the battle, and for his widow and his orphan, to do all which may achieve and cherish a just and lasting peace among ourselves, and with all nations."

XXXVI
PREPARING A DIFFERENT WAR

During the five weeks which remained to Lincoln on earth, the army was his most obvious concern. He watched eagerly the closing of the enormous trap that had been slowly built up surrounding Lee. Toward the end of March he went to the front, and for two weeks had his quarters on a steamer at City Point. It was during Lincoln's visit that Sherman came up from North Carolina for his flying conference with Grant, in which the President took part. Lincoln was at City Point when Petersburg fell. Early on the morning of April third, he joined Grant who gives a strange glimpse in his Memoirs of their meeting in the deserted city which so recently had been the last bulwark of the Confederacy.(1) The same day, Richmond fell. Lincoln had returned to City Point, and on the following day when confusion reigned in the burning city, he walked through its streets attended only by a few sailors and by four friends. He visited Libby Prison; and when a member of his party said that Davis ought to be hanged, Lincoln replied, "Judge not that ye be not judged."(2) His deepest thoughts, however, were not with the army. The time was at hand when his statesmanship was to be put to its most severe test. He had not forgotten the anxious lesson of that success of the Vindictives in balking momentarily the recognition of Louisiana. It was war to the knife between him and them. Could he reconstruct the Union in a wise and merciful fashion despite their desperate opposition?

He had some strong cards in his hand. First of all, he had time. Congress was not in session. He had eight months in which to press forward his own plans. If, when Congress assembled the following December, it should be confronted by a group of reconciled Southern States, would it venture to refuse them recognition? No one could have any illusions as to what the Vindictives would try to do. They would continue the struggle they had begun over Louisiana; and if their power permitted, they would rouse the nation to join battle with the President on that old issue of the war powers, of the dictatorship.

But in Lincoln's hand there were four other cards, all of which Wade and Chandler would find it hard to match. He had the army. In the last election the army had voted for him enthusiastically. And the army was free from the spirit of revenge, the Spirit which Chandler built upon. They had the plain people, the great mass whom the machine politicians had failed to judge correctly in the August Conspiracy. Pretty generally, he had the Intellectuals. Lastly, he had—or with skilful generalship he could have—the Abolitionists.

The Thirteenth Amendment was not yet adopted. The question had been raised, did it require three-fourths of all the States for its adoption, or only three-fourths of those that were ranked as not in rebellion. Here was the issue by means of which the Abolitionists might all be brought into line. It was by no means certain that every Northern State would vote for the amendment. In the smaller group of States, there was a chance that the amendment might fail. But if it were submitted to the larger group; and if every Reconstructed State, before Congress met, should adopt the amendment; and if it was apparent that with these Southern adoptions the amendment must prevail, all the great power of the anti-slavery sentiment would be thrown on the side of the President in favor of recognizing the new State governments and against the Vindictives. Lincoln held a hand of trumps. Confidently, but not rashly, he looked forward to his peaceful war with the Vindictives.

They were enemies not to be despised. To begin with, they were experienced machine politicians; they had control of well-organized political rings. They were past masters of the art of working up popular animosities. And they were going to use this art in that dangerous moment of reaction which invariably follows the heroic tension of a great war. The alignment in the Senate revealed by the Louisiana battle had also a significance. The fact that Sumner, who was not quite one of them, became their general on that occasion, was something to remember. They had made or thought they had made other powerful allies. The Vice President, Andrew Johnson-the new president of the Senate-appeared at this time to be cheek by jowl with the fiercest Vindictives of them all. It would be interesting to know when the thought first occurred to them: "If anything should happen to Lincoln, his successor would be one of us!"

The ninth of April arrived and the news of Lee's surrender.

"The popular excitement over the victory was such that on Monday, the tenth, crowds gathered before the Executive Mansion several times during the day and called out the President for speeches. Twice he responded by coming to the window and saying a few words which, however, indicated that his mind was more occupied with work than with exuberant rejoicing. As briefly as he could he excused himself, but promised that on the following evening for which a formal demonstration was being arranged, he would be prepared to say something."(3)

The paper which he read to the crowd that thronged the grounds of the White House on the night of April eleventh, was his last public utterance. It was also one of his most remarkable ones. In a way, it was his declaration of war against the Vindictives.(4) It is the final statement of a policy toward helpless opponents—he refused to call them enemies—which among the conquerors of history is hardly, if at all, to be paralleled.(5)

"By these recent successes the reinauguration of the national authority—reconstruction—which has had a large share of thought from the first, is pressed more closely upon our attention. It is fraught with great difficulty. Unlike a case of war between independent nations, there is no authorized organ for us to treat with-no one man has authority to give up the rebellion for any other man. We simply must begin with, and mould from, disorganized and discordant elements. Nor is it a small additional embarrassment that we, the loyal people, differ among ourselves as to the mode, manner and measure of reconstruction. As a general rule, I abstain from reading the reports of attacks upon myself, wishing not to be provoked by that to which I can not properly offer an answer. In spite of this precaution, however, it comes to my knowledge that I am much censured for some supposed agency in setting up and seeking to sustain the new State government of Louisiana."

He reviewed in full the history of the Louisiana experiment From that he passed to the theories put forth by some of his enemies with regard to the constitutional status of the Seceded States. His own theory that the States never had been out of the Union because constitutionally they could not go out, that their governmental functions had merely been temporarily interrupted; this theory had always been roundly derided by the Vindictives and even by a few who were not Vindictives. Sumner had preached the idea that the Southern States by attempting to secede had committed "State suicide" and should now be treated as Territories. Stevens and the Vindictives generally, while avoiding Sumner's subtlety, called them "conquered provinces." And all these wanted to take them from under the protection of the President and place them helpless at the feet of Congress. To prevent this is the purpose that shines between the lines in the latter part of Lincoln's valedictory:

"We all agree that the Seceded States, so called, are out of their proper practical relation with the Union, and that the sole object of the government, civil and military, in regard to those States, is to again get them into that proper practical relation. I believe that it is not only possible, but in fact easier, to do this without deciding or even considering whether these States have ever been out of the Union, than with it Finding themselves safely at home, it would be utterly immaterial whether they had ever been abroad. Let us all join in doing the acts necessary to restoring the proper practical relations between these States and the Union, and each forever after innocently indulge his own opinion whether in doing the acts he brought the States from without into the Union, or only gave them proper assistance, they never having been out of it. The amount of constituency, so to speak, on which the new Louisiana government rests would be more satisfactory to all if it contained 50,000 or 30,000, or even 20,000 instead of only about 12,000, as it does. It is also unsatisfactory to some that the elective franchise is not given to the colored man. I would myself prefer that it were now conferred on the very intelligent, and on those who served our cause as soldiers.

"Still, the question is not whether the Louisiana government, as it stands, is quite all that is desirable. The question is, will it be wiser to take it as it is and help to improve it, or to reject and disperse it? Can Louisiana be brought into proper practical relation with the Union sooner by sustaining or by discarding her new State government? Some twelve thousand voters in the heretofore slave State of Louisiana have sworn allegiance to the Union, assumed to be the rightful political power of the State, held elections, organized a State government, adopted a free State constitution, giving the benefit of public schools equally to black and white and empowering the Legislature to confer the elective franchise upon the colored man. Their Legislature has already voted to ratify the constitutional amendment recently passed by Congress abolishing slavery throughout the nation. These 12,000 persons are thus fully committed to the Union and to perpetual freedom in the State—committed to the very things, and nearly all the things, the nation wants—and they ask the nation's recognition and its assistance to make good their committal.

"Now, if we reject and spurn them, we do our utmost to disorganize and disperse them. We, in effect, say to the white man: You are worthless or worse; we will neither help you nor be helped by you. To the blacks we say: This cup of liberty which these, your old masters, hold to your lips we will dash from you and leave you to the chances of gathering the spilled and scattered contents in some vague and undefined when, where and how. If this course, discouraging and paralyzing both white and black, has any tendency to bring Louisiana into proper practical relations with the Union, I have so far been unable to perceive it. If, on the contrary, we recognize and sustain the new government of Louisiana, the converse of all this is made true. We encourage the hearts and nerve the arms of 12,000 to adhere to their work, and argue for it, and proselyte for it, and fight for it, and feed it, and grow it, and ripen it to a complete success. The colored man, too, in seeing all united for him, is inspired with vigilance and energy, and daring, to the same end. Grant that he desires the elective franchise, will he not attain it sooner by saving the already advanced steps toward it than by running backward over them? Concede that the new government of Louisiana is only to what it should be as the egg is to the fowl, we shall sooner have the fowl by hatching the egg than by smashing it.

"Again, if we reject Louisiana, we also reject one vote in favor of the proposed amendment to the national Constitution. To meet this proposition it has been argued that no more than three-fourths of those States which have not attempted secession are necessary to validly ratify the amendment I do not commit myself against this further than to say that such a ratification would be questionable, and sure to be persistently questioned, while a ratification by three-fourths of all the States would be unquestioned and unquestionable. I repeat the question: Can Louisiana be brought into proper practical relation with the Union sooner by sustaining or by discarding her new State government? What has been said of Louisiana will apply generally to other States. And yet so great peculiarities pertain to each State, and such important and sudden changes occur in the same State, and with also new and unprecedented is the whole case that no exclusive and inflexible plan can safely be prescribed as to details and collaterals. Such exclusive and inflexible plan would surely become a new entanglement. Important principles may and must be inflexible. In the present situation, as the phrase goes, it may be my duty to make some new announcement to the people of the South. I am considering and shall not fail to act when satisfied that action will be proper."

XXXVII
FATE INTERPOSES

There was an early spring on the Potomac in 1865. While April was still young, the Judas trees became spheres of purply, pinkish bloom. The Washington parks grew softly bright as the lilacs opened. Pendulous willows veiled with green laces afloat in air the changing brown that was winter's final shadow; in the Virginia woods the white blossoms of the dogwood seemed to float and flicker among the windy trees like enormous flocks of alighting butterflies. And over head such a glitter of turquoise blue! As lovely in a different way as on that fateful Sun-day morning when Russell drove through the same woods toward Bull Run so long, long ago. Such was the background of the last few days of Lincoln's life.

Though tranquil, his thoughts dwelt much on death. While at City Point, he drove one day with Mrs. Lincoln along the banks of the James. They passed a country graveyard. "It was a retired place," said Mrs. Lincoln long afterward, "shaded by trees, and early spring flowers were opening on nearly every grave. It was so quiet and attractive that we stopped the carriage and walked through it. Mr. Lincoln seemed thoughtful and impressed. He said: 'Mary, you are younger than I; you will survive me. When I am gone, lay my remains in some quiet place like this.'"(1)

His mood underwent a mysterious change. It was serene and yet charged with a peculiar grave loftiness not quite like any phase of him his friends had known hitherto. As always, his thoughts turned for their reflection to Shakespeare. Sumner who was one of the party at City Point, was deeply impressed by his reading aloud, a few days before his death, that passage in Macbeth which describes the ultimate security of Duncan where nothing evil "can touch him farther."(2)

There was something a little startling, as if it were not quite of this world, in the tender lightness that seemed to come into his heart. "His whole appearance, poise and bearing," says one of his observers, "had marvelously changed. He was, in fact, transfigured. That indescribable sadness which had previously seemed to be an adamantine element of his very being, had been suddenly changed for an equally indescribable expression of serene joy, as if conscious that the great purpose of his life had been achieved."(3)

It was as if the seer in the trance had finally passed beyond his trance; and had faced smiling toward his earthly comrades, imagining he was to return to them; unaware that somehow his emergence was not in the ordinary course of nature; that in it was an accent of the inexplicable, something which the others caught and at which they trembled; though they knew not why. And he, so beautifully at peace, and yet thrilled as never before by the vision of the murdered Duncan at the end of life's fitful fever — what was his real feeling, his real vision of himself? Was it something of what the great modern poet strove so bravely to express —

"And yet Dauntless the slughorn to my lips I set,

And blew: Childe Roland to the dark tower came."

Shortly before the end, he had a strange dream. Though he spoke of it almost with levity, it would not leave his thoughts. He dreamed he was wandering through the White House at night; all the rooms were brilliantly lighted; but they were empty. However, through that unreal solitude floated a sound of weeping. When he came to the East Room, it was explained; there was a catafalque, the pomp of a military funeral, crowds of people in tears; and a voice said to him, "The President has been assassinated."

He told this dream to Lamon and to Mrs. Lincoln. He added that after it had occurred, "the first time I opened the Bible, strange as it may appear, it was at the twenty-eighth chapter of Genesis which relates the wonderful dream Jacob had. I turned to other passages and seemed to encounter a dream or a vision wherever I looked. I kept on turning the leaves of the Old Book, and everywhere my eye fell upon passages recording matters strangely in keeping with my own thoughts—supernatural visitations, dreams, visions, etc."

But when Lamon seized upon this as text for his recurrent sermon on precautions against assassination, Lincoln turned the matter into a joke. He did not appear to interpret the dream as foreshadowing his own death. He called Lamon's alarm "downright foolishness."(4)

Another dream in the last night of his life was a consolation. He narrated it to the Cabinet when they met on April fourteenth, which happened to be Good Friday. There was some anxiety with regard to Sherman's movements in North Carolina. Lincoln bade the Cabinet set their minds at rest. His dream of the night before was one that he had often had. It was a presage of great events. In this dream he saw himself "in a singular and indescribable vessel, but always the same... moving with great rapidity toward a dark and indefinite shore." This dream had preceded all the great events of the war. He believed it was a good omen.(5)

At this last Cabinet meeting, he talked freely of the one matter which in his mind overshadowed all others. He urged his Ministers to put aside all thoughts of hatred and revenge. "He hoped there would be no persecution, no bloody work, after the war was over. None need expect him to take any part in hanging or killing these men, even the worst of them. 'Frighten them out of the country, let down the bars, scare them off,' said he, throwing up his hands as if scaring sheep. Enough lives have been sacrificed. We must extinguish our resentment if we expect harmony and union. There was too much desire on the part of our very good friends to be masters, to interfere and dictate to those States, to treat the people not as fellow citizens; there was too little respect for their rights. He didn't sympathize in these feelings."(6)

There was a touch of irony in his phase "our very good friends." Before the end of the next day, the men he had in mind, the inner group of the relentless Vindictives, were to meet in council, scarcely able to conceal their inspiring conviction that Providence had intervened, had judged between him and them.(7) And that allusion to the "rights" of the vanquished! How abominable it was in the ears of the grim Chandler, the inexorable Wade. Desperate these men and their followers were on the fourteenth of April, but defiant. To the full measure of their power they would fight the President to the last ditch. And always in their minds, the tormenting thought-if only positions could be reversed, if only Johnson, whom they believed to be one of them at heart, were in the first instead of the second place!

While these unsparing sons of thunder were growling among themselves, the lions that were being cheated of their prey, Lincoln was putting his merciful temper into a playful form. General Creswell applied to him for pardon for an old friend of his who had joined the Confederate Army.

"Creswell," said Lincoln, "you make me think of a lot of young folks who once started out Maying. To reach their destination, they had to cross a shallow stream and did so by means of an old flat boat when the time came to return, they found to their dismay that the old scow had disappeared. They were in sore trouble and thought over all manner of devices for getting over the water, but without avail. After a time, one of the boys proposed that each fellow should pick up the girl he liked best and wade over with her. The masterly proposition was carried out until all that were left upon the island was a little short chap and a great, long, gothic-built, elderly lady. Now, Creswell, you are trying to leave me in the same predicament. You fellows are all getting your own friends out of this scrape, and you will succeed in carrying off one after another until nobody but Jeff Davis and myself will be left on the island, and then I won't know what to do—How should I feel? How should I look lugging him over? I guess the way to avoid such an embarrassing situation is to let all out at once."(8)

The President refused, this day, to open his doors to the throng of visitors that sought admission. His eldest son, Robert, an officer in Grant's army, had returned from the front unharmed. Lincoln wished to reserve the day for his family and intimate friends. In the afternoon, Mrs. Lincoln asked him if he cared to have company on their usual drive. "No, Mary," said he, "I prefer that we ride by ourselves to-day."(9) They took a long drive. His mood, as it had been all day, was singularly happy and tender.(10) He talked much of the past and the future. It seemed to Mrs. Lincoln that he never had appeared happier than during the drive. He referred to past sorrows, to the anxieties of the war, to Willie's death, and spoke of the necessity to be cheerful and happy in the days to come. As Mrs. Lincoln remembered his words: "We have had a hard time since we came to Washington; but the war is over, and with God's blessings, we may hope for four years of peace and happiness, and then we will go back to Illinois and pass the rest of our lives in quiet. We have laid by some money, and during this time, we will save up more, but shall not have enough to support us. We will go back to Illinois; I will open a law office at Springfield or Chicago and practise law, and at least do enough to help give us a livelihood."(11)

They returned from their drive and prepared for a theatre party which had been fixed for that night. The management of the Ford's Theatre, where Laura Keene was to close her season with a benefit performance of Our American Cousin, had announced in the afternoon paper that "the President and his lady" would attend. The President's box had been draped with flags. The rest is a twice told tale — a thousandth told tale.

An actor, very handsome, a Byronic sort, both in beauty and temperament, with a dash perhaps of insanity, John Wilkes Booth, had long meditated killing the President. A violent secessionist, his morbid imagination had made of Lincoln another Caesar. The occasion called for a Brutus. While Lincoln was planning his peaceful war with the Vindictives, scheming how to keep them from grinding the prostrate South beneath their heels, devising modes of restoring happiness to the conquered region, Booth, at an obscure boarding-house in Washington, was gathering about him a band of adventurers, some of whom at least, like himself, were unbalanced. They meditated a general assassination of the Cabinet. The unexpected theatre party on the fourteenth gave Booth a sudden opportunity. He knew every passage of Ford's Theatre. He knew, also, that Lincoln seldom surrounded himself with guards. During the afternoon, he made his way unobserved into the theatre and bored a hole in the door of the presidential box, so that he might fire through it should there be any difficulty in getting the door open.

About ten o'clock that night, the audience was laughing at the absurd play; the President's party were as much amused as any. Suddenly, there was a pistol shot. A moment more and a woman's voice rang out in a sharp cry. An instant sense of disaster brought the audience startled to their feet. Two men were glimpsed struggling toward the front of the President's box. One broke away, leaped down on to the stage, flourished a knife and shouted, "Sic semper tyrannis!" Then he vanished through the flies. It was Booth, whose plans had been completely successful. He had made his way without interruption to within a few feet of Lincoln. At point-blank distance, he had shot him from behind, through the head. In the confusion which ensued, he escaped from the theatre; fled from the city; was pursued; and was himself shot and killed a few days later.

The bullet of the assassin had entered the brain, causing instant unconsciousness. The dying President was removed to a house on Tenth Street, No. 453, where he was laid on a bed in a small room at the rear of the hall on the ground floor.(12)

Swift panic took possession of the city. "A crowd of people rushed instinctively to the White House, and bursting through the doors, shouted the dreadful news to Robert Lincoln and Major Hay who sat gossiping in an upper room. . . . They ran down-stairs. Finding a carriage at the door, they entered it and drove to Tenth Street."(13)

To right and left eddied whirls of excited figures, men and women questioning, threatening, crying out for vengeance. Overhead amid driving clouds, the moon, through successive mantlings of darkness, broke periodically into sudden blazes of light; among the startled people below, raced a witches' dance of the rapidly changing shadows.(14)

Lincoln did not regain consciousness. About dawn his pulse began to fail. A little later, "a look of unspeakable peace came over his worn features"(15), and at twenty-two minutes after seven on the morning of the fifteenth of April, he died.

BIBLIOGRAPHY

It is said that a complete bibliography of Lincoln would include at least five thousand titles. Therefore, any limited bibliography must appear more or less arbitrary. The following is but a minimum list in which, with a few exceptions such as the inescapable interpretative works of Mr. Rhodes and of Professor Dunning, practically everything has to some extent the character of a source.

Alexander. A Political History of the State of New York. By De Alva Stanwood Alexander. 3 vols. 1909.

Arnold. History of Abraham Lincoln and the Overthrow of Slavery. By Isaac N. Arnold. 1866.

Baldwin. Interview between President Lincoln and Colonel John B. Baldwin. 1866.

Bancroft. Life of William H. Seward. By Frederick Bancroft. 2 vols. 1900.

Barnes. Memoir of Thurlow Weed. By Thurlow Weed Barnes. 1884.

Barton. The Soul of Abraham Lincoln. By William Eleazar Barton. 1920.

Bigelow. Retrospections of an Active Life. By John Bigelow. 2 vols. 1909.

Blaine. Twenty Years of Congress. By James G. Blaine. 2 vols. 1884.

Botts. The Great Rebellion. By John Minor Botts. 1866.

Boutwell. Reminiscences of Sixty Years in Public Affairs. By George S. Boutwell 2 vols. 1902.

Bradford. Union Portraits. By Gamaliel Bradford. 1916.

Brooks. Washington in Lincoln's Time. By Noah Brooks, 1895.

Carpenter. Six Months at the White House with Abraham Lincoln. By F. B. Carpenter. 1866.

Chandler. Life of Zachary Chandler. By the Detroit Post and Tribune. 1880.

Chapman. Latest Light on Abraham Lincoln. By Ervin Chapman. 1917. The Charleston Mercury.

Chase. Diary and Correspondence of Salmon Chase. Report, American Historical Association, 1902, Vol. II.

Chittenden. Recollections of President Lincoln and His Administration. By L. Chittenden. 1891.

Coleman. Life of John J. Crittenden, with Selections from his Correspondence and Speeches. By Ann Mary Coleman. 2 vols. 1871.

Conway. Autobiography, Memories and Experiences of Moncure Daniel Conway. 2 vols. 1904.

Correspondence. The Correspondence of Robert Toombs, Alexander H. Stephens, and Howell Cobb. Edited by U. B. Phillips. Report American Historical Association, 1913, Vol. II.

Crawford. The Genesis of the Civil War. By Samuel Wylie Crawford. 1887.

C. W. Report of the Joint Committee on the Conduct of the War. 1863.

Dabney. Memoir of a Narrative Received from Colonel John B. Baldwin, of Staunton, touching the Origin of the War. By Reverend R. L. Dabney, D. D., Southern Historical Society Papers, Vol. 1. 1876.

Davis. Rise and Fail of the Confederate Government. By Jefferson Davis. 2 vols. 1881.

Dunning. Essays on the Civil War and Reconstruction and Related Topics. By William A. Dunning. 1898.

Field. Life of David Dudley Field. By Henry M. Field. 1898.

Flower. Edwin McMasters Stanton. By Frank Abial Flower. 1902.

Fry. Military Miscellanies. By James B. Fry. 1889.

Galaxy. The History of Emancipation. By Gideon Welles. The Galaxy, XIV, 838-851.

Gilmore. Personal Recollections of Abraham Lincoln and the Civil War. By James R. Gilmore. 1899.

Gilmore, Atlantic. A Suppressed Chapter of History. By James R. Gilmore, Atlantic Monthly, April, 1887.

Globe. Congressional Globe, Containing the Debates and Proceedings. 1834-1873.

Godwin. Biography of William Cullen Bryant. By Parke Godwin. 1883.

Gore. The Boyhood of Abraham Lincoln. By J. Rogers Gore. 1921.

Gorham. Life and Public Services of Edwin M. Stanton. By George C. Gorham. 2 vols. 1899.

Grant. Personal Memoirs. By Ulysses S. Grant. 2 vols. 1886.

Greeley. The American Conflict. By Horace Greeley. 2 vols. 1864-1867.

Gurowski. Diary from March 4, 1861, to November 12, 1862. By Adam Gurowski. 1862.

Hanks. Nancy Hanks. By Caroline Hanks Hitchcock. 1900.

Harris. Public Life of Zachary Chandler. By W. C. Harris, Michigan Historical Commission. 1917.

Hart. Salmon Portland Chase. By Albert Bushnell Hart. 1899.

Hay MS. Diary of John Hay. The war period is covered by three volumes of manuscript. Photostat copies in the library of the Massachusetts Historical Society, accessible only by special permission.

Hay, Century. Life in the White House in the Time of Lincoln. By John Hay, Century Magazine, November, 1890.

The New York Herald.

Herndon. Herndon's Lincoln. The True Story of a Great Life: The History and Personal Recollections of Abraham Lincoln. By W. H. Herndon and J. W. Weik. 3 vols. (paged continuously). 1890.

Hill. Lincoln the Lawyer. By Frederick Trevers Hill 1906.

Hitchcock. Fifty Years in Camp and Field. Diary of Major-General Ethan Allen Hitchcock, U. S. A. Edited by W. Croffut. 1909.

Johnson. Stephen A. Douglas. By Allen Johnson. 1908.

The Journal of the Virginia Convention. 1861.

Julian. Political Recollections 1840-1872. By George W. Julian. 1884.

Kelley. Lincoln and Stanton. By W. D. Kelley. 1885.

Lamon. The Life of Abraham Lincoln. By Ward H. Lamon. 1872.

Letters. Uncollected Letters of Abraham Lincoln. Now first brought together by Gilbert A. Tracy. 1917.

Lieber. Life and Letters of Francis Lieber. Edited by Thomas S. Perry, 1882.

Lincoln. Complete Works of Abraham Lincoln. Edited by John G. Nicolay and John Hay. 2 vols. New and enlarged edition. 12 volumes. 1905. (All references here are to the Colter edition.)

McCarthy. Lincoln's Plan of Reconstruction. By Charles M. McCarthy, 1901.

McClure. Abraham Lincoln and Men of War Times. By A. K. McClure. 1892.

Merriam. Life and Times of Samuel Bowles. By G. S. Merriam. 2 vols. 1885.

Munford. Virginia's Attitude toward Slavery and Secession. By Beverley B. Munford. 1910.

Moore. A Digest of International Law. By John Bassett Moore. 8 vols. 1906.

Newton. Lincoln and Herndon. By Joseph Fort Newton. 1910.

Nicolay. A Short Life of Abraham Lincoln. By John G. Nicolay. 1902.

Nicolay, Cambridge. The Cambridge Modern History: Volume VII. The United States. By various authors. 1903.

Miss Nicolay. Personal Traits of Abraham Lincoln. By Helen Nicolay. 1912.

N. and H. Abraham Lincoln: A History. By John G. Nicolay and John Hay. 10 vols. 1890.

N. P. Official Records of the Union and Confederate Navies. First series. 27 vols. 1895-1917.

O. P. Official Records of the Union and Confederate Armies. 128 vols. 1880-1901.

Outbreak. The Outbreak of the Rebellion. By John G. Nicolay. 1881.

Own Story. McClellan's Own Story. By George B. McClellan. 1887.

Paternity. The Paternity of Abraham Lincoln. By William Eleazer Barton. 1920.

Pearson. Life of John A. Andrew. By Henry G. Pearson. 2 vols. 1904.

Pierce. Memoirs and Letters of Charles Sumner. By Edward Lillie Pierce. 4 vols. 1877-1893.

Porter. In Memory of General Charles P. Stone. By Fitz John Porter. 1887.

Public Man. Diary of a Public Man. Anonymous. North American Review. 1879.

Rankin. Personal Recollections of Abraham Lincoln. By Henry B. Rankin. 1916.

Raymond. Journal of Henry J. Raymond. Edited by Henry W. Raymond. Scribner's Magazine. 1879-1880.

Recollections. Recollections of Abraham Lincoln. By Ward Hill Lamon. 1911.

Reminiscences. Reminiscences of Abraham Lincoln, by Distinguished Men of his Time. Edited by Allen Thorndyke Rice. 1886.

Report of the Joint Committee on Reconstruction, first session, Thirty-Ninth Congress.

Rhodes. History of the United States from the Compromise of 1850. By James Ford Rhodes. 8 vols. 1893-1920.

Riddle. Recollections of War Times. By A. G. Riddle. 1895.

Schrugham. The Peaceful Americans of 1860. By Mary Schrugham. 1922.

Schure. Speeches, Correspondence and Political Papers of Carl Schure. Selected and edited by Frederick Bancroft. 1913.

Scott. Memoirs of Lieutenant General Scott, LL.D. Written by himself. 2 vols. 1864.

Seward. Works of William H. Seward. 5 vols. 1884.

Sherman. Memoirs of William T. Sherman. By himself. 2 vols. 1886.

Sherman Letters.

Letters of John Sherman and W. T. Sherman. Edited by Rachel Sherman Thorndike. 1894.

Southern Historical Society Papers.

Stephens. Constitutional View of the Late War between the States. By Alexander H. Stephens. 2 vols. 1869-1870.

Stoddard. Inside the White House in War Times. By William O. Stoddard. 1890.

Stories. "Abe" Lincoln's Yarns and Stories. With introduction and anecdotes by Colonel Alexander McClure. 1901.

The New York Sun.

Swinton. Campaigns of the Army of the Potomac. By William Swinton. 1866.

Tarbell. The Life of Abraham Lincoln. By Ida M. Tarbell. New edition. 2 vols. 1917.

Thayer. The Life and Letters of John Hay. By William Roscoe Thayer. 2 vols. 1915.

The New York Times.

The New York Tribune.

Tyler. Letters and Times of the Tylers. By Lyon G. Tyler. 3 vols. 1884-1896.

Van Santvoord. A Reception by President Lincoln. By C. J. Van Santvoord. Century Magazine, Feb., 1883.

Villard. Memoirs of Henry Villard. 2 vols. 1902.

Wade. Life of Benjamin F. Wade. By A. G. Riddle. 1886.

Warden. Account of the Private Life and Public Services of Salmon Portland Chase. By R. B. Warden. 1874.

Welles. Diary of Gideon Welles. Edited by J. T. Morse, Jr. 3 vols. 1911.

White. Life of Lyman Trumbull. By Horace White. 1913.

Woodburn. The Life of Thaddeus Stevens. By James Albert Woodburn. 1913.